SULLA T̶̶ ̶̶̶̶̶̶̶̶̶̶̶

Frontispiece.

Lucius Cornelius Sulla Felix

SULLA THE FORTUNATE

ROMAN GENERAL AND DICTATOR

G. P. BAKER

Cooper Square Press

First Cooper Square Press edition 2001

This Cooper Square Press paperback edition of *Sulla the Fortunate* is an
unabridged republication of the edition first published in London in 1927.

Published by Cooper Square Press
An Imprint of the Rowman & Littlefield Publishing Group
150 Fifth Avenue, Suite 817
New York, New York 10011

Distributed by National Book Network

Library of Congress Cataloging-in-Publication Data

Baker, G.P. (George Philip), 1879-1951.
  Sulla the fortunate : Roman general and dictator / G.P. Baker.—1st Cooper
Square Press ed.
    p. cm.
  Unabridged republication of the edition originally published: London :
J. Murray, 1927.
  Includes index.
  ISBN 0-8154-1147-2 (pbk. : alk. paper)
    1. Sulla, Lucius Cornelius. 2. Rome—History—Republic, 265-30 B.C. 3.
Statesmen—Rome—Biography. I. Title.

DG256.7.B3 2001
937'.05'092—dc21
[B]   2001017094

♾™ The paper used in this publication meets the minimum requirements of
American National Standard for Information Sciences—Permanence of
Paper for Printed Library Materials, ANSI/NISO Z39.48-1992.
Manufactured in the United States of America.

PREFACE

THERE are many reasons why Lucius Cornelius Sulla should be of particular interest to us to-day. His life was a remarkable one ; his personality was still more remarkable ; his significance in the history of politics makes the story of his career not only apposite, but even topical. Not to know who Sulla was, or what he did, is to be ignorant of one of the crucial episodes of history : an episode which neatly illustrates the problems of our own age.

Next to Gaius Julius Caesar, he was the greatest individual produced by ancient Rome. He has been eclipsed by the figure of Caesar, who undid his work, overshadowed his fame, and based his own career to a great extent upon the methods of his predecessor. . . . He was as great a soldier as Caesar ; as great a statesman, though a less successful one ; and if the stray fragments of his lost autobiography, surviving embedded in the books of later historians, are any guide, he was a writer whose experiences were as interesting as Caesar's own. And he was the Great Dictator ; and he died in his bed.

Not until the idea of Dictatorship became a living contemporary issue was any one likely to see either interest or meaning in Sulla's career. We shall look in vain for any authoritative biography of Sulla from the great Victorians. There is none. There is not even any sign that they knew what he was, or meant.

But with Mussolini dominating Italy, Primo del
Rivera ruling Spain, and Pilsudski Poland, and with
a Dictatorship of the Proletariat reigning in Russia,
and likely to go on doing so—with all these present
actualities, we can look at Sulla with fresh eyes and
suspect that he had more meaning than our fathers
imagined. And he had. He did mean more than
they thought. But there was nothing in the circumstances of their own days to reveal what that meaning
was. We can understand Sulla better, because we
live in an age more like his own.

There is a proverb that " History repeats itself."
There is just this much obvious truth in it, that the
history of social institutions is a kind of biology ; for
the collective life of man, like his individual life,
develops by a definite law. We know the series of
changes through which the physical body goes.
Everything we can say about it we can similarly say
of the changes through which civilisation passes.
Both have definite stages. At seventeen, a man
probably falls in love ; at thirty, he may marry some
one else ; at forty-five he is liable to put on flesh ;
at sixty he goes grey ; " three-score and ten years
are the life of a man." . . . The course of civilisation can be predicted with no less—and no more—
certainty. The traditions of our race have never left
us in doubt on that head. Plato knew that aristocracy precedes oligarchy, and that democracy follows
it ; the compilers of the Old Testament knew all
about the development of the tribal system into the
first (or primitive) form of monarchy. But so long
is the wave length of history, that it is only now,
after another two thousand years, that we realise that
what followed Plato and the Old Testament was a
logical development which is very likely to repeat

itself. We have gone the round afresh. After the last Augustus—or Augustulus—the tribes reappeared, and monarchy followed ; and aristocracy once more came on the heels of monarchy, and oligarchy on the heels of that ; but we erred in imagining that the democracy which succeeded was the last, final, never-to-be-changed form of political organisation. . . . It has all happened before. . . . On the last journey round, Sulla followed Tiberius Gracchus as Mussolini has followed Mazzini.

Sulla was thus a very modern man—far more modern, more one of ourselves, than Alfred the Great or Cesare Borgia. Sulla faced most of the problems which a modern statesman has to face. He was familiar with the decay of religious faith, the failure of aristocracy, the rise of Bolshevism, the industrial revolution, and the power of international finance. He was accustomed to the modern woman ; he was an ardent play-goer ; he was involved in the problem of the ex-service man. It is an advantage to see all these things set on a different stage, detached from our own circumstances, isolated from our interests and prejudices, and made more dramatic by their completeness. We do not know the issue of our own actions ; but we know the issue of Sulla's. We cannot tell what the Logic of Events may do with us ; but we know what it did with Sulla's world. . . . This is doubtless a wise age, and Sulla's was a foolish one. " But how dieth the wise man ? Even as the fool."

Sulla did not exactly invent the policy of dictatorship, for under the Roman constitution the dictatorship in times of emergency was a legal and constitutional office, and in the Greek cities, at a certain stage of political evolution, dictators were as common as mushrooms ; but he was the first statesman who applied the idea systematically, intelligently, and on a scale sufficiently large to be instructive to us. His life story is one of the very few available to us which give us a working model of a great civilisation like our own, struggling with our own difficulties. . . . It may possibly be helpful if it leads some people to realise that dictatorship is a known stage in political growth. . . . Not every one falls to the common ailments. Some states may avoid dictatorship. But none avoids the necessity of growing up.

Hence there is much in this narrative that will not be, or may not be, true of our own age. Sulla saw civilisation move a step ahead of its " furthest north " ; with average luck, we may pass that limit. For we do move ; though we move rather in social things than in things peculiar to the individual and his capacities.

This book, therefore, has all the faults and failings of a book intended to be useful, and based upon the lives of actual men who worked, suffered, died, and have something of real human urgency to tell us as a result.

The sources for Sulla's life are well-known and well-trodden ground—perhaps too well-trodden. Nothing can be added to facts long familiar. The only opportunity for originality lies in the reading of the facts. In this, a biographer who is not a professional scholar has a great advantage. He is not bound by any of the responsibilities which make a professional scholar chary of embarking on some kinds of adventure. In the present case the facts have been read according to the probabilities familiar to us in modern life. The assumption which underlies the whole book is that Sulla was an ordinary human being of extraordinary achievements ; that all his friends and foes were ordinary human beings ; and that the stuff of human life and motive is everywhere and always much the same —only the fashions vary. Human beings are so inherently interesting that to praise them or blame them is unnecessary ; all that is needed is to understand them.

G. P. B.

ELMER, SUSSEX,
1927.

CONTENTS

CHAP.   PAGE

PREFACE   5
Importance of Sulla—The key to Sulla lost—" Re-
capitulation " in social development—Modernity of
Sulla—Dictatorship—The parallel only approximate
—Sources—The unknown is to be interpreted by the
known.

I   SULLA   19
State of Europe—Britain—The Frisians—The Baltic
—Germany—Gaul—The small political unit—Limita-
tion of energy—Rome the real centre of interest—Rome
in Sulla's day—An age of transition—Ancestry of Sulla
—Sulla's person—Eccentricity of his appearance—His
early days—His family poor—The lady Nicopolis—His
stepmother—His Bohemian tastes—The drama—
Complexity of his character—His passivity—His
conventionality—Limits of his conventionality—His
caution—He was an opportunist on principle—The
theory of " Fortune."

II   THE ANTECEDENTS OF SULLA'S WORLD . .   40
" Mediterranean " civilisation—The city state—Evolution of the tribe—Larger political units the ideal—The
state rationalised—The abolition of kingship—Political
control made responsible—Development of Rome—
Law brought under the control of the state—The
aristocracy controlled by law—Abolition of privilege
—The state strengthened by the changes—The war of
Hannibal—The Roman state proof against force—Ruin
of the peasantry—The problem of action—Tiberius
Gracchus—Economic action to be controlled by the
state—Impatience of Tiberius—He is murdered—Gaius
Gracchus—The bankers support Gaius—The state to be
controlled by economic forces—The financiers privileged—Projected extension of the Roman franchise—
Gaius a revolutionary—Drusus the elder—The electors
detached from Gaius—Force employed—The movement suppressed—Consequences of the suppression.

III   SULLA'S WORLD   65
Sulla aet. 17—The prestige of law damaged—Import-
ance of Rome—Objections to the Gracchan policy—
Importance of the aristocratic tradition—Difference

11

between the oligarchy and the aristocracy—The aristocracy and wealth—Divorce of political and economic power—The roots of Roman rule—The Romans possessed the gift of association—The aristocracy originated it—Decay of aristocracy—Educative effect of aristocracy—The expansion of Rome a consistent process—Difficulties consequent—Necessity of unity in the control—The bankers and merchants—Parallel with the nineteenth century—Insecurity of the state—The problem of popular rights—Power of the economic control—Economic effects of slavery—The European character—Variability of the European type—Disqualifications of the European as a master—Political control necessary—The aristocratic policy the only practicable one—Sulla's relation to these theories—His conduct explained by them.

IV THE RISE OF SULLA TO FORTUNE . . . 86

Character of Gaius Marius—Marius tribune, 119 B.C.—Marius praetor, 115 B.C.—Propraetor in Spain, 114 B.C.—He marries into the family of Caesar—The trouble in Africa—Jugurtha—Revival of the *Populares*—The African war—Trouble in the North—Competence of the oligarchy in question—Marius in Africa, 108 B.C.—Marius Consul I, 107 B.C.—The army reforms of Marius—Sulla quaestor aet. 31—Marius commander in chief in Africa, 106 B.C.—Difficulties of the war—Sulla arrives in Africa—The problem of King Bocchus—Sulla sent to Bocchus—Sulla receives the ambassadors—The embassy in Rome—Sulla's second mission to Bocchus—Danger on the road—Sulla reaches Bocchus—The official conference—The secret conference—Sulla successful—Bocchus and Jugurtha—Capture of Jugurtha, 105 B.C.

V THE TRIUMPH OF MARIUS 113

Fresh danger—The Cimbri and Teutones—Party position in Rome—Caepio in Gaul—Defeat at Arausio—Panic in Italy—Demand for Marius—The crime of Caepio—Marius Consul II, 104 B.C.—His triumph—Sulla legate under Marius—The new army—Marius Consul III, 103 B.C.—Doubts of Marius—Marius Consul IV, 102 B.C.—Sulla takes work under Catulus—Movements of the Cimbri and Teutones—Battle of Aquae Sextiae—Marius Consul V, 101 B.C.—Catulus in retreat—The Cimbri—Battle of Vercellae—Sulla's version of the battle—Dispute on the field.

VI THE POLITICAL STRUGGLE 133

Problems of the peace—Electoral campaign, 101 B.C.—Sulla's political position—Criticisms of Marius—Sulla's view of Marius—Catulus—Relation of Catulus and Sulla—Metellus Numidicus—Marius as a politician

CHAP.   PAGE

—Marius Consul VI, 100 B.C.—The cabal against
Marius—Saturninus and the Senate—Difficulties of
Marius—" The Catonic pose "—The *equites* go over—
Elections for 99 B.C.—Triumph of the oligarchy—The
Italians—Marius travels in Asia—The Italians and the
franchise—Scaevola : lex Licinia Mucia—The eques-
trian courts again—Hesitation of the oligarchy—The
" group "—Scaevola's administration in Asia—Rutilius
impeached—Sulla praetor, 93 B.C., aet. 45—Rutilius
condemned—Exiled—Condition of Asia—Character of
Mithradates—Asiatic despotism—Policy of Sulla—
Results—The gold plaque—Impeachment dropped—
Drusus the younger—The programme of Drusus—
Difficulty of his policy—His success—His failure—
His murder—Revolt of the Italians.

VII THE MILITARY STRUGGLE IN ITALY .   .   . 163

The Social War, 90 B.C.—The opposing forces—Change
in character of Rome—The Italians apprehend the true
nature of the war—The Varian tribunal—Sulla in Campania—Roman reverses—Marius in central Italy—
Success of Marius—Dissensions in Rome—Problem
of the franchise—Change of opinion—Italians weakened
by the concessions made to them—Changes in command, 89 B.C.—Sulla commands in Campania—The
reversion of the Asiatic command—Second year of the
war—Sulla and his army—Sulla's raid into Samnium
—His success—The war a military defeat but a moral
victory for the Italians—Consequences of the war—
News of Mithradates—The massacres in Asia—Italy
seriously damaged by the Social War—Alarm of the
equites—Sulpicius Rufus—Sulla Consul I, 88 B.C., aet.
50—" Fortune "—His marriage to Caecilia Metella—
Lampoons against Sulla—Sulla's action against
Sulpicius—Sulla is assaulted and intimidated—The
eastern command offered to Marius—Sulla prepares
to enforce his claims—Murder of the tribunes—
Sulla's march on Rome—Entry into the city—Escape of
Marius—Death of Sulpicius—Audacity of Sulla's act
—Its justification—His intentions—His measures of
pacification—He leaves for the east.

VIII SULLA IN GREECE 189

Situation in Greece—Sulla's advance—Lucullus—the
siege of Athens—Difficulties of supply—Requisition
of the treasures of Delphi—The siege drags—Ill
news from Rome—Athens taken by assault—The
army of relief—The journey of Lucullus—Reaction
against Mithradates—Sulla in Boeotia—Arrival of the
Pontic army—Sulla occupies the fords—The entrenched position—Battle of Chaeronea—The Pontic
left wing broken—Rout of the Pontic army.

CHAP.   PAGE
IX THE VENGEANCE OF MARIUS AND THE RETENTION
      OF ASIA 207
      Italy unsettled—The *equites* dissatisfied—Cinna acts for
      them—Blundering of Octavius—Civil war—Arrival of
      Marius—He takes Ostia—The Senate surrenders to
      Cinna—Mental condition of Marius—The Marian
      proscription—Impossibility of controlling him—Marius
      Consul VII, 86 B.C.—Death of Marius—The *Populares*
      supreme—Their intellectual impotence—The refugees
      flee to Sulla—Flaccus sent to supersede Sulla—Sulla
      and Flaccus—They part—Sulla at Orchomenos—The
      new Pontic army—Sulla's engineering—Archelaus
      attacks the ditches—Sulla's complete success—Flight
      and death of Flaccus—The war goes against Mithra-
      dates—Negotiations—Sulla drafts terms—Attempt to
      modify the terms—Sulla's interview with Mithradates
      —The terms ratified—The army disappointed—
      Fimbria—The Fimbrian army melts—Attempt to
      assassinate Sulla—Suicide of Fimbria—Settlement of
      Asia—Sulla's financial diplomacy—Legal position of
      Sulla—He writes to the Senate—Cinna murdered.

X   SULLA COMES HOME 237
      83 B.C., Sulla, aet. 55—Sulla's rest in Greece—Difficul-
      ties of invading Italy—His undertakings—He lands in
      Italy—The March to Campania—Defeat of Norbanus
      —Accessions to Sulla—Crassus—Pompeius—Sulla
      meets Pompeius—Negotiations with Lucius Scipio—
      Sulla alleges an agreement with the Consul—82 B.C.
      Sulla, aet. 56—Sulla's plans—Advance of Metellus
      Pius—Sulla's advance—The troops worn out—Battle
      of Sacriportus—Praeneste invested—Murder of
      Scaevola—Sulla's advance on Carbo—The arrival of
      the Samnites—Carbo flees—Samnites resolve to destroy
      Rome—They are delayed by a sally—Battle of the
      Colline Gate—Sulla's troops broken—Panic—Crassus
      successful—End of the battle of the Colline Gate.

XI THE DICTATORSHIP OF SULLA 254
      State of Rome—Sulla's triumph—" Sulla Felix "—
      His policy—The problem of restoration—The logic of
      events—Massacre of the prisoners—Praeneste taken
      —Fate of other towns—The Dictatorship—Its terms—
      Samnium devastated—Financial difficulties—The
      " Capital levy "—Principle of the Sullan proscription
      —Doubts of his friends—The lists—Views of the
      proscription—Scandals—Sulla unable to prevent abuses
      —The auctions—Success of the proscription—Sulla's
      creative measures—Poverty of material for a new
      aristocracy—Sulla's practical reforms—The franchise
      confirmed to the Italians—Local government—The
      franchise partly ineffective—Land colonisation—The

CHAP.   PAGE

equites—Legal reforms—The Senate—Civil and
military power separated—Sulla's aim the repression
of monarchy—Reasons against monarchy—Sulla Consul
II, 80 B.C., aet. 58—Sulla ignoring the real truth—
His inconsistency.

XII THE DEATH OF SULLA 281

Pompeius in Sicily—His tolerance—Sulla disappointed
in him—Pompeius recalled—Pompeius and the opposition—Breach between him and Sulla—The turn of
the tide—Sulla contemplates failure—The Opimian
wine—Death of Metella—Valeria Messalla—Ofella—
The parable of the husbandman—Lepidus—Sulla's
verdict on Pompeius—Sulla resigns—He retires—
Attacked by sickness—His commentaries—He bursts a
blood-vessel—His death, 78 B.C., aet. 60—Pompeius
protects the dead man—The funeral.

XIII THE DEATH OF SULLA'S WORLD . . . 295

Reaction—Sulla's success temporary—The oligarchy—
Mithradates—Sertorius in Spain—Spartacus—Fall of
Sertorius—Pompeius burns the correspondence of
Sertorius—Weakness of the *Populares*—Rise of Crassus
—Consulship of Pompeius and Crassus—Sulla's
constitution cancelled—Lucullus in Asia—Caesar—The
memory of Marius revived—Lex Gabinia, 67 B.C.—
Lex Manilia, 66 B.C.—Caesar financed by the bankers
—The trophies of Marius restored—Dissensions
among the *Populares*—Conspiracy of Catilina—Caesar
in sole control of the *Populares*—The first Triumvirate,
60 B.C.—Caesar goes to Gaul—The Triumvirate re-
newed, 56 B.C.—Results of the murder of Caesar—The
empire—Review of Sulla's work—Realism of Caesar
—The empire a new type of monarchy—Aristocracy
cannot be deliberately created—The oligarchy neglected
ability—The army becomes a guild—Political power
controls all others—The change beneficial to the
economic power—The empire ended the political
evolution of Rome—Defects of Caesar's policy—
Christianity necessary as a counterbalance—Christianity a " political " organisation—Dualism of allegiance
unsatisfactory—Faults of Sulla—Sulla's work a stage in
our own evolution.

INDEX 318

ILLUSTRATIONS

BUST OF L. CORNELIUS SULLA FELIX   *Frontispiece*

                                              FACING PAGE
PORTRAIT OF SULLA; AND KING BOCCHUS DELIVERING
    JUGURTHA TO SULLA 86

PORTRAIT OF GNAEUS POMPEIUS MAGNUS . . . 281
    After the Palazzo Spada, Copenhagen and Naples busts

PORTRAIT OF GAIUS JULIUS CAESAR 295
    After a bust in the British Museum

MAPS AND DIAGRAMS
                                                    PAGE
GENEALOGY OF THE SULLA FAMILY 30

MAP OF THE CIMBRIAN WAR 112

PLAN OF THE FORUM ROMANUM 132

MAP ILLUSTRATING THE SOCIAL WAR 162

PLAN OF THE BATTLE OF CHAERONEA 188

MAP OF THE WAR IN GREECE 206

MAP OF THE ITALIAN CAMPAIGNS OF SULLA . . . 236

GENEALOGY OF THE CAESAR FAMILY 268

SULLA THE FORTUNATE

CHAPTER I

SULLA

I

A NARROW street, paved with cobbles : soaring tenements, straight, ugly, many-windowed : a distant roar of traffic : *Rome*, twenty-one centuries ago. A strongly built, middle-sized man, with startling blue eyes, a purple-and-white complexion, and a shock of golden hair : *Sulla*, whose tale this is.

II

Glance over the Europe in which Sulla dwelt. Take your stand on Ludgate Hill—a smooth slope rising up from the undulating ground north of the Thames, overlooking the marshes. There, already, probably, stood Ludd's Dun, a fortress of great earthworks crowned with timber walls, and stocked with its sheds of munitions and supplies : from which continued the town of little wooden houses to the other earthwork on what is now Tower Hill, guarding the way east. It was no great town then— chiefly the river-port that kept the more important town, which is now St. Albans, in touch with the sea.

The salmon-haunted, silver old Thames was a

wide, shallow, marsh-bordered stream, which had
hardly time in summer to drain off the winter flood-
water. Vast forests filled the Kent and Sussex
wealds, which are now cleared and cultivated, while
the now wooded hills were bare. It was a wild
land of hill emerging smooth from thick woods
scored by flooded streams and determined swamp—
a savage, pioneer land to which civilisation had not
yet come ; the hills dotted with ringed villages that
were ramparted with high turf walls and wicker
battlements, wherein long-haired, scarlet-clad tribal
chiefs with wonderfully decorative but soft-bladed
swords ruled in rural splendour over the common
people who still used the flint knife to shear the sheep
and ring the bull : a pastoral people, fishing and
bird-trapping in the marshes, and hacking out
scanty allotments of corn-land on the hill-sides.

Britain was a land of local diversity and local
government ; its rulers suspicious and exclusive.
It could be traversed only by certain roads—and
these so well watched that the traveller could not
easily escape being examined and turned back, unless
his credentials were uncommonly good. Productivity was low : population thin, and somewhat
scattered. There was no national organisation
either public or private. Education was in the
hands of a Druid church of distinctly theosophical
colour. Trade was restrained, not only by the low
productivity of industry, but by the degree to which
all enterprise was repressed by the exclusive mono-
poly of the local tribal groups. Nothing could be on
a large scale.

The northern trade was largely in the hands of
Frisians, who brought in furs, amber, fish and eggs,
and took in return the tin that came from Cornwall,

and a certain amount of gold from Ireland : returning home to sell the tin and the gold to the men who
came down, laden with more amber and furs of the
Baltic, in many-oared whale-boats steered by cold-
faced, blue-eyed kings who let no stranger into their
countries. The Frisians held this trade because it
was dangerous to cross the North Sea, and in all ways
safer to steer by the coast and come over the narrow
sea to the Thames mouth, or on to the ports of Gaul.

Not much was known of the Baltic. The Frisians
kept that market in their own hands, and the North-
men in these times did not care to come further
down themselves, although it is possible that in
earlier times their whale-boats had traded as far
south as Brittany and Spain. Germany was backward and disunited, having been swept by repeated
devastating wars ; but in other respects was the
same predatory, militaristic Germany with which we
have been familiar : and Germany formed a barrier
which prevented any easy access by land to the
North. But the Baltic lands were then, as now, progressive and intelligent—their artificers expert metal
workers who could cast trumpets and bronze chains,
and forge and inlay iron, though not, as yet, temper
it. On the whole, north-western Europe was in a
state of transition and decadence—fallen off from
many of the splendours of an earlier age, and not yet
risen to its new future.

The central fact was, perhaps, that north-western
Europe still lingered in a definitely tribal stage of
social organisation, in which great social and
economic unities were impossible. Men were
limited and hindered by this fact, and were awaiting
some fresh form of organisation in which their
energies could be safely unleashed. Such develop-

ments do not come in a day ; but events were
already moving, though the news came through
slowly and sporadically. The coast of Denmark
gave way and let in the sea, as in later ages it broke
into Holland and formed the Zuyder Zee. The
Cimbri and Teutones were swamped out, and began
to look for new homes : and there was local trouble
and war, and movement as far south as the Rhine.
The Goths of Sweden were crossing over to the
south coast of the Baltic, and colonising the valley
of the Vistula. Something was impending over
Europe. The Etruscan augurs declared that a new
age was beginning—whatever that might mean.

III

Amid this confinement and restriction of energy,
the attention of an onlooker would almost insensibly
wander to the real centre of interest ; and the way
would have been to strike the Tin Road, the Pil-
grim's Way, which led to Winchester, and by a side
road to Southampton. There sea-going ships with
leathern sails and iron anchors would take the
traveller (fare uncertain and fixed by private treaty)
over into the ports of the Loire. The tin and gold
went by that trade route, either up the rivers, or
overland, southward, in return for the iron of Gaul.
In Gaul, at first, it would seem much as it was in
Britain ; but there was a leaven at work ; the social
unit was perhaps greater ; the hills might be higher,
and the marshes vaster, but certainly the villages
were larger, and the ringed forts bigger. Cattle-
breeding was the chief occupation ; but a good trade
was done in iron and metal work. The Gaulish
craftsmen were the first to invent enamelling, and
to discover the processes of tinning and silvering.

The further south one went, the richer the land became : till one came to the Cevennes, and walked straight into a new world.

The vine and the olive began at the Cevennes, and a road or two, and landed estates, and all the first signs of civilisation. And going forward, one would meet more roads, and farms and vineyards, and country houses, and so come at last to the outer villages, and then to the subordinate towns, and then to the suburbs, and then to the walls, of a roaring city of civilisation with factories, and shops, and working men, and middle-classes, and millionaires, and old aristocratic families—labouring, idling, trading, speculating, swindling—doing all those things which, for good or evil, civilised men do. Her harbours were full of ships, her banks full of money. This, you ask, was Rome ? So any intelligent Briton, who got so far, would reverentially ask. No—it was Marseilles. But here " Rome " began.

And now all was changed. There were surveyors and civil engineers in the Roman world. It was not indeed until a hundred years later that they linked up the Italian road system with the roads of Transalpine Gaul, and built the solid graded highway that ran from Marseilles, with bridge, bank, and causeway as necessary, forking at Aquae Sextiae, round, past and over the barrier of the Alps to Pisa, along the old track-way between the mountains and the sea. So in these days it was still the simplest course to take ship direct to Pisa. And at Pisa was another great city ; and here, in Italy, the world was civilised. Social problems, political disputes, administrative systems ; public baths, water supply, drainage, rates and taxes ; theatres, circuses, and other less respectable places of entertainment—all were here. It was not

long since a political crisis. Another crisis might
come to pass at any time. You could have enjoyed
an intelligent conversation with any respectable
person as to whether the Dole was really a just and
an expedient policy, and whether Catulus or Metellus
would succeed in gaining the second place in the
consular elections : and why Italians should not have
the vote. You could have been introduced into a
political or a social club : you could have put up
in lodgings or in an hotel. True, these things were
not in all cases shaped in precisely our way : the
fashion was different : but the substance was there
in full measure. Italy, in Sulla's day, was socially
nearer to us than the England of 1600.[1]

And all these things depended on a certain order
of man. By degrees he might be identified : a more
or less prosperous, pushing, confident man with a
chin, who took the pavement of every one—a Roman,
whatever mysterious significance that term might
have. And there was a mystery attached to it.
You would hear the name and fame of Rome and yet
see no police and no soldiers. It was a civilisation
conducted without the gendarme. The court of
justice sat, and recorded its judgments ; but there
was no obvious reason why they should be respected.

Take the road from Pisa—the great Via Aurelia
that ran south, passing through ancient cities,
between the Apennine and the sea, down through the
rich cultivation of old Etruria, where the chain-gangs
worked in the vineyards, and the chained shepherd
watched his flocks by night—amid the signs of ever

---

[1] The absence of machinery—the most obvious difference
—was due to an economic cause : slave labour was so cheap
that the sinking of capital in machinery was not commercially
profitable.

growing wealth, of transcendent prosperity. It is a
Whig civilisation of vast estates and huge isolated
country houses—a world of the *nouveau riche* who
is already nearly an aristocrat, and soon will be.
Thicker become the houses ; you pass miles of grave-
stones set up beside the road, and reflect on the
quaintness of foreign customs ; you come to the
Pons Aurelius ; you cross it——

And there is Rome !

Not the Rome of eighteenth-century classical
idealism, nor even the Rome of the Palladian
renaissance (which resembled it rather less than
Sir Edward Burne Jones's pictures resembled the
Middle Ages), but the real Rome, with its temple of
Capitoline Jupiter still flaring with Etruscan colour,
and its senators still clad in purple-edged mantles
and scarlet shoes ; a Rome rammed together tight
within walls too small to hold her tremendous traffic
and roaring life ; the poorer quarters built tenement
above tenement, and packed room over room, beside
narrow streets ; an unimproved, old-fashioned
Rome, like the London of the 'sixties, with, in one
way, all the world at her feet, and, in another, with
all the world before her : a seething, wood-and-brick
Rome, over-brimming with a life just cut loose from
the trammels of old decorum and old incredible
religion, not yet provided with Higher Thought,
Oriental Mysteries, or the Artistic Life : a Rome with
the remembrance of wonderful deeds of human
courage and iron heart, but no idea, as yet, what to
do with the results. It was a Rome as much unlike
the later Rome as the London that any man of middle
age can still remember, before they pulled down
Holywell Street and began to build the Bush Building, is unlike modern London. It would have

repaid the trouble of wandering through its streets and examining its life.

IV

It was an age of rapid change, when one world was coming to an end, and another was beginning. Men, manners and modes—the economic system, the spiritual tension, the necessity, the ideal—were all simultaneously altering. Economic changes sent the Roman landholder into the city to live, and to Campania for his holidays, while a bailiff or agent took over the practical charge of his estates ; increasing business kept the Roman financier there ; growing wealth enlarged their houses and their households. The dour old Kruger-like farmer was a disappearing species—except when the type was revived as a pose—and his descendant was a washed, manicured person, with a study, and a secretary, and perhaps a room full of scribes (typists being as yet unborn) : who might collect objects of art, might write poetry (as Lucullus did), and betrayed his ancestry only by a certain robustness of neck. The *nouveau riche* was plentiful. And he, whose father had sat at the foot of the table in the old farm-house, might now boast of his butler and his expensive cook, and all the other details of the fashionable life, which were pretty much then what they are now ; while he whose fathers had sat at the head as lord and master might be living in lodgings—as Sulla did.

For Sulla sprang of the great Cornelian house whose origin went back, not to any equivalent of a Norman Conquest, but to an age of gods and heroes, lost in an infinite antiquity. He belonged to the branch called Rufinus, which, some century and a half before, had acquired instead the name Sulla. Lucius Cornelius Sulla was his full name. And he indeed lived in lodgings, though the magistracies of Rome, from the beginning, had been filled by innumerable Cornelii.[1]

V

But first of Sulla himself as a person. If his portrait be authentic, be belonged to the same Roman type as Julius Caesar—the old Roman aristocratic type, which was as distinctive as the Norman. Any one who walks down the gallery of busts of Roman emperors in the British Museum may obtain a profitable lesson in some historical facts. They are, most of them, to a modern eye, extraordinarily wide in the face. Perhaps the type culminates in Nero, whose broad jaw and upturned chin are startling in their peculiarity and distinctness. It was the typical face of the Roman governing class in the days when the old aristocracy was dying out, or dead. Nero was of the plebeian family Domitius. Walk on a step or two to the end of the gallery. There, last of all the busts, stands that of the founder of the empire, Gaius Julius Caesar. And it is far more startling than Nero's—but in this case because of its human splendour. The head is vast, a gigantic brain-case, magnificently modelled, above a face thin, finely boned, aquiline of nose, with a small firm jaw and a large but thin-lipped mouth curled into proud repose. Nero's face gives one the impression of a human soul struggling dim through the mountainous tyranny of appetite and

[1] Of 140 patrician consuls between 366 B.C. and 173 B.C., 30 (equivalent to 21·3 per cent) were Cornelii. The Valerii, who came next, were somewhat less than 13 per cent.

physical dominance. Caesar's looks out as through
a mask of crystal. Every line of it speaks of power,
refinement, and quietude. It may (we do not know)
have been the most splendid of its kind. It was
certainly almost the last of its kind.

Sulla belonged to that type. He had the same
shape of brain-case, immense in capacity, yet beautifully moulded—the same fine, silky hair, very slightly
wavy ; fairer than Caesar's, which was reddish.
Sulla's mouth was smaller, and instead of the passion-
less repose of Caesar, the ghost of a sad wounded
spirit haunts the lips. The lower lip is thicker.
The Creator of mankind has not struck off many
faces nobler than these. . . . The modelling
throughout is remarkably decisive. Compare the
portrait of Lucius Lucullus, who was of a plebeian
family. Lucullus had a kindly and pleasant mouth ;
he had no particular sort of nose, and no particularly striking head ; his flesh is dimpled where
Sulla's, like Caesar's, is hewn in smooth definite
planes. Men of the type of Nero made much
money, and were powerful men ; but the men like
Sulla and Caesar conquered the world.

VI

The complexion of Sulla raises some curious
questions. It was a prominent fact to his contemporaries ; they have handed down express notice
of the peculiarity of his appearance ; and yet,
whether through delicacy or carelessness the description is not sufficiently definite to tell us what it was.
It cannot have been the well-known symptom of
cardiac disease, for Sulla was a very vigorous and
active man, who lived to a good age and died of
something very different. The overwhelming prob-

ability is that he was disfigured by a birth-mark.
If so, it scarred his soul as well as his body. Every
one who knew Sulla knew that he was oddly incalculable, liable to fits and starts of sudden resentment—
capable of cruelty, yet easily moved to tears—until
those who recorded his actions did not know whether
he were a good-humoured man who was sometimes
vindictive, or a vindictive man who was usually
cheerful. He certainly had the touch of perversity
which (as in the case of Byron) is apt to belong to
those who are irresistibly conscious of carrying a
peculiarity they hate. The atrocities of the sack
of Athens probably owed much to certain Greek
verses chanted on the wall, reflecting on Sulla's
appearance : he wiped out the insult in blood which
ran out of the city gates. Some of his incalculable
cruelties may have turned on a self-conscious expression, an unwise stare, a betrayal of noticing that
which was not to be noticed. If he worshipped
Pompeius, it was partly because Pompeius had all
the silly perfection of which Fortune had deprived
Sulla. . . . We know the nature of men. The
great Julius himself was ashamed of being bald.

VII

The lodgings in which Sulla lived during his
early days were tenements obeying the economic
law governing all great cities. The influx of the
wealthy sent up the price of land and houses ; so for
those of modest means there arose great blocks of
flats, floor upon floor, suitable for all purses. The
ancient Romans called them " insulae "—islands.
They were probably ugly, and certainly uncomfort-
able. In later centuries, when Rome had been
greatly improved, the traffic was deafening by day,

GENEALOGY OF L. CORNELIUS SULLA FELIX

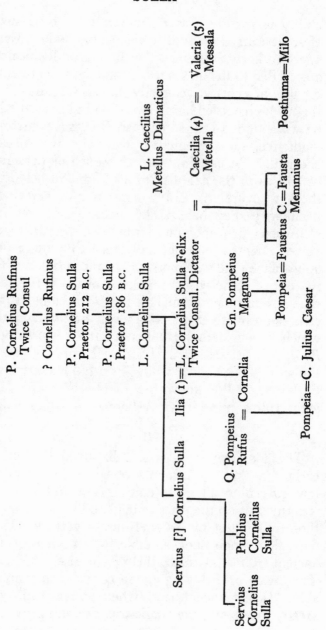

and the vehicles which were not allowed to enter
during the day, made sleep an impossibility at night.
Gaius Gracchus, as befits a reformer, voluntarily
occupied a house in one of the humbler districts ;
but Sulla's domicile had the additional discomfort
of necessity. He could not even boast of being a
" Settlement." He was that most embittering of
things—an out-at-elbows aristocrat.

Sulla paid £26 a year for a flat in the lower floors :
having for neighbour overhead a freedman who paid
£17. The authority for this is not Sulla but the
freedman, who, when in later years thrown off the
Tarpeian Rock for concealing political offenders,
publicly called attention to his old acquaintance with
the Dictator. Sulla possibly did not enjoy the recol-
lection ; or possibly (as so often happens) he had
old scores to wipe out with his neighbour overhead ;
for at any rate the reminder did not save the freedman. It is a pity that we do not know his name, and
have not the benefit of his further recollections.
Who called upon Sulla in those days ? How did he
occupy his time ? What had the freedman to put
up with, in the way of bachelor parties ? We do
not know. We only know that Sulla was a poor man
of aristocratic descent, who lived in obscure lodgings
while laying the first foundations of his career.

VIII

That career must, of course (if it were to exist
at all), be political and military. No other was
open to a man of noble birth, unless he chose to
declass himself : no other was conceivable. But
to begin it, money was necessary, and Sulla had
none. His family had never been rich. Only one
of his ancestors had reached the highest honours

—Publius Cornelius Rufinus,[1] who had been consul.
But disaster had overtaken Publius. He had been
convicted by the censors of possessing more than
ten pounds of silver plate above the legal maximum,
and had been expelled from the Senate. His
family, burdened with this scandal, had continued
more or less in proud obscurity. Sulla, however,
had lived it down, we may believe. It is not likely
that he retained any silver plate : and besides,
public opinion was changing. Silver plate, even in
large quantities, was no longer regarded as altogether
scandalous.

But as to the funds necessary for beginning a
career, Sulla had been blessed with striking rather
than engaging looks : he was not like his friend in
later life, the young Pompeius, from whom Flora,
the courtesan, could never part without biting him.
Nobody ever wanted to bite Sulla, save in the way

[1] P. Cornelius Rufinus was consul in 290 B.C. with the famous
Manius Curius Dentatus : fought in Samnite wars, and was
granted a triumph : consul again in 277 B.C. : fought the Samnites and South Italian Greeks, and captured Croton. He was
expelled from the Senate in 275 B.C. on the grounds alleged by
the Censors G. Fabricius and Q. Aemilius Papus. His grandson
was the first to assume the name " Sulla."
These particulars have suggestiveness in view of the career
of his descendant. M. Curius Dentatus, moreover, was a
grand old Roman—a hard-bitten fighter and countryman, whom
the Samnite ambassadors found sitting over his hearth roasting
turnips. He told them that he preferred ruling over men who
possessed gold, to possessing it himself. He also built the old
Anio aqueduct, and drained the lake Velinus, thereby first
creating the falls of Terni. If Sulla possessed any ancestral
images, he may often have surveyed Publius Rufinus with interesting side thoughts about his eminent colleague, who resembled
in many respects an even more famous contemporary of Sulla's
own.

of unkindness. The deficiency needed to be made good, and the obvious way was by cultivating a charm that should compensate, as it so often does, for lack of beauty. And who so liable to fall victims to charm without beauty as those with neither ?— especially when aristocratic birth is thrown in to weight the scale.

Sulla therefore began his career by paying court to a rich plebeian lady who was not accepted in the best society. Without the details, now lost, we can reconstruct her in imagination : probably plain, possibly deeply interested in occultism and the contemporary forms of spiritualism and higher thought : delighted to find a poor but proud youth of high descent, who listened patiently and never failed with the appropriate compliments. It may have been then that Sulla first discovered his Fortune, his occult friend. . . . He never failed in any of his serious undertakings, and this must have been a very serious one. . . . In due time the lady Nicopolis died, leaving Sulla heir to the whole of her fortune. We may believe that Sulla promptly moved out of his £26 flat, and that the freedman on the floor above saw him no more as a neighbour.

Sulla's father (of whom we know little else, though the indications point to a somewhat Micaw-berish person) was also co-operating in building up the family fortunes. He married again, and this time made a wealthy match. Sulla made him-self so agreeable to his stepmother that " she loved him as if he were her own son " : and when she died, he was found to be her heir. The foundations of a career were now, from a business point of view, thoroughly well laid. Sulla had the means

C

necessary for advancement : that is, for life, adventure, the society of his equals, and whatsoever Fortune could perchance add to these.

The essence of Sulla's quality is shown in these early incidents. He had the gift, when he chose to exercise it, of attracting real affection. . . . This is a gift not always meant to be exercised for its own sake. In later life he used it to control a fierce mercenary soldiery and to get his way with difficult and dangerous men ; but he first practised the art, as most men do, with women.

IX

But he had his disinterested interests. While he was being thus acceptable in appropriate quarters, he was cultivating others which were acceptable to him. He never tired, even as an elderly man, of the more Bohemian side of things. He thoroughly enjoyed the company of immoral persons of both sexes. He maintained a lifelong friendship with Metrobius, the actor, and was deep in the company of dancers, mimes, and actresses. The testimony to Sulla's looseness of life is sufficiently emphatic, for it to be recorded as a fact ; but it is a fact of which we cannot estimate the precise value. We are not told, nor is there any evidence, that he was an indiscriminately loose person ; the gravamen of the charge is that he mixed much, and very intimately, on cordial and kindly terms, with people of the stage.

No doubt he took their colour and shared their code of manners, which have never coincided with those of the more austere sections of the community. Besides this, he must have shared their interests. He may well have known them first when he had nothing to offer them except appreciation and friendship ; and if actors are alike in all ages, he may in those days have owed them more than they owed him. He was certainly a good amateur singer, and wrote comedies of his own for private performance.

A deep and genuine passion for the stage is consistent with the rest of his character. Possibly it appealed to some part of his mind which craved for it as a necessity ; there may have been some hunger in him for the artistic perfection of impersonation, the dramatic completeness of episode, which nothing else could give. The art of the stage has qualities which bring it nearer the sympathies of the man of action than the cool, contemplative, static art of the sculptor or painter, Many of Sulla's ways of thought and action suggest (as we shall see later) something of this interest in the theatre. A dozen times in his life he solved the problem of a difficult situation by a bold dramatic improvisation ; he certainly had a flair for a good " curtain." The question is even suggested, whether the Sulla Felix, from whom we shall part at the end of this book, were not, to some extent, a dramatic invention.

The proof that Sulla's life was a loose one is found, not in any testimony, but in his own character. He was obtuse on some points of conduct, in a way which shows that he had dulled his fineness of perception. He was five times married ; his first two wives, Ilia and Aelia, of whom little is known, may be mentioned as belonging to his early life. His three later marriages all have some anecdote attaching to them, illustrative of some inherent quality in him which struck even his contemporaries as being

open to criticism. And there were other incidents
bearing on the same point. Nothing that has been
recorded of him shows the spirit of his great successor, Gaius Julius Caesar, who refused to divorce
one wife for political reasons, and of another,[1]
whom he did divorce, made the famous remark :
" Caesar's wife should be above suspicion " : which,
whether perfectly sincere or not, illuminates the
mental attitude of the man who made it.

X

Sulla was, therefore, a man of double nature :
a Roman aristocrat, with all the hereditary qualities
of power and leadership, which his hard-bitten
ancestry had given him, built into the fabric of his
character : but a different kind of man dwelt in
the fabric—a cultivated, emotional man, who loved
an emotional art, and mixed with unconventional
people, and did unorthodox things [2] : and this
second man was human, cheerful, vainglorious,
easily moved by imagination, cynically witty, almost
childishly hopeful. These two sides to his mind
were not antagonistic, so far as action was concerned ; indeed, so far from warring together, they
co-operated in building up his amazing career and
his striking personality. But there was a certain
sphere where the two did clash and become irrecon-
cilable. It became visible only towards the close
of his life, when events were moving to their dramatic
consummation, and death and judgment (at least,

[1] She was Sulla's own granddaughter, Pompeia. See
Genealogy, p. 30.
[2] He was a good Greek scholar, just as in modern times
similar tastes would make it probable that a man would know
French.

the judgment of mankind) were at hand. It
probably did not affect his youth.

There are all kinds of avenues to success, and
many kinds of success. It depends on the man,
and on suiting the means to the end. It may
come through hard work, or dexterous steering
through troubled waters ; but it may (given the
kind of man) come through a studied negligence,
an almost careful carelessness, a wise drift with
angry currents. Such a course suited Sulla very
well. We know that in after years he never reckoned
too closely. He gave full scope to the operations
of that force which men call chance, or luck, or
fortune ; his task was to grasp opportunities rather
than to create them. We know that—as the story
will show—he could not only act promptly, but
wait patiently. It is an easy deduction that he
went by this rule from the first : if anything, we
may infer that he avoided long plans and rigidly
fixed projects, preferring to let the drift of things
carry him passively until the chance of action came
into view. This would explain why, when he first
appears upon the scene as a political person, he
has power and influence without the snare of attach-
ments. He had spent his time in the simple task of
becoming socially accepted.

There was discernment in this. Men—any men,
all men, but especially rich and official classes—
distrust ideas and plans. They just as instinctively
trust those who do what every one else does, without
putting forth any set projects or noticeable bias.
Hence, as soon as he had the means to enter their
circle, Sulla became gradually known to all the men
of his class : they met him, did business with him,
caroused with him, knew his secrets, and let him

know theirs, for he was one of them. Nor could
Sulla have forged that passport to acceptance.
He was indeed one of them. His protective
coloration was genuine enough.

XI

But let us note that Protective Coloration with
closer attention. If he conformed to type, was it
from the same motives as his friends ? We may
doubt it. Their conformity sprang from ignorance.
They knew nothing—neither what they did, nor the
approaching results of their deeds—and accordingly
few of them survived the days shortly to come.
There were probably not many who could have distinguished between the outward form and the inward
nature of aristocracy : most would have thought
the distinction a dangerous one to make. Sulla's
conformity was not from ignorance but from
indifference. When we have traced to the end the
career he was now about to begin, we shall see
that his respect for forms (and he did respect them)
was intelligent and qualified : he never hesitated
to break through them when he thought fit ; and
his conduct in this respect compels us to believe
that he had the power of distinguishing between
the spirit and the letter, though possibly his judgment was not infallible. A man with this power
will never violate forms wantonly, without cause.

At the beginning of his career it is clear enough
that he did not wantonly transgress them. He
drifted with the current so unobtrusively that even
when his career was well advanced, his contemporaries did not realise him for what he was. He
seemed so very ordinary a person that they were
inclined perhaps to deprecate his first extraordinary

successes. He was not considered quite a fitting match for Caecilia Metella, though old Metellus, who is not likely to have been a bad judge in these matters, evidently thought otherwise.

To this extent, of course, Sulla was an opportunist : but his principles forbade him to be otherwise. The instinctive suspicion, which clung to Gaius Julius Caesar all his life, that he had some deep consistent plan in his mind, and some far-seen objective continually in view—this suspicion never attached to Sulla. And the reason for this was that Caesar, by the nature of the case, really had such a consistent plan, whereas Sulla, on principle as well as by temperament, had none, for a man who is intending to initiate a new departure in policy needs to have that policy very clearly formulated in his mind, while a man who merely wishes to renew, reform, and conserve, requires only to seize favourable moments—he will be a devotee of Fortune.

And such a devotee Sulla was. He was destined to go from one incident to another—each a dramatic surprise and each a stirring episode ; and when he came to look back, he could see a connection and coherence that struck his intelligence as being rational. But when at last he towered immense and dominating over the Roman world, he had only one explanation to give his contemporaries and posterity. Something other than himself had put him there.

It was Fortune.

CHAPTER II

THE ANTECEDENTS OF SULLA'S WORLD

I

SULLA'S world was composed of a very ancient and highly developed civilisation—known to us as " Mediterranean "—which after many vicissitudes had arranged itself round the dominant spirit of Rome.

The difference between modern and ancient civilisation has often been described : ancient civilisation was based upon the City State, while modern civilisation is based upon the Nation. It was as difficult for men in that age to think politically, apart from the city, as it is for us to imagine away the nation as the unit of political life. The point of importance about Rome in a political sense is that she represented the final stage of the City State, and she formed, in her later ages, the transitional step from the city to the nation. Her history has a particular interest for us on this ground alone, even if we neglect its many other claims upon our attention. It is worth while to review the development of Rome, both in order to illustrate the career of Sulla, and in order to envision the precise nature of the experiment he made.

II

A fair conception of what a City State was, can be formed by observing the ancient earthworks which still survive on the hills throughout England. Their purpose at once suggests itself : they were places of refuge in war time for the primitive tribes who occupied the district. There is an almost continuous chain of links between the " British Camps " and such cities as Athens and Rome. These fortifications, first stockaded and then walled, formed centres at which grew up the first activities of men as they emerged from the purely tribal bonds of blood-kinship to the condition of political and economic relationship in which the connection is one of mutual interest rather than of common origin. This is what we mean by a " political " state of any kind : one in which interest, not blood-relationship, is the nexus between men.

The earliest form of government was tribal, usually circling round the headship of the Father, who was King and Priest in one. In Asia he was frequently more priest than king ; in Europe, rather more king than priest. Families multiplied and branched ; tribes joined in alliance for common purposes : the " father " became a somewhat formal and official kind of father ; the pressure of business separated kingship and priesthood ; " tribes " became, by the legal expedients of adoption and ascription, mere technical expressions. Since there was adequate protection, the fortified township naturally became a market, as we see in the Middle Ages. Some failed in the struggle for existence, and remained the turfed mounds and ditches, the mysterious walls we still see ; others succeeded in unequal degrees. And, as frequently happens, those which were first in the field were often beaten by the late-comers. The cities of Mesopotamia rose early into wealth and influence, with the result that they never grew free of a certain primitive stamp. Their governments remained archaic in type, while the cities of Greece developed advanced conceptions of politics which allowed greater social progress. But still the unit of politics remained the city. Any government was conceived of as the government of a city; a citizen was literally a citizen—the freeman of a municipality.

III

But the development of wealth, art and intelligence which was rendered possible by the political city state, instead of making men permanently content, revealed to them further potentialities of still vaster development if the comparatively narrow scope afforded by the city could be extended by the creation of larger political units. For very many centuries the problem of creating such larger units seemed insoluble to the statesman. When tentatively created, nothing would make them stable.

The rise of the Greek cities ought to have found its logical consummation in the empire of Alexander the Great, but from various causes Greek political conceptions proved unequal to the task of expanding the City State to form a larger political unit. Alexander's empire proved to be founded on a political basis insufficient to sustain it ; the organisation was weak, the discipline immature, and the great empire broke up again into chaos. It might well have been wondered then, as it has been wondered since, " whether the human animal, as he exists at present, is capable of solving the social problems raised by his own aggregation."

But those attempts which are enforced on men by real necessities are not abandoned after one failure, nor two. They are repeated, through the steady pressure of the necessity, until the result is at last achieved. The fundamental condition required for success was not mere genius, nor sheer will, but the creation of a political organism strong enough to stand the strain of widely extended government without being disrupted.

Rome evolved a political organism sufficiently strong for this purpose. She was the first state to do so.

IV

When Rome first emerges into the dawn of its history, the City State was already beginning its last phase. There was a widespread movement throughout the European cities : everywhere the ancient kingly system of government, older than Egypt and Babylon, was giving way before a new conception. The change was at first one of mental attitude. The State began to be conceived of, not as a single authority, issuing its commands without responsibility, and interpreting an unalterable and divine law, but as a composite authority whose commands were arrived at by the negotiation of the various classes or elements which constituted it. In the Hellenic cities a series of principles was put into practice long before they could be defined or understood. Authority was questioned, and its nature analysed ; methods of political creation were investigated. It was not an accident that the Greeks, as the most enterprising commercialists of the age, had an interest in the development of free and secure intercourse. Political and economic speculation naturally go hand in hand.

The State therefore tended to follow the economic

interests of men—it went into the market-place,
whither kings had some difficulty in following it.
Government became a public matter. The Romans
had a word for it which we still, with a difference,
retain—*respublica*. A torrent of political experiment began to flow through the European cities.
Most of it failed—some of it tragically, some of it
brilliantly, but perhaps none of it fruitlessly. There
is no reason to disbelieve the tradition that the
Romans noted, and learnt from the Greek experience. The soundness and correctness of many of
their measures hint that they were not acting
altogether in the dark. We have here only to
consider the experiment which finally succeeded—
that of Rome.

v

It was perhaps an advantage to the political
development of Rome that her last kings were
foreigners—Etruscans whose expulsion was as much
a patriotic as a political reaction. The Romans
were no exception to the rule that the City States
which went over to the new form of government
were marked henceforth by a deep, ineffaceable,
most bitter hatred of kings. But the issue had
been so far obscured that the reaction spent itself
on the personal character of the last of the kings,
rather than on the policies they embodied. The
kings left the plebeians an organised power in the
State, capable of negotiating as a solid body with
the patricians who claimed to be the only true and
original Roman citizens. Later ages attributed this
organisation of the plebeians to the last King but
one, Servius Tullius. It turned the patricians,
from being the true and only Roman citizens, into

a special class of Roman citizens—it made them an aristocracy.

Throughout the City States influenced by the new movement, the determining motive was a desire for greater freedom of action. The aristocracy—always a rigidly conservative force—could not forgive the king's betrayal of tradition, his concessions to the plebeians, and felt that they could fight that battle better alone ; while the plebeians—who were not wrongly described as a party of innovation—no doubt justly felt that the abolition of kingship was the irrevocable confirmation of the breach with tradition ; and they trusted to themselves to hold their ground against the aristocracy. Hence Rome started not with the victory of one tendency over the other, but with both the old tradition and the new aspirations fully represented in her political life. The change abolished the king without abolishing his power. The power was transferred intact to two elected magistrates who held office for one year. As both were absolute, each had a complete veto on the actions of his colleague ; they could act only when agreed, and they had to answer for their acts when, at the end of their year of office, they laid down their government, and divested themselves of the protection it conferred. They had the power of nominating a Dictator in times of public emergency, who held the whole regal power : but his period of office expired with theirs. It is hardly possible to combine all the advantages of every system of government more neatly than by the institution of annual Consuls. Had Rome remained, from that day to this, exactly the same city which elected the first Consuls, Consuls might be ruling her yet.

An institution does not fall or change necessarily from weakness ; it may simply be outgrown, or may become inapplicable. Rome did not, and could not, remain permanently the same city. She fought the Etruscans ; she formed a new league of Latin cities to strengthen her position : excited jealousy and distrust : was sacked and burnt by the Gauls, while her allies supinely stood by : rebuilt her city, and for her own protection transformed the Latin League into a complete system of dependence upon Rome. It was a question of going forward or going under ; and no race of men ever clung to life with more unbending obstinacy than the Roman. Constant war meant the frequent calling out of the citizen army ; and the strain fell hardest on the least rich. Ten years after the abolition of the kings, the plebeians revolted, and left the city in a body. This was the famous " Secession to the Sacred Mount." It had prompt effect. The aristocracy listened to reason.

The complaints of the plebeians were simple : they amounted, in sum, to this, that the power of the consuls was unfairly used to the prejudice of the plebeians, who were subjected to the main stress of military service while possessing the least resources to meet it : while the patricians so domin- ated the electoral assembly that they could prevent any plebeian control over the magistrates. The reforms accordingly arranged were so remarkable as to deserve attention. The aristocracy did not compromise on its own main principle—its control of executive government—but it gave the plebeians what amounted to an absolute and unlimited pro- tection against the abuse of its power. The plebeians were granted the legal right to elect two inviolable

magistrates—tribunes—who had the power of veto-
ing any administrative action of the consuls. They
had no other power of any sort. They had purely
and simply this negative right of an absolute veto
upon the acts of the executive.

The essential nature of the political conflict
between the aristocracy and the plebeians was from
beginning to end of this kind. The aristocracy
aimed at preserving in their own hands the power
of *action*. The plebeians hardly disputed this
right : they sought to protect themselves against
the *abuse* of the power of action. Out of this
conflict arose a number of important by-products.

VI

It soon became evident that the power of the
tribunes was not, in itself, sufficient for the purpose
for which it had been designed. A mere right of
veto, while perfectly effective up to a certain point,
left some spheres almost untouched. One of these
was the sphere of law.

The early law of Rome was what we know, in
mediaeval history, as " customary law " : it was
a law of pure tradition, handed down verbally
from father to son among the original Roman
clansmen. Every tribune of the plebs was liable
to be entangled in the endless intricacies of a web
which must often have nullified the effects of his
veto. The plebeians therefore demanded the
definite fixing of this elusive web. After a vigorous
struggle they carried their claim : the law was
investigated by a commission, the Decemvirate,
and its main heads codified and published on twelve
tablets which were fixed up in the Forum for all
men to see.

But to touch the law was to change the nature of the struggle.

The plebeians were organised in tribes that were little more than legal fictions for convenience of administration. But the patricians were genuine tribesmen, and their law was tribal law which governed their own corporate life as well as the Roman State. To fix, define and codify this law, even in part, was to set a precedent for the State to interfere with other significant aspects of it—in fact, to control the aristocracy. Hitherto the aristocracy had not admitted that the plebeians were Roman citizens in the full sense : they had dealt with them as if they were a separate community— as in fact they were—with which the aristocracy negotiated as with a foreign nation. The plebeian had no right to hold a magistracy, and therefore could not enter the Senate : more, a plebeian could not contract a legal marriage with a patrician. . . . The richer plebeians—the financial and mercantile men—had hitherto stood by their brethren faithfully ; they now obtained their reward.

The impossibility of intermarriage was the first to go. It became at last possible for the descendants of a plebeian to enter the patrician circle, and to inherit the property and privileges of a patrician parent. The way was thus paved for something more. In the same year the first proposal was made to legalise the election of plebeians to the consulship. It was successfully resisted : but the aristocracy conceded the election of Military Tribunes with consular power. That they foresaw the possibility of plebeian success is proved by the institution of the Censorship, by which the power of revising the lists of Senators was removed from the Consuls and given to elected Censors who must be patricians. The task of the Censors was to fill up periodically the vacancies of the Senate, and to remove from its ranks those who were not qualified for their position. They became, by degrees, peculiarly important magistrates, by whose action the Senate was constantly watched and kept under the control of the aristocracy.

For nearly fifty years the plebeians never succeeded in gaining election to the Military Tribunate. Seventy-nine years passed before they won, after a determined struggle of ten years, not only the right of election to the consulship, but the legal right that one consul should always be a plebeian. Another sixty years passed, at the end of which the plebeians were politically on an entire equality with the patricians. The Consulship, the Dictatorship—every magistracy whatever of any political value—became open to them. By the year 300 B.C. the aristocracy had ceased to exist as a political fact. The equalisation of the orders was complete.

Nor was this all. By degrees the Assembly of the plebeians, in which the Tribunes were elected, had become the legislative assembly of the Roman State. It is almost true to say that the plebeians had won not merely political equality but political supremacy. The aristocracy had become a tradition —a number of families still united by sympathy and custom, but no longer politically privileged. Plebeians were enabled to take magisterial office, to pass into the Senate, to hold and enjoy any dignity they thought it worth while to occupy. On the other hand, the old aristocracy had no share in the legislative Assembly, which was still wholly composed of plebeians.

Several points are to be noticed in this process.
First, it was a steady process which occupied fully
two hundred years. Secondly, it was accomplished
without bloodshed or civil war, by almost purely
peaceful means. The Secession to the Sacred
Mount was the nearest approach to organised
violence that took place, and it was, as far as we
know, utterly bloodless. We can give no higher
praise to any people than to say that such political
changes as these took place without violence.

VII

We have no means of knowing precisely what
private hopes and fears men had of the possible
results of these changes : but whatever they may
have been, the real consequences probably were not
what any one expected : certainly not what we
should expect, if we were ignorant of the results
that actually followed. The plebeians neither over-
turned the State, nor did they enter upon a long
millennium of peaceful industry in which every man
dwelt in content under his own vine and fig-tree.
The old aristocracy neither disappeared, nor lost
its practical power. On the contrary, it proved
that the possession of political privileges is unnecessary to an aristocracy which knows its business : a discovery of the utmost importance. The
magisterial offices continued to be filled by a long
succession of aristocratic candidates : the plebeians
who gained office merged into the old aristocracy,
took its colour, adopted its ways and habits, and
imitated its character. The men who, in the year
300 B.C., may have gone home in despair, anticipating
the early ruin of the State, lived to see Rome no
longer fighting with the enemy at the door, but

mistress of Italy and supreme in dominance. The very young men who, in that year, may have rejoiced in the advent of freedom, may have lived to see, as very old men, what was to Romans " The Great War," the catastrophe which marks a dividing line in Roman history.

That war was the Second Punic War—the war of Hannibal : the grand test to which the Roman State, the fruit of two hundred years of political struggle, was now to be submitted. Rome had fought down her Italian enemies, planted colonies of military settlers in their midst, and established a hegemony over the Italian City States—a system of alliances of which she was the head. What she had so far created was not a new form of State, but a league of States, who all submitted their external relations to her guidance. The process brought the Romans into contact with the great Semitic power of Carthage, then the commercial centre of the western world, and the mistress of the seas.

Thus far, then, Rome had done nothing that Athens had not done ; for the Confederacy of Delos and the Athenian empire were just such things as this. But now a trial was to be made, not of the external aspect of the Roman hegemony, but of its inward quality. The Spartans had shaken down the Athenian empire. A greater man than Lysander now advanced to shake down the Roman.

The Hannibalic war is strangely revealing. We may be misled as to the detailed facts of the story of the Roman constitution, and the personalities who built it up, but we cannot be far wrong as to the manner of men who fought Hannibal. To the irresistible force of a man of military genius as great as Alexander or Napoleon, the Romans opposed the immovable object of unbending resist-ance. Never, perhaps, before or since, has the virtue of mere unbendingness been shown on so huge a scale, or carried to such a degree. For ten years the Romans hardly fought a battle they did not lose. For ten years Hannibal was victorious whithersoever he went—victorious in a demoralising, disheartening way, as if he had only to look at a Roman army in order to beat it. The Roman defeats included two—Lake Trasimene and Cannae —which were first-class disasters, either of which might have been the downfall of any ordinary State. One of the most brilliant individuals known to history pitted his power against the moral quality of a ring of rather commonplace men ; but the commonplace men stood the punishment and lasted out the war. They kept up their hearts against the enemy abroad, and they kept their tempers with one another at home. When the Senators, after Cannae, solemnly met the surviving consul, Varro—the man directly responsible for the defeat, and their political enemy—to thank him " for not despairing of the State," they carried mere patience and public spirit to the height of moral heroism.

The formidable men who showed that spirit were the descendants of those who, through two centuries of embittered struggle, shaped the Roman State without a revolution, without civil war, without, finally, any permanent scar of partisan hatred.

If the Roman State, so composed and reconciled in its parts, could not be broken by Hannibal, neither could he disrupt the great league of cities of which Rome was the head. The political organisation of Rome remained perfectly intact.

When the Hannibalic war was over, Rome had not merely survived, she had increased. She had reduced Carthage to the level of a provincial town, had acquired Spain and part of Gaul, and was watching the conduct of the exiled Hannibal in Asia. She had proved that, whether or not her political system were as ideal as the Athenian, it had one virtue that the Athenian did not possess : it could live.

Rome had invented something as wonderful as printing or steam, or tool-steel or wireless telephony : a State that could resist any known force. And from that time onward the politics of the City States of the Mediterranean basin, many of them far older, maturer, and more cultivated than Rome could claim to be, surrendered to the superior politics of Rome.

VIII

The Second Punic War was a grand turning-point in her career. The price she paid for victory determined her future.

The war fatally damaged the class of small farmers who hitherto had been the main substance of the Roman people and their Italian allies. It had swept them away in hundreds of thousands, and devastated their lands by fire and sword. Those who survived were in many cases crippled by debt. Much land went back permanently into uncultivable wilderness. The failure of the Roman State to comprehend the nature of what had happened to it is the central failure of Roman civilisation—the grand test which it failed to pass. Those who had capital bought up the small farms and ran them by slave-labour, a form of enterprise which grew ever

more profitable : and through the competition of
the great slave-worked estates, both at home and
in the provinces, the small farmer was still further
damaged. The new land-holders were soon so
thoroughly established, and so powerful in virtue of
their possessions, that they dominated both the
political and the economic side of Roman life.

We must not confuse this fact with the quite
different idea that Roman agriculture was decaying.
Economically, Rome was improving : cultivation
was better, production greater. The old Rome,
struggling with its constitution and with the Samnite,
had been a poor, ignorant, backward State, not for
a moment to be compared with the Rome into
which poured all the fruits of conquest—the science
and art of the Greeks, the trade of the East, the
cheap and muscular slave-labour of all the lands of
the Mediterranean. What had happened to Rome
was not an economic, but a political disaster. Her
citizens of all classes were diminishing in numbers
under the stress of war, and were being separated
from the agriculture which had been the source of
their strength. The rich landowners of the Senatorial class, and the rich capitalists of the middle
class, were rapidly becoming richer ; at last they
became intoxicated with the wealth that flowed
into their hands. They did not know what to do
with it ; but all seemed well to them while the
stream of riches rose like a torrent in spate.

The stage was now set for a new act in the drama
of Roman history. There were weaknesses in the
Roman which had not, so far, betrayed themselves.
Confronted with concrete necessity, the Roman had
acted : hammered in war, he had borne punishment
with unflinching endurance. And now he was to

be hammered no more ; no concrete necessity was
to spur him to action ; he was to stand, as it were,
in a void, in which he must act upon intelligent
principles of right, without compulsion. . . . And
a kind of prolonged pause fell over the Roman
world. . . . No man acted in a way corresponding
to the purely intellectual necessity that had arisen.
It seemed as if the Roman, the most successful of
men, had shot his bolt, and was incapable of adjust-
ing himself to the new circumstances, or of generating
action out of himself.

IX

The man who at last stepped forward—Tiberius
Sempronius Gracchus—had precisely the combination of qualities which marks so many earnest
modern reformers. The gens Sempronia was one
of the wealthy and distinguished plebeian houses
which were now mingling on equal terms with
the old patriciate, and forming the oligarchy which
replaced the old aristocratic government. He himself was one of the most brilliant young men of his
generation, and among the first Romans to be really
influenced by Greek intellectual culture, as distinct
from the pure old Roman tradition. His supporters
were drawn from both elements in the State. In
the struggle he waged, his principal ally was his
father-in-law, the Appius Claudius of the day. It
would have been impossible to hunt out a name
more securely enshrined in the heart of Roman
aristocracy than the Claudian, which was distinguished among the aristocratic families by its
tradition of political intelligence and strongly individual character. An Appius Claudius had been
the chairman of the great commission which codified

the Roman law. Among the sympathisers of
Tiberius was also Publius Mucius Scaevola, the
Pontifex Maximus—the representative of a great
plebeian house, the most famous lawyer of his day,
a mighty ball-player in his youth, and the father of
a jurist even more famous than himself. It is
necessary to recollect this, and to be quite clear
in our minds respecting the origin of the party he
was destined to found. A great gulf separated
him both from the earlier aristocracy, and from the
later popular leaders of the type of Saturninus.

The plan of Tiberius was to restore the small
agriculturist to the soil by enforcing the neglected
law limiting the amount of Roman State-owned
land which could be legally held by any one person ;
and by distributing the consequent surplus among
those citizens who had no land.

The proposal was the signal for dissensions such
as had hardly torn the Roman State before. It was
successfully, and even enthusiastically passed,
though only after a constitutional crisis. Gaius
Octavius, a fellow-tribune, interposed his veto ;
whereupon Tiberius solemnly proposed, carried
and enforced a law deposing any tribune who
should act against the interests of the people.
The reasons he gave for the step were certainly
logical ; but it was a Greek rather than a Roman
kind of logic, and the action was, as we should
phrase it, unconstitutional. It showed a spirit of
haste and impatience in disturbing contrast with
the patience with which the claims of the plebeians
had once been enforced. It was, if nothing else,
a distinct breach with political tradition. More
than this, Tiberius, in order to superintend
the practical execution of his plans, illegally

stood again for the tribunate in the following
year.

When it was clearly seen that his re-election
was a certainty, partisan fury broke all bounds.
Scaevola, who was consul that year, refused to
intervene, so illegality was answered with illegality.
The Senators themselves, under the leadership of
Publius Scipio Nasica, arming themselves with
broken benches, attacked Tiberius and his supporters. Tiberius was clubbed to death : his
body was cast into the Tiber. The spell was
broken : blood had now been deliberately shed in
a political quarrel : and the blood was that of a
man whose purity of character was without speck
or flaw.

If the oligarchy imagined that it had swept away
the proposals of Tiberius Gracchus, it was singularly
mistaken. It had changed nothing, saved nothing,
avoided nothing. His successor was not long in
arriving, in the person of a man even greater than
he—namely, his younger brother, Gaius Gracchus.

X

When Gaius Gracchus, nine years after his
brother's death, came forward as a candidate for
the tribuneship, it was in a very different spirit.
It was no longer merely in order to pass a particular
limited scheme of reform, but with the aim of conducting a constitutional revolution. He first of all
legalised the possibility of the re-election of a tribune.
He re-enacted the laws of Tiberius, extending them
to include a scheme of active re-colonisation both
in Italy and Africa. He then went further, and
introduced two laws whose influence was never to
die out while the Roman State survived.

Of these, one was the institution of the Corn
Dole, by which any Roman citizen was entitled to
a supply of corn at a rate fixed below the market
value. He was, in short, to be entitled to a pension
or subsidy. When the first applicants for the Dole
lined up, it was noticed that an elderly noble,
Lucius Calpurnius Piso, had taken his place in the
queue : but whether the motives of Calpurnius
were political or economic, the fashion did not
spread. Gaius Gracchus intended the impoverished
citizen, who was unable to return to agriculture, at
any rate to have maintenance—and to find it near
the polling booths.

The second was a still more far-seeing measure.
Gaius attracted the support of the moneyed middle
class by removing the control of the law courts
from the Senators to the commercial and financial
men—the *equites*. This was politically a master-
stroke. It based the tribune upon an almost
unassailable foundation. No influence that the
senatorial class could exercise was powerful enough
to overcome a combination between the capitalists
and the reformers.

It may at first sight seem to have been a trifling
concession, hardly calculated to achieve the object
of transferring to the reformers the support of the
moneyed class ; but in the circumstances of Roman
political life the change was revolutionary. Hitherto, the magistrate against whom complaints were
levelled at the expiry of his term of office had been
indicted and tried before juries composed of members of his own class, who shared, generally speaking, his own point of view, which was that of an
Italian landholder legally excluded from trade.
He was in future to be tried before men dominated

by a totally different class of interest—the bankers and merchants whose main financial commitments were in the provinces. The disadvantage to the Senators was considerable. Instead of the indulgent review of their friends (any of whom might have to stand a similar trial) they had to face the inspection of men who cared nothing for their particular difficulties and ideals, and were unaffected by their especial interests. And, on the other hand, the advantage to the *equites* was immense. For the first time the minority of moneyed men, hitherto able to influence government only by constitutional means, were given a leverage on the policy of the provincial governors. He would be a bold man in future whose conduct as an administrator went against the moneyed class.

Gaius Gracchus gave the financiers an equally practical " retainer " for their political support when he dealt with the reorganisation of the Asiatic provinces. Asia was to a large extent a peasant country ; the peasants paid their taxes in kind, in the form of a percentage on their production. These taxes were put up to auction at Rome, and sold to the highest bidder, who could then collect the produce. . . . The exploitation of these taxes was a concession of immense value, which could only be acquired by great Roman financial corporations. As the moneyed men had now the control of the courts, it was little likely that the agents of the corporations could be successfully sued for extortion or any other form of maladministration. Asia was practically handed over to the tender mercies of huge and highly capitalised corporations, while the power of the legal governor was tied hand and foot.

All these measures were blows at the power of the senatorial oligarchy which had hitherto ruled Rome and had murdered Tiberius Gracchus. But some of the less spectacular policies of Gaius gave rise to even greater searchings of heart.

The great Roman roads hitherto had been purely military roads. Gaius put in hand plans for the construction of new roads of a less military type, which, instead of striking straight from one strategic centre to another, should connect the towns and villages of Italy. This was necessary in the interests of the small landholders, who needed easy means of communication by which to put their produce upon the market : for it had been cheaper, up to then, for the Sicilian and African plantations to ship corn to Italy by sea, than for the Italian farmer to transport his produce to Rome. The new roads were a prominent feature of the second tribunate of Gaius Gracchus. They were pushed forward with all the energy of an expert administrator. . . . They had another possibly conceivable object. It became realised that vague schemes of extending Roman citizenship to the Italians at large were likely to find their culmination in a legislative project. The new roads might be the convenient means by which the new voters might gain ready access to Rome.

The mere idea spread panic through the ranks of the oligarchy : and not without reason. The tribunate of Gaius Gracchus showed every sign of becoming a perpetual magistracy, which he would retain indefinitely : he would become a kind of king. He was rapidly transforming the tribunate into an administrative office conducted on the most business-like lines : he was already the centre of a vast network of activity which he carried on with energy and adequacy. If, in addition to the hold he possessed over the Roman voter, and the moneyed men, he were to add myriads of Italians to the electoral roll, the oligarchy could no longer keep any grip over the State. Its days would be over : a vast revolution would have been effected, and Rome would be governed by a perpetual tribune before whom all other magistrates were shadows.

The suggestion was far from being the product of mere partisan enmity. The policy of Gaius did undoubtedly tend to such an end. He felt that it was his duty to avenge the death of his brother ; and the vengeance was to be political. . . . Spurred to some kind of action, the oligarchy attempted to break up the *bloc* which Gaius had formed. The *equites* were too closely involved to be effectually reached, but the Roman voter might be of softer stuff. Besides, the voter was, in a sense, the strategic point to attack, for if once Gaius lost his hold over the electorate, he need no longer be feared. It was therefore to this consummation that the oligarchy directed its counter-attack.

The particular wedge which was used to split the *bloc* was the reforming enthusiasm of Marcus Livius Drusus. We know little in detail of his aims and character, but from that little it is fairly easy to reconstruct the man. He was a wealthy and even an enlightened man, firmly convinced of the advantages of aristocracy, and even of oligarchy, but keenly anxious to remove the scandals which hindered its success as a political force. His friends, who had doubtless often been intolerably bored by his zeal for reform, pushed him forward as a rival to Gaius Gracchus.

The schemes of Drusus, who was not a practical

administrator, far outshone those of Gaius. He proposed to found twelve new colonies, in which provision was to be made for the very poor as well as for the more prosperous class of emigrant : and he proposed that both his own colonies and those of Gaius should be exempt from taxation. The Senate indulgently assented to these measures. Drusus also brought in specific measures to remove the grievances of the Italians, many of whom preferred his programme to the extension (which had its drawbacks as well as its advantages) of the franchise. Even among the Italians, public opinion was as yet far from solid on the question of the franchise, so that an adequate measure for the practical reform of abuses had ample effect in the way of detaching supporters of the Gracchan policy.

The oligarchy secured the election as consul of a man of type widely different—Lucius Opimius, a vigorous reactionary of questionable character. The plans, adroitly laid by some skilful intriguer, matured. Gaius Gracchus failed to secure re-election.

The first step taken by his enemies was the repeal of the law for the founding of the colony of Carthage. At the meeting of the Assembly Gaius appeared in the Forum with a strong band of supporters whose enthusiasm was more certain than their object. They were, at least, there to defend him. Probably every one was excited ; for a person named Antullius, an attendant of the consul, spoke words supposed to be insulting, and made a gesture towards Gaius imagined to be threatening. Antullius was at once slain by the loyal enthusiasts. In his anxiety to disclaim the action of his followers, Gaius illegally interrupted the proceedings of the Assembly. The consul had now ample excuse for action. The city hardly slept that night. A political thunderstorm was about to break over Rome.

Opimius occupied the Capitol with troops, and convoked a meeting of the Senate. It declared a state of emergency, and summoned Gaius, and his lieutenant Fulvius Flaccus, to answer for their actions. They prudently declined. Flaccus urged resistance to what was coming : Gaius had no ardour for any such course. Flaccus, however, entrenched himself on the Aventine, whither Gaius, for safety, accompanied him. Gaius was still anxious to avoid violence, and negotiations continued ; he even proposed to accept the terms offered by Opimius. But on both sides the extremists had gained the upper hand, and neither Gaius nor the more enlightened Senators could make their voices heard. Opimius attacked the Aventine. With the help of Cretan archers the stronghold of the Gracchans was successfully stormed ; Flaccus was hunted down and slain in his hiding-place, while Gaius, who had taken no part in the civil strife, was hurried away by two friends. As he went, he is said to have prayed that the people of Rome, as a punishment for their fickleness, might never be free from their slavery. . . . His prayer—if he ever made it—was fulfilled.

He and his personal servant were found dead together in the grove Furrina. . . . In the proscription which followed, three thousand Gracchans perished by the hand of the executioner. . . . Their crime was rebellion ; their status, that of public enemies outside the pale of the law.

XI

That year, a splendid summer was followed by a warm autumn. The vintage in Italy was a wonder ; the " Opimian wine " became a thing the memory of which lasted for centuries.

XII

If the death of Tiberius Gracchus had broken a spell, that of Gaius marked the first political proscription in Rome. Sentimentality and idealism can be of many kinds. They can attach as easily to the policies of repression as to the policies of reform. It is dangerous, in a civilisation governed by public opinion, to defy that opinion. And the real, though silent, verdict it passed was singularly definite. The Gracchi expanded giant-like into a kind of political apotheosis. Many men paid daily sacrifice to their images. All they had done, all they stood for, became suddenly sanctified and irrevocable. Opimius and Nasica,[1] thinking that they had destroyed the Gracchi, had made them eternal.

The Gracchi were dead. And now their deeds arose and marched.

[1] The fate of both Opimius and Nasica is curious. Nasica, although Pontifex Maximus, and therefore bound to reside in Italy, was sent abroad by his friends in the Senate, on some convenient excuse. He never returned. Opimius (like his father before him, a bad character) became involved in scandals over the Jugurthan war, and was obliged to abscond. He died in poverty in Epirus.

CHAPTER III

SULLA'S WORLD

I

SULLA was seventeen years old in the year in which Gaius Gracchus fell : amply old enough to have known, and even to have seen, those great events which marked the beginning of new and catastrophic days for Rome. The age of seventeen is an impressionable age, at which a young man is occupied, not so much in forming opinions, as in being moulded by impressions which he can neither govern nor repel.

It is likely enough that Sulla saw the great tribune, and knew the familiar stories told of him. Gaius Gracchus had been a new kind of man—almost the first Roman who administered a whole State as an alert and competent business man. Sulla had at any rate the opportunity of seeing, by direct observation, how a purely civic government could be conducted. There were, of course, consuls to watch ; but consuls were mere magistrates, going through a routine that called for no indispensable intelligence. Gaius had been a creative ruler. . . . And ever since Sulla was able to notice anything at all, he had had before his eyes the spectacle of embittered political strife—the hint, the threat, of vast changes—the example of men who swayed multitudes by that subtle art which prevails upon

many obstinate individuals to think and act alike.
He had seen the unreliability of popular support,
the easy way in which the voter can be hoodwinked,
diverted from his allegiance, and caused to sacrifice
his real but remote interests to his immediate but
imaginary ones. The fall of Gaius Gracchus can
hardly have failed to produce on the minds of young
men the impression that it was perilous to base
hopes on the electorate. The people are fickle. A
crop of youthful sceptics must have been the natural
result.

But something deeper was shaken in the minds of
young men by the fall of the Gracchi. Hitherto,
obedience to the law had been a habit, a religion,
even a superstition ; men had contested political
issues, but always—as befitted Romans—within the
bound of law. Now this superstition was exploded,
the religion questioned, the habit broken. Murder,
proscription, and the straining of legal right had
become accepted political weapons. . . . This
Nemesis pursued the oligarchy. It had every reason
to dread force, since it was few in number, and its
power based chiefly on moral prestige ; yet it had
itself invoked force.

II

A young man who merely watches the events of
the day is seldom idle, even though he may be
inactive. He has enquiries to make, curiosity to
satisfy ; he has a whole education to go through,
preparatory for the day when he is at last to act.
And here was a whole world in crisis, providing
ample intellectual food for the musings of any
intelligent youth who required explanations.

It was certain, for one thing, that this Rome, in

which Sulla lived, was especially important ; for she governed the world, and was the only political power capable of moulding and controlling mankind. If she broke down, there was nothing to take her place ; nothing else had demonstrated the possession of sufficient tensile strength to stand the strain. She was civilisation ; but she might be admitted to be an imperfect civilisation. Every one, in Sulla's day, was as full as we are now of a general sense that the condition of the world was unsatisfactory ; and then, as now, the problem was not whether the world were perfect, but in what way it could be improved with any likelihood of success.

In thinking over such a question, a young man in Sulla's position had not only reason to go upon but strong instincts to reckon with. Both converged upon the conclusion that whatever might be the right method of improving the world, it would turn out to be a development and improvement of the Roman system. The Gracchi themselves had never doubted this. . . . But were the lines they had followed the right ones ?

Political reactions are not blind. They have a rationale as much based upon the facts as the policies which provoke them. A great deal could be said against the Gracchi. Some facts were too obvious to be overlooked. Had either of the Gracchi any clear conception of the ultimate developments to which they would be committed ? Their most express fault was an unwillingness to accept the logical consequences of their actions. Granting, for the sake of argument, that they had been right in their methods and aims, they had nevertheless shrunk from the task of safeguarding them. There

was serious weakness in this ; and if their hesitation
proceeded from some secret element of doubt in
their own minds, was it not obvious that to bring
about any improvement a more consistent and
defensible policy must be thought out ? The first
necessary step was the adoption of a severer con-
sistency.

In such a search, however casually it might be
undertaken, a young aristocrat who was repelled
from the Gracchan policy would naturally look with
especial interest at the political tradition of his own
class. It might be the repository of principles
which had been forgotten, but which nevertheless
retained their inherent power. Nor was an aristocrat committed, by such a fancy, to endorsing the
methods of Opimius and Nasica. They and their
foes the Gracchi, alike, were no more than members
of a mixed oligarchy partly descended from plebeian
families. If one went further back, it was possible
to make important distinctions. The failure of the
Gracchi, it might be contended, was due to an inherent weakness in the common people, who produced politically nothing positive, nothing creative ;
and the negative quality in the oligarchy, typified by
Opimius and Nasica, which merely resisted action
without itself generating it, was in all likelihood
derived similarly from a plebeian mentality. Whatsoever was positive seemed to come from the old
aristocracy. This, then, was a clue which might
lead to definite results.

Any one who reviewed the case in the light of such
thoughts could easily criticise the governing class,
and analyse it into component elements of widely
different origin and character. The oligarchy which
ruled Rome in the days of Sulla's youth was by three

great revolutionary epochs removed from the age when the genuine old Roman aristocracy had been supreme. The plebs had entered it in virtue of their wealth and business faculty, bringing with them qualities and instincts by no means necessarily identical with those of the old families. They were a different type of man, bred under different conditions. The essential quality of the old Roman aristocrat had been a grim, austere, unflinching devotion to the community. He observed—and carried sometimes to an almost insane excess—the awful principles of law and discipline. Individualism had been his abhorrence—the cultivation of personal will, of independent being, had been to him as the Great Whore of Babylon to the Puritan. Nothing existed for him but the State. Nothing was impossible to him, when that great principle was invoked. Valour beyond human valour ; firmness beyond the conception of self-indulgent weaklings ; the self-immolation of a martyr—the self-assertion of a confessor : these were the virtues of the authentic patrician. Such at least was the legend he had created around himself. The wealthy plebeians, with their enterprise, their commerce and commercial adaptability, had introduced a streak of weakness into the class they joined. They mimicked, rather than acquired, its characteristics. The oligarchy might be conceived of as only a parody of the aristocracy. It was capable of anything except self-sacrifice.

The old aristocracy had hardly valued itself as a mere aristocracy ; it had not, to any great degree, been conscious of its existence as such. What it had been acutely aware of was the sacredness of the charge it held. It opposed the plebs not because it feared for itself, but because it feared for its charge. When compelled at last, in the public interest, to surrender, it had surrendered without bloodshed, that the sacred charge might be still intact. . . . The oligarchy could not make this distinction. It thought itself the sacred charge : it imagined its own private interests to be the precious thing it had in custody. But a member of the great Cornelian house might be excused for some quickness in perceiving that an Opimius or even a Nasica was under a delusion in such a belief.

This oligarchy, then, was not the old patrician order. The patrician houses were, of course, parts of it ; but the plebeian element was an increasing one. The way was always open to wealth. The older patricians still despised wealth. The younger men, who grew up with Sulla, took rather a different view. They were ceasing to feel that it was necessary to reject riches in the interest of moral example (a state of mind only convenient when one possessed ample landed estates on which to conduct the austere life). For one thing, the moral example did not seem to work ; for another, it was probably much wiser to set an example of the right use of riches. We cannot truthfully say that either Sulla or Caesar was a model to be followed in the right use of wealth ; but it is certainly true that a change for the better came about, and that rich men began to use their money for more beneficial ends. Men like Augustus and Maecenas, and a whole host of lesser men during and after their era, if they did not always accumulate wealth in the best possible way, were nevertheless much more enlightened in its expenditure than those of the age of Lucullus. No man is absolutely disinterested. Their enlightenment may have been enlightened selfishness, but it was enlightenment.

III

The young aristocrat who cast about for political convictions was thus likely to attribute more importance to the peculiar and unique qualification he himself possessed, than to the secondary qualification he might succeed in sharing with rich contractors and successful freedmen—and yet to appreciate the function played in all government by the control of wealth. In the earlier ages of Rome, political power and economic power had been united in the same hands. The political power remained clear and definite in the hands of the public magistrates ; but economic power was slipping into the hands of private and irresponsible persons, and the two forces conflicted. Society was ceasing to have its old solidity, and was becoming divided into rival spheres of power. The instinct of the aristocrat would be to side with the political power.

And for this there were reasons, connected with the conditions under which the two kinds of power were acquired. The range of qualities which, in a highly civilised state, make a man rich, do not certify him to possess the faculty of government. They do not, indeed, deny him the great qualities of an administrator : but we mean something more than this by government and by politics, and to illustrate the point, let us consider the inward construction of the power which gave Rome her dominance.

There are two explanations of the spread and the permanence of Roman rule, or of any rule like it. One is, that it was a tyranny imposed by brute force

on an innocent world. This explanation is very
unlikely, and it is in any case an explanation that
needs further explaining : for how can that brute
force possibly have been evolved ?—and what was
that innocent world like ? There is a second
explanation which, while somewhat more complicated, is the more credible one.

The first element of human morality, which gives
to the other elements the only value they ever can
have, is the power of social co-operation : not merely
mutual help, though that is a necessary corollary,
but the faculty of unswerving loyalty to a common
aim, the gift for being members of a society or
community which is wholly at one—for putting the
benefit of this society before the individual benefit of
its members—the power of blending many human
personalities into a kind of collective personality.
No rule of ordinary morality has any validity or even
any sense, except in the light of this first great law :
and the absolute and binding nature which these
other rules can and do possess is created by the power
they have of riveting men together into this unity.
The whole idea of the Ten Commandments is, that
if we break them, we break the unity of the society.
And if the society is broken, there are but so many
feeble men wandering helplessly on the earth,
instead of standing in the firm strength of their
unity.

And to the degree to which men possess this gift
of association, to that degree is their strength.

Hence the mystery of Roman dominion is only
the fact that certain men (vaguely denominated the
" Romans ") had to a transcendent degree the gift of
association, and that other men had less of it. No
Romans known to us were bigger men or wiser men

than those of other nations. They did not exceed—
nor even equal—the Celt or the German in physical
strength, nor the Greek in intellectual acuteness ;
their one gift was the gift of mutual loyalty. At the
root of Roman dominion was some unbendable,
unbreakable power against which the Celt, the
German, the Greek and the Semite hurled themselves in vain. It was the power of association.

But who were these " Romans " ? The answer
is, that they were the old Roman aristocracy—the
circle of ancient families which had constituted the
first, original Rome, round which the Rome of later
ages had aggregated a concealing mask of derivatory
classes. It was these men who had first possessed
it, and from whom it proceeded. These men—the
Fabii, Valerii, Quintii, and others—were legendary ;
their tales are stories of stern, unswerving devotion.
They had no gift for explaining their virtues vividly
to an admiring world ; they were only partly conscious of those virtues, and what consciousness they
had slipped out, not in the form of rational explanation, but in the form of a fierce pride. Other men
(they seemed to say) were but dogs—" canaille "—
dregs of humanity little above the level of beasts :
they themselves were the men, and the only men.
They bore the Ark of the Covenant, the secret of
all secrets, the holy of all holies—the gift of loyalty.
They were the *Optimates*—the " Best " : best not
in individual brilliance but in collective power.

When, therefore, we see woven into the fabric of
Roman life a thin but all-powerful thread of this
pride, we must recollect that it was not the casual
vanity of a few wealthy speculators recently retired
from successful business. It was not casual ; it
was not vanity ; those who entertained it were often

not wealthy; they were not speculators; their
"business" was that of Scaevola, Cincinnatus and
Camillus. And what they sought to preserve was
the original power out of which everything else in
the Roman State had proceeded.

But the Roman aristocracy was growing thinner
and more attenuated, as every aristocracy does. It
is inherent in the nature of an aristocracy to die
out through the very operation of its own powers.
When Quintus Curtius jumps into the gulf, there
is an end of Quintus Curtius : and hence war,
devotion and self-sacrifice had left the ancient
aristocracy but a leaven in the midst of an oligarchy
of wealthy capitalists striving hard to copy its
virtues, but usually succeeding only in imitating its
vices. . . . But if it could be revived and
strengthened, the State itself would be so far
strengthened.

Here we have a key to Lucius Cornelius Sulla.

IV

We have not exhausted the qualities of the Roman
aristocracy by naming this gift of association. This
indeed came before all else, for without it their
other qualities would have availed little ; but they
had other virtues and powers, which came into
successful operation under its protection.

The Roman aristocratic families were the origin-
ators of even the spirit which resisted them. They
possessed from the first, and never lost, the quite
peculiar and uncommon gift of stamping their own
spiritual impress upon all who were for any length
of time in contact with them : to be near them was
to become like them. How such a gift can be created
we do not know : we only know that certain rare

types of men possess it, and that the Roman patricians did. The political methods invented by the aristocracy educated the Roman people so effectively that they acquired the same characteristics which the aristocracy possessed. Precisely how deep the likeness went might be a matter of opinion. A copy is usually capable of being distinguished from the original. That the likeness existed there can be no question : the question was only of its degree. And this Roman spirit went on spreading, and absorbing alien elements into the fabric of the Roman world, until the aristocracy was lost out of sight under the mass of them. But the aristocracy was still there : still invincibly sure that *it* was Rome—the only Rome that really signified.

The expansion of Rome to wide dominion was thus a perfectly smooth and logical development of the same process that expanded her from a group of villages to a united city. The exclusion of plebeians from government, and the retention of all political rights in the hands of the patricians, was in no way a different kind of fact from the exclusion of Italians and provincials, and the restriction of citizenship to Romans. Once on a time the patricians had been the only Romans ; then the plebeians had gained entrance into the charmed circle ; the Italians now claimed admission ; and the turn of the provincials would come next, as in actual fact it did. The Gracchi, being practical statesmen, had grasped the logic of the position. Rome would always be educating her outer ring of non-citizens up to the standard of citizenship. The process was inevitable.

But (and this was the difficulty !) the results, while they would be the same in their effect upon the minds and interests of men, would not be the same in their effect upon the system of government. There may be a great deal of difference between what is possible, when men live in close neighbourhood, each knowing all by familiar daily contact, and what is necessary when men dwell hundreds of miles apart, and scarcely see one another at all. The similarity of men is produced by their constant association. When they live altogether apart, they naturally diverge and become different. There must accordingly be, in every widely extended State, some artificial point of contact, by which all the parts can be made to conform to a common trend. Lacking this, a large State falls to pieces because of the progressive divergence of its constituent elements.

The consequence was foredoomed. Dimly, in the minds of the ablest men, the necessity began to be felt for some new method, by which the Roman dominion might be given unity. Two solutions were to hand ; but before we discuss them, a third possibility must be noticed.

v

A large class of Roman citizens neither knew nor cared about any such alleged necessity. Their attitude was perfectly simple. The aim of expansion was, in their eyes, exploitation. They organised themselves for the express purpose of exploiting the provinces, without regard for consequences. This aim, as an entirely unpolitical aim, and one that was opposed to political control, brought them naturally into conflict even with the oligarchy. They were, after all, the very men whose interests and ideals had first started the search after the Great State, the large political unit. What index could point out to them the stage at which their policy began to defeat its own ends ? They wished for the advantages of government without its restrictions. Their proceedings gave rise to the appalling series of slave-insurrections which were the scandal of this period of Roman history, and several times imperilled the State. The possibility always existed that these men might succeed in actually destroying the political control of Rome altogether, and in originating a series of independent economic powers. Their policy was self-defeating because they could not maintain even their own position without the frequent intervention of the State ; and their shrift in independence would have been short. But their attempts to dissolve the control of the political State which upheld them were constant. The policy of Gaius Gracchus had increased their power. It is essential to bear in mind the existence and character of these men, for the problem to which they gave rise rapidly became the dominating factor in Roman life.

The age of Sulla bore typical resemblances to the nineteenth century. Then, as later, there had been a great expansion of political control over an immense area of potential wealth ; then, as later, a new class, often of low birth and little education, had come forward to exploit it ; then, as later, the governing class, partly from laziness, partly from a sense of its own private advantage, tolerated proceedings incompatible with sound government. Industrial and financial enterprise, when allowed to run to an unqualified, unrestrained extreme, are always incompatible with sound government. In this case, the extreme in question was connected with the use of slave-labour, and the standard it set. Vast planta-

tions were the order of the day; and we may
sympathise with that much maligned man, Mr.
Legree, when we consider how tenderly, even
sentimentally, compared with the Roman planter,
he treated his human property. The labour was
cheap, and there was plenty of it. It was driven to
the last extremity, scrapped, and replaced. It was
held down by the spy and the torture-chamber.
Every advantage the Roman citizen possessed in the
way of legal privilege was ruthlessly employed to his
own advantage. The influence of the standard so
set up penetrated into every corner of Roman
industrial life. If ever the cry of a wronged,
oppressed, and frustrated humanity rose up to
heaven, it did so in the days of Sulla's youth.
Revolts, however great in scale, could be put down
by the military forces of the government; but who
could prevent the volume of that cry penetrating,
or disturbing, vaguely and worryingly, the deepest
withdrawn mind, as if on some wireless current that
could not be entirely cut out?

VI

Rome was thus the first civilisation which
developed far enough politically to reach a problem
of popular rights. The Greek civilisation did
attain the stage of democracy; but the problem
was badly stated and left unsolved when the Hellenic
world broke up. What Rome had reached in the
early days of Sulla was something much more
important. Greece had merely fought over the
problem whether the sheer human right of the
individual citizen, however poor, should place him
politically on an equality with the rich man of
property. This, however important and interesting,

is a narrow problem. Rome faced the more general question whether a crowd of human beings of all sorts—slaves, freedmen, poor plebeians, impoverished aristocrats, and wealthy men of liberal tendencies—could somehow sway the State against the will of the rich owners of property. If so, how could they do it ? What were the methods ?

The difficulties were very old. For one thing, the rich man has a vast advantage, owing to the weakness of human nature, with its liability to be bought up, to be terrorised, or to be flattered. The Roman man of wealth was, moreover, a particularly tough person to tackle. He was as hard and resolute as man can be ; and such religion as he possessed had no tabus on certain forms of human action. He had no ten commandments. His Lares and Penates—when he had any—did not threaten him with eternal damnation if he removed his neighbour's landmark—nor that the dogs should lick his blood because of the blood of Naboth. So he was free to do many things to his personal advantage if he could—and he often could. He could—and did—do many things that the hardest modern rich man would shrink from doing. The existence of slavery was a fact which gave the rich man a tremendous pull over his fellows. He had control just where the modern rich man has none. He could—and did—set his gangs of club men, his armed gladiators, on the street, and keep a firmer finger on them than any American boss or German junker.

Slavery, as an economic fact, worked to a similar result ; but its merely economic consequences were not so extensive as we are apt to imagine. They were pretty much the consequences of the unregulated Factory System—namely, a great waste of life, great cheapness of production, bullying and hustling, work that was done without pleasure or conscientiousness, a sapping of the moral independence of those who were under it ; and, on the other hand, the gradual growth of a certain unity among the victims of the process, a spontaneous league of interests and sympathies : for where interests and sympathies lie in one common direction, there unity will grow in the grain.

But these difficulties had existed in all former civilisations : what was new were the factors which stood against them. There was the quality of the people concerned. The intelligence of the Greek and the Asiatic, when repressed by subjection, reappeared in a cunning which their masters recognised, but could not grapple with. Moreover, the European was then two thousand years nearer his beginnings, with so much the less modification of his tremendous aboriginal qualities.

Considered merely as a beast, the European has not had justice done him. He has been one of the finest beasts turned out by nature, and when he came fresh from the forests he was a bigger, hardier, fiercer, more dangerous beast than the negro, the Red Indian, or the Polynesian—with notably strong predeterminations, and immense capacity for toning down into a philosopher or etherealising into a saint. It took him, however, some seven hundred years more to make the mental and nervous rearrangements necessary for philosophy or saintship : at the beginning he was essentially a man of action. The Gaul, the German, the Iberian, the Illyrian, the Latin, the Samnite were not thinkers but doers, easily exploded into action. And these were the men who confronted the Roman rich man.

More than this, the European races vary more, and more suddenly ; they produce a high human average, and a still higher quality of " sport." Every now and then, quite incalculably, they throw up something gigantic in the way of a man : a Sulla, a Caesar, a Charlemagne, a Cortes, a Drake, a Napoleon. This variability, this tendency to throw up " sports," works against the interests of the rich, who require, for their advantage, an order of society stable, settled, and calculable, without anything out of the common either for or against them. It is as awkward for them to have Sulla to defend them as to have Caesar to attack them. In the wars of the supermen, the merely rich are always losers. Tranquillity should be their chief aim.

The Egyptian, wise beyond the wisdom of most men, understood this law : calm was the essence of his creed—and because he preserved tranquillity in Egypt, he reigned for millenniums, in great glory and wealth, until repeated war broke up his power. But the Roman was himself a European : he too had the itch for action which prevented him from this wise calm : his people were not Egyptian, and neither was he. They could not be levelled out into Egyptian bondage, nor could he level them, being the wrong sort of man to do it : so that in all things, however much it might be against his real material interests, drama would creep in, and with drama, of course, excitement and upset, and the flaming-up of the European temper into general strife, to the disturbance of all those serene processes by which money is made and kept in security.

All these conditions being present, and the rich

being positively unable to refrain from those actions which exasperate men at large—the problem was to find a method of fighting the merely rich.

VII

Faced by these intricate problems, for whose solution only reason, and not experience, was as yet available, any intelligent young man, reacting from the Gracchan policy, might well feel that the first indispensable condition was the firm maintenance of political control at any cost. And this obviously meant the maintenance of the aristocratic tradition around which the whole political scheme was entwined. The unity which the Roman world wanted was (this was the first and most obvious theory probable upon the face of it) dependent upon the preservation of a circle of like-minded men whose policy would be constant and whose temperament was uniform, and who would carry to the provinces during their terms of office one invariable tone of mind.

The opposing theory—if it can be called a theory at this early stage, when it was unformulated, and had scarcely been definitely envisioned—was a perpetual magistracy, such as Gaius Gracchus had attempted to develop. Against it, the arguments were overwhelming. It was directly opposed to Roman tradition ; and it had nothing to show for itself in the way of pattern or example. What experience could be called in to aid showed nothing more fruitful in the way of perpetual magistracies than oriental despots and Greek tyrants. If a modern man could at this point have intervened with the suggestion of a central representative assembly, the arguments against it would have seemed conclusive alike to Optimates and Populares. It would not have secured the unity required ; above all, an assembly can seldom be an active means of government, save under circumstances, such as those of earlier Rome or mediaeval Venice, entirely unlike those in which Rome found herself at this time.

The idea of a perpetual magistracy, if it ever came to anything, would need to be evolved in practice before it could be entertained as a hypothesis. Hence a new policy, different from that of the Gracchi, more hopeful as to its possible good results, could only be an aristocratic policy, and one which approached the problems of the day in a spirit of caution, certainly not conceding without necessity any change which might weaken the main principle at stake. . . . And this, which has here been reasoned out, represented the point of view which Sulla actually did take up, when he came to the age in which action was possible. At every point, he acted as though this were the principle he had in mind.

On no occasion do we find Sulla stickling about particular measures of legislation. He invariably accepted accomplished facts, when they were the fruit of a genuine political opinion. He accepted the Italian franchise, when it at last became law. What he sought after was something different—namely, a particular species of man in government. Once granted that kind of man, measures were a question of expediency, to be taken on their own intrinsic merits. The apparent inconsistency and cynicism of Sulla are considerably modified if we judge him by this test. His cynicism was a mannerism—sometimes a desperate mannerism, most

decided when he was most pressed, and most in
earnest. It was not any form of insincerity.

VIII

But there was a feature of his character which
impressed his contemporaries quite as strongly as
his cynicism, and that was his unexpectedness.
He had a considerable gift for holding his tongue,
and when he spoke or acted, he was liable to take
friends and foes alike by surprise. Yet in this too
he was consistent. He put forward no personal
propaganda, no novel ideas. While he was in a
subordinate position, he accepted orders with complete obedience, and sank himself in his class as
dutifully as any ancient Roman father. Not until
command was legally and rightfully his did he
reveal any views of his own ; and then his views
were startling and even, to some, incomprehensible.
But his attitude in this respect was a logical one.
It was a consistent interpretation of the principle
of aristocracy. He obeyed, until he was entitled
to command.

And again, that opportunism, that habit of waiting patiently on events, which may have been
partly temperamental in origin, had its roots partly
in the considerations we have been describing.
A reaction from the Gracchi meant a return to the
old aristocratic habit of allowing events to shape
the conduct they provoked. There are obvious
difficulties in the way of positing a necessary scheme
of action, and then applying it to events without
regarding whether it fits them or not. Sulla and
his contemporaries lived in a world which, having
progressed further in some respects than any
preceding period, had no experience exactly adapted

to its own situation : and Sulla took this into
account.

IX

He was right. Events came in disguise. Two
years after the death of Gaius Gracchus, when Sulla
was nineteen, an obscure officer, one Gaius Marius,
a man of low birth, stood for the tribuneship, and
was elected. And neither Sulla nor any one else
could have imagined that the occasion possessed
importance. No slow music greeted his advent :
yet one of the mighty protagonists had stepped
upon the stage. Sulla was still awaiting his cue,
but Gaius Marius had entered.

CHAPTER IV

THE RISE OF SULLA TO FORTUNE

I

GAIUS MARIUS was a man very different from
Sulla. He was a man of humble family.
His father, a resident at Arpinum (where the great
Cicero also was born), was entirely obscure—one of
those Roman farmers whose numbers were decreas-
ing year by year, but who had formed the driving
force of the mighty armies which had made Rome
supreme. Young Marius had the peculiar characteristics of the rank from which he sprang. He
was dour, hardy, and of extraordinary determination—an unbending, immalleable man, once his
mind was made up. But he had to be dealing with
subjects he understood before this quality in him
came clearly forth. He had nothing of Sulla's easy
instinct. Sulla was no beauty—but Marius, like
the Duke of Wellington, erred rather on the side
of a forbidding strength. He had " a damn'd dis-
inheriting countenance " ; and the fact is an index
to the spiritual difficulty he had in adapting himself
to complex or unfamiliar circumstances. All was
clear to Marius when the road was straight ; he
pushed on like a bull ; but he lost himself in any
kind of maze—and then his weakness came out,
and he proved an angry, obstinate, blundering man,
seeking to beat down what he should have gone

PL. II.

Fig.2.
King Bocchus delivering
Jugurtha to Sulla,
from the coin issued by Faustus
Cornelius Sulla in B.C. 62.

Fig.1.
Portrait of Sulla
from the coin issued by Quintus
Pompeius Rufus in B.C.57.

round. And Marius had a temper which rose before opposition, as water does behind a dam. When it broke through, it became a devastating flood.

So much of those characteristics in him which functioned as faults. His virtues were remarkable. Even through the cloud of calumny which his political opponents shed over him, we can perceive that he was a man of iron courage, who never fled from any danger through fear ; a man sincerely, though somewhat crudely, desirous of justice ; but a man above all animated by that thorough sympathy with common people which we have nowadays learnt to call " democratic." Marius was quite happy doing rough work, sharing rough quarters, and bandying rough words with rough men. Over and above this he had the indefinable quality of genius—a capacity for perceiving and carrying out tasks beyond the competence of mere ability. He had the Cromwellian touch without the modifying influence of Cromwell's religion and Cromwell's subtlety. In such a character as this are the potentialities of great success and of great catastrophe. He had both, before he ended.

Marius and Sulla present a contrast in another respect, not uncommon in human life. Sulla, nominally a holder of old tradition, was in his private mind a somewhat advanced person, interested in unconventional ideas and people, and utterly unfettered by rules. Marius, nominally a revolutionist and an upsetter of established usage, was a perhaps narrowly conservative man, strict in his private life, with the decorum and adherence to convention which professional soldiers are especially liable to develop. He embodied all the characteristics of the old-fashioned Roman.

II

Marius spent his early years on his father's small farm, working vigorously with his hands, and was a grown man before he ever saw a city. His entrance into military service was as a soldier in the ranks, whence he rose on his merits until he attracted the favourable notice of the great Scipio Aemilianus. That Scipio thought highly of him is shown by a curious anecdote. Some one ingratiatingly asked Scipio at dinner where they should find again a general such as he : whereupon he turned playfully to Marius, who sat next to him, clapped him on the shoulder, and answered : " Here, perhaps ! " . . . The prophecy (though true words are often spoken in jest) was less to the point than the fact that Marius sat next to the famous man.

The encouragement of Scipio induced Marius to take the first steps towards the political career which alone could open to him the higher military commands. The family of the Metelli had been friendly to him and his father ; and by the interest of L. Caecilius Metellus Dalmaticus, who was standing for the consulship, Marius was elected tribune—an office proper to an undistinguished plebeian. He made a success of the office very illustrative of his whole political career. He introduced a bill to amend the regulations which governed the voting in elections ; and since the proposed measure seemed to weaken the oligarchic interests, it was opposed by the senior consul Cotta, who carried the senate with him. Marius was not in the least intimidated. He promptly threatened the consul with the exercise of his tribunician authority, which meant imprisonment for Cotta : and turning to his friend, Metellus, required his support. Metellus was obliged to explain that he shared the views of his colleague : whereupon Marius committed Metellus into custody. Metellus appealed to the other tribunes, but they refused to intervene, and Marius triumphantly carried his bill, to the admiration of the people. But having in this manner stood up to the rich and powerful, Marius went on to prove his incapacity as a demagogue by successfully resisting a proposal for a new Corn Dole to the electorate. As a small farmer, he hated the laws which undercut the price of Italian-grown corn. He ended his year of office respected and disliked by both parties.

To achieve a military command, however, he needed to hold one of the higher magistracies, to which the tribuneship had been merely an introduction : and he had endangered his chances. He was defeated in his candidature for an aedileship. Undiscouraged, he lifted his aim higher, entered for the praetorship, and was successful by a very narrow margin. It illustrates an inherent weakness in the Roman political constitution that it had no better means of getting a great soldier forward than making him a chief justice !

His unpopularity was sufficient to cause an attempt to unseat him on a charge of bribery. Marius fought his case with determination, and with typical candour. Finally the judges, influenced by his defence, and still more by his personality, voted a tie, and the case was dismissed. Had he lost, he might never have been heard of again : by such very narrow margins is history made !

Marius passed an uneventful year as praetor. He probably left all the serious work to his better instructed subordinates. At the end of it, when the provincial commands were distributed among the retiring magistrates, he obtained Further Spain for his share. Marius was now launched.

Never very successful as a political intriguer, he was thoroughly in his element in Spain. His energy, honesty and strictness gave him precisely the increased reputation which his political efforts never gave him. He cleared the province of a plague of banditti who, as in some Latin countries of later date, had the respectful sympathy of the populace ; and his general conduct was rewarded by a social advance which was to prove of very great importance to him. He married a daughter of the great Julian house of Caesar, a sister of the Gaius Julius Caesar who was to be the father of another of the same name, the conqueror of Gaul, and the founder of the empire. To be accepted as a son-in-law and brother-in-law by one of the great aristocratic houses was an enormous step for the son of the poor farmer of Arpinum. It meant that henceforward nothing need be impossible to him.

III

Sulla was waiting ; Marius had arrived ; and now the two clouds arose on the horizon which were the harbingers of the coming storm. Human history is so much the tale of the unexpected, that we need not be surprised to see the course of events not only influenced, but even to some extent created, by factors which seem external, and almost accidental. In rapid succession Rome had to deal with two problems of an unforeseen nature.

One was the African problem, which rose slowly into importance through a series of years. There

never would have been any African question except
for Jugurtha. Africa was settled, organised, and
done with ; the subject was closed. Jugurtha
reopened it. He was an illegitimate nephew of old
King Micipsa of Numidia ; and, as frequently
happens, the love-child proved an infinitely greater
man than the legitimate heirs, Hiempsal and Adherbal, with whom he shared the old man's kingdom.
Jugurtha was a magnificent example of the type of
mind which is that of a great statesman if it be
successful, and of a great criminal if it be un-
successful. In a series of dramatic events he slew
his two cousins and became sole King of Numidia.

His actions, however, involved serious questions
of Roman policy which promptly divided Rome
into two camps. Hiempsal and Adherbal had
been under Roman protection ; many Roman
traders had lost their lives when Adherbal fell ;
and the question immediately arose, how far Rome
could tolerate the proceedings of Jugurtha. The
oligarchy was against intervention : the *Populares*
took a contrary view. The controversy aroused in
a fresh form all the party passions that smouldered
unquenched from the Gracchan days : and they
sprang into life now over questions in which domestic
issues were not involved. The *Populares* freely
charged the oligarchy with being in the pay of
Jugurtha. The Senate, on the other hand, had an
accurate perception of the practical difficulties
involved in any attempt to bring Jugurtha to heel.
Whether they were bribed or not, they were right
in this view. An African war would be an enterprise of immense difficulty and doubtful success,
which no body of prudent statesmen would lightly
undertake.

But here entered, as a serious element in the situation, the domestic distrust which had been the result of the proceedings against the Gracchi. The policy of the oligarchy was wise, but it was a policy of secret diplomacy and private negotiations. It caused a violent outburst of popular opposition to the whole political trend of the oligarchy : and Rome was involved in an African war to which no definite end could be foreseen.

While the controversy was still proceeding, the second cloud arose. Roman punitive expeditions against the half-wild Celtic tribes of the Danube region had been fairly frequent, and presented little difficulty. No serious pressure on that frontier was felt. But in 113 B.C. some unaccountable movement was visible. The Celts were being attacked from the unknown north, and through them rolled an immense invading army which spread right up to the Alps and the passes into Italy.

The consul Gnaeus Papirius Carbo turned it back (not without damage) from Aquileia, and the strangers, whoever they were, disappeared into the fastnesses. They evidently wandered along the northern side of the Alps, for two years later they began to cross the Rhine. They were an immense body of people, a whole nation migrating—men, women and children, flocks and herds, moving, as every European migration moved, with covered wagons and nightly laager. By degrees they came south, and at length reached the Roman frontier, where they asked the authorities for land on which to settle. It was a somewhat alarming demand, difficult to satisfy. That a modern government is never confronted by such a situation is no reason for us complacently to underrate its seriousness.

This year was therefore marked by two disturbing incidents. The Roman expedition in Africa was completely and disgracefully defeated, and compelled to make most humiliating terms with Jugurtha ; while the consul M. Junius Silanus, endeavouring to turn the northern invaders back from the Roman frontier in Gaul, met with catastrophe. The invaders spread themselves over northern and central Gaul, reducing the country under their own control.

The whole motive, policy and competence of the oligarchy were now involved. It must stand or fall by its ability to grapple with a situation it had done nothing to create, under a watchful criticism it had embittered by its treatment of the Gracchi. Steps were at once taken to put the African war on a satisfactory basis. The consul Quintus Caecilius Metellus, a man of accepted probity and ability, the brother of Marius's old friend, was given the command. Great sums were voted ; the levy was put into force ; men of ability were selected to accompany him ; and with Metellus, as officers of his staff, sailed Gaius Marius and Publius Rutilius Rufus.

IV

The competence of Metellus was beyond question. He reorganised the Roman army in Africa, entered and occupied Numidia, and defeated Jugurtha. But the end of the war was not brought appreciably nearer : Jugurtha merely disappeared into the desert and raised another of those elusive and interminable armies which African deserts produce. The problem was shifted. Something more than the corruption of an alleged scandalous oligarchy was clearly involved.

The new problem was nothing less than the character and efficiency of the Roman army itself. Marius had flung himself with vigour into his new duties, and was not only a first-rate commander, but a man extremely popular with the rank and file. He shared their food and labours, spoke their language, was with them and among them constantly, and organised his work with the system and adequacy which were his own peculiar gifts. But he could not shut his eyes to obvious facts. The whole system of army organisation was radically wrong. However well fitted it may have been to an earlier stage of Roman civilisation, it no longer fitted the requirements of the day. The men were not always suitable ; they were selected without a proper regard for either justice or military value ; they were citizen soldiers with private interests at home to worry them, and with a training inadequate to draw the best out of them. The officers were frequently incompetent. And when Metellus had obtained from Jugurtha the surrender of the Roman deserters in his hands, the disciplinary action of the commander-in-chief can hardly have aroused the enthusiasm of such a man as Marius. Some had their hands cut off ; some were buried in earth up to their waists, shot at with arrows, and finally burned to death. To one who knew and loved and felt with the common man, such deeds must have seemed both monstrous and unjust. . . . A breach began between Marius and his commander.

Marius seems to have come to the conclusion that the whole system of organisation needed revision, on every ground. He had the vigorous support of the Roman capitalists settled in Africa. They may not have realised precisely the military reasons for his views ; they themselves, it is probable, were chiefly concerned with the prospect of an unending war, dragging on indefinitely ; but whatsoever reasons may have had most weight with them, they supported Marius. Glowing accounts of him began to circulate in Rome.

The storm broke when an old personal and family friend of Metellus—T. Turpilius Silanus—allowed the important station of Vaga to fall into the hands of Jugurtha. Turpilius himself was sent back in safety—the only Roman to escape the massacre. Marius made a stand over the matter. He accused Turpilius of deliberate treason, and carried his point so successfully that Metellus was obliged to bow to public opinion, and to visit his friend with the military penalty of death. He never forgave Marius.

The accusation against Turpilius was subsequently denied, and said to be disproved ; but it is certain that Marius never altered the opinion he had formed, and expressed emphatic satisfaction with his own share in the incident. But it meant a further breach with the oligarchic party. Marius had quarrelled successively with two brothers, both of them important and influential men to whom, by ordinary worldly standards, he owed a great deal. They and their friends are hardly likely to have taken any but a black view of his character and conduct.

Marius thereupon made the characteristic resolution of standing for the consulship himself. Unlikely as success might seem (for men outside a certain ring of very old or very wealthy families seldom achieved the chief magistracy), there were factors in his favour. Metellus did his best, by ridicule and opposition, to prevent the candidature. Marius obtained the necessary leave of absence only twelve days before the elections, and at once made a dash for home. He reached Utica after a journey of whirlwind haste ; the auguries were favourable—and so (more important still) was the wind. He arrived at Rome seven days after he had left the army, found that his reputation had preceded him, and was triumphantly elected consul for the first time.

There must have been much discussion, not only far away in Africa, round the dinner table of Metellus, but around the dinner tables nearer at hand in Rome. The election of Marius meant even more than his enemies imagined.

v

The schemes which Marius must have been turning over in his mind, and discussing with his friends for some time previously, he now began to develop ; and the oligarchy discovered with horror and amazement that the most terrifying of all portents to an oligarchy had appeared upon the political stage—a man with great ideas. Sulla began his political career that year, succeeding in a comparatively humble candidature for the quaestorship, and he was therefore associated from the beginning with the drafting and execution of the military reforms which his consul put into operation.

Their substance consisted in the creation of a regular army, a voluntary army. Hitherto the Roman armies had been citizen armies, levied upon the qualified Roman electors and Italian allies on a property basis. Marius carried through the sweeping revolution of abolishing this old system, and

calling for voluntary recruits who were prepared
to take up arms as a profession. It is only by
approaching this policy from the political angle
that we can seize the true perspective of it ; and
then we can see that, though nominally a military
reform, it was in fact a revolution which followed
logically upon the policy of Gaius Gracchus, and
paved the way for all the constitutional changes
that he had first foreshadowed, and that were to
transform the Rome of Marius into the Rome of
Augustus. . . . Here the obtuseness of Marius
came to his aid. He was not an imaginative man ;
he had no intellectual culture, and it is improbable
that he could or would enter with any sympathy
into deep (and to him, no doubt, remote) constitutional questions. He was concerned solely with
the creation of an adequate military force, and in
this aim he cared for no distinctions of mere political
theory. Yet the objections which might be felt to
his policy on grounds of principle were neither
few nor trifling. He was tearing up the military
arrangements of King Servius Tullius on which
the Roman political constitution rested, and from
which it had originally grown. He was dividing
the soldier from the citizen, and creating an instrument which might easily place the control of the
State into hands not responsible to the constitutional
government. Classical statesmen knew well enough
the means by which military tyrannies were founded.
There must have been many men who, though not
prepared for opposition to valuable practical reforms,
watched intently for opportunity to divert the
possible consequences.

On the other hand, Marius, with the instinct of
the purely practical mind, had grasped a logic that

was in the situation itself rather than in the ideas and principles entertained by men. Had he failed or flinched, a necessary step in the political evolution of Rome would never have been taken, and the " large political unit " towards which civilisation was working would have died before it had developed to the end. He was doing that thing which creates more real revolutions than any idealism does—he was adapting institutions to the practical necessities of the day.

Such questions of principle were alone enough to divide the parties sharply ; but Marius, in his public speeches, showed a candour and a supreme self-confidence which may have been justified as to its substance, but was indiscreet. He undertook to take Jugurtha dead or alive. He told the electors in his rough way that he had wrested the consulship as spoil of war from the incompetent hands of the rich : and that he gloried in the wounds he had received in the cause of Rome as much as some men gloried in the images of their famous ancestors —this latter an allusion to a sacred aristocratic custom which must have offended its devotees as deeply as a somewhat similar allusion would offend a modern Catholic. And he asked whether those famous ancestors would not have preferred a descendant such as himself, to the fools who wor- shipped them. . . . These things were first-rate electioneering, and were enormously popular ; but they were not forgotten. . . . What Sulla thought of them we are not informed.

VI

At the close of his year of office, Marius refused the offer of the Gallic campaign, and insisted on superseding Metellus. The new army, being destined for Africa, was therefore of no benefit to his colleague, L. Cassius Longinus, who, undertaking the operations in Gaul, was lured into an ambush in which he himself fell. The Gallic question must wait. Marius transported his army to Africa. Sulla was detained in Italy by the special work of raising and equipping a large cavalry force. He may, therefore, have seen the return of Metellus, who was accorded by his friends a welcome not free from the suspicion of being a political demonstration against Marius and the *Populares*. The Senate granted a formal triumph, in which Metellus anticipated any hopes of Marius by securing to himself the honorary title of " Numidicus." It is not likely that Sulla, on the point of leaving for Africa, was neglected by the great men of his own party.

We do not possess any contemporary narrative of the African campaigns of Marius written from a sympathetic standpoint. Sallust, who was a political sympathiser, wrote much later, and his record may, for all we know, have been insensibly coloured by the accounts of hostile authorities. The whole subject rapidly became involved in party animus. The enemies of Marius declared (apparently with some truth) that he had undertaken a task which he was unable successfully to finish. It seems certain that Marius carried out some wonderful military operations, beyond the capacities of Metellus ; but it is equally certain that they brought the war no nearer its end. There was, in fact, only one way of ending it, and that was by the capture of Jugurtha.

Marius had the kind of intelligence which, while

comparatively narrow in its scope, is extraordinarily deep and efficient. His movements were secret to the last—so secret that sometimes the secret has failed to survive—swift, and very long. He drove Jugurtha out of his strongholds, struck at and took Capsa far in the south, and when Sulla at length arrived with his cavalry, was in the far west of Numidia, on the borders of Mauretania, five hundred miles from his base. Thither Sulla proceeded, and joined his commander.

Marius was not enthusiastic. The quaestor was his chief of staff, the next man in rank and authority to himself : and Marius had no taste whatever for a dissipated young scion of an impoverished aristocratic house, who added to his vices the doubtful virtues of Greek culture. But Sulla did not prove to be the kind of person anticipated. He was soon popular ; his manners were easy and simple ; he was ready to do a good turn wherever he could ; and even Marius thawed before proof of the only quality he was prepared to acknowledge as acceptable—the virtue of military efficiency. Sulla brought with him something else, not so obvious : namely, a thorough acquaintance with the point of view of the Optimates concerning the African war.

Sulla was singularly fortunate in beginning his career under the command of the man who was before all others the greatest general of his age. Bluff and rough as he was, Marius was a great organiser—a man who worked, and saw that others also worked. The quaestor must have had much to learn ; and to judge from his subsequent career he learnt it well. The tone of Marius's army was something worth acquiring. It may have been there that the young aristocrat picked up the art

of an unbending familiarity with the common man :
that subtle mingling of human equality and personal
authority of which Marius was the chief exponent.
Sulla had to learn—and did learn—to stand upon
his own feet, relying not upon any social rank or
artificial support, but on his own power of managing men. For this his earlier life had prepared
him. A devotion to the drama may not be useless
to an intelligent man. Sulla had the faculty of
making the most of a situation, of seeing it from
the spectators' point of view, of giving a certain
artistic turn to occasions which increased their
value. . . . And here he was, on the spot, to see
for himself the results of the military reforms of
Marius, and the true inwardness of the political
controversy over the African war.

VII

Marius had come to the Mauretanian frontier to
overawe King Bocchus, and to prevent a junction
of forces between him and Jugurtha. The expedition was one of those which give rise to acute
differences of opinion. Marius reduced the frontier
fortresses, disregarding the claims of Bocchus that
he was trespassing on Mauretanian territory. He
was conducting a war a large part of the results of
which could only be moral. What counted was
the state of mind he could create. He certainly
created considerable apprehension in the mind of
Bocchus. It gave the king much to think of to see
a Roman army penetrate successfully to his frontiers,
and there carry on military operations : but it was
not a case in which solid fighting and definite
results could be looked for.

When the time came for retirement, and Marius

started on the long march back to his base, it was the signal for a cloud of Mauretanian horsemen to emerge from the frontier. Jugurtha had been busy. He had proposed to Bocchus to cede one-third of Numidia to the king in exchange for his help ; the bargain to be effective if the Romans were driven out of Africa, or if a treaty were made with them which left Numidia intact in Jugurtha's hands. Bocchus agreed. Marius had impressed him with the long military reach of Rome ; it might be well now in any case to impress Marius in turn. If the importance of Bocchus could be suitably made clear to the Romans, the king would be in a better position to negotiate with them in the event of Jugurtha's failure.

The march of Marius was uninterrupted until he was near home. Then the blow fell ; and the rest of the journey became a nightmare of desperate fighting Three times the Romans fought a pitched battle ; they were unceasingly on guard. Throughout the march, Sulla was the right-hand man of Marius, and on two occasions his rapidity and discernment had much to do with the safety of the army. The losses of the Moors and Numidians were heavy. In close fighting they were no match for Roman troops.

With the safe return of the Roman expedition, a change took place in the whole situation. It became clear to Bocchus that the Romans could not be driven out of Africa, and that he could expect little from Jugurtha. Five days later his envoys arrived to sound Marius : and now Marius, who had hitherto been grimly bent on prosecuting the war to a bitter end, unexpectedly lent a friendly ear. How far Sulla's private conversation was

responsible for the alteration in the opinions of
Marius it is impossible to guess ; the military
situation alone might well carry conviction to a
soldier. The threatening situation in Gaul had
also to be reckoned with. However the facts
might stand, Sulla was one of the two representatives whom Marius despatched to conduct conver-
sations with Bocchus. On the way, he talked his
colleague over to his own point of view, and it was
agreed that Sulla should conduct the negotiations.

VIII

Sulla was aware of many facts which it is not
absolutely certain that Marius knew : or, if Marius
knew, appreciated. Before vacating the African
command, Metellus had been in touch with Bocchus,
and had gained from the king what amounted to
a cautious assent to the idea of a friendly relation
with Rome. Metellus was in no way obliged to
report his proceedings to Marius, with whom, in
any case, he was not on friendly terms : and the
strong probability is that Marius was ignorant of
the correspondence. It would be to the Senate
that Metellus would report, or, even more probably,
to his private and political friends. In this case,
Sulla might very well know far more than Marius,
who, when approached, shortly after his arrival,
by Bocchus, had dismissed with scepticism the
king's advances, which he imagined to be diplomatic
trickery. On their present renewal, for the third
time, Sulla realised (as he naturally would, if his
knowledge were complete) that the king had been
repeatedly making advances which had not been
received with ardour. It was now time to show a
certain amount of enthusiasm.

Without waiting for the king to broach the
subject, Sulla spoke of the pleasure which he and his
friends felt that Bocchus had recognised that peace
was preferable to war. He assured the King that
Rome had at all times sought friends rather than
subjects, and valued the loyalty which was voluntarily given far higher than that which was extorted
by compulsion. The friendship of Rome was an
advantage, not a burden, to a man in the position
of Bocchus. His remoteness would render unlikely any conflict of interests ; but no man was
too remote to be reached by the gratitude of
Rome.

Finding that, far from having to humiliate himself,
he was accepted with joy, Bocchus expanded under
the cordiality of Sulla. He explained that he had
not been actuated by any hostile feeling against
Rome : he had fought to protect his country ;
and he repeated his statement that the border-lands
in which Marius had operated were not in Jugurtha's
territory, but in his own. He also recalled, as
evidence of his own good will, an embassy he had
formerly sent to Rome, several years previously,
which the Senate had refused to receive. He would
like to send another embassy. . . . The envoys,
subject to the consent of Marius, agreed. . . .
These were the official transactions. . . . Bocchus
was well aware that a Roman commander had no
plenary authority, and that any binding agreement
must be made with the Senate. Sulla knew that
the Senate, anxious to terminate the war, would
lend a more favourable ear than a general of the
Populares, if approached in the right manner.

As soon as Sulla and his colleague had left,
Bocchus received the representatives of Jugurtha,

who made a determined attempt to prevent the defection of the Mauretanian king. His careful consideration of Jugurtha's claims did not prevent the proposed embassy from setting out. It included five of his oldest and most trustworthy friends, on whom he could thoroughly rely. . . . The embassy, having fallen into the hands of hostile tribesmen, arrived penniless, disreputable, and without their credentials, at the Roman head-quarters, expecting to be treated as tramps and impostors, and to be turned away from the door.

Marius, luckily, was away, and Sulla in command. He received them with dignified and lavish hospitality, on their mere word as to who they were, supplied them with a fresh outfit, and showed all that charm which came so easily to him when he would. He entertained them, instructed them carefully in what to say, and in how to say it, and explained to them the official formulas, mystifying to the literal mind, which must be employed in the negotiation. On the return of Marius a council was summoned ; the envoys were introduced, and the question was debated. Strong opposition was raised ; but Sulla had prepared the ground and was successful in obtaining an armistice for Bocchus, and leave for the envoys to proceed to Rome. He had coached them well. They made the correct expression of humble penitence on behalf of their master, and prayed for the friendship of the Roman people. The resolution of the Senate expressed, in the recognised form, its acceptance of his repentance, and its willingness to grant a treaty and the name of friend to Bocchus, when he had proved that he deserved the grant.

If in any way Bocchus had come to an under-

standing as to how he was to " deserve the grant,"
few hints of it have survived. Yet as soon as the
official answer of the Senate was communicated to
him he wrote to Marius asking that Sulla should be
sent to discuss with him some matters of common
interest to himself and Rome. Sulla, with his
commander's approval, at once set out.

IX

Sulla's mission was of crucial importance, and
as dangerous a mission as any man ever undertook.
If the " matter of common interest " could lay his
hands on Sulla, it was improbable that he would
hesitate. A cohort of Italian troops, together with
auxiliaries lightly equipped for rapid travel, accompanied the quaestor. On the fifth day of their
journey, an apparently immense body of cavalry
was seen ahead. They were wild horsemen of the
desert. On their approach, they proved to be an
escort under the command of Volux, the son of
Bocchus, sent to meet Sulla and conduct him safely
to the king. For two more days Sulla journeyed
in company with Volux. On the evening of the
second day the scouts brought in word that Jugurtha
was near.

Volux begged Sulla to leave the camp with him,
under cover of night. Sulla refused ; he would
not desert his men. Volux suggested a night march,
to which Sulla consented. At daybreak, weary
with marching and want of sleep, they found
Jugurtha two miles in advance of their position.
First a panic, then something like a mutiny broke
out in the Roman force, and Sulla, himself suspicious,
had to intervene to prevent his men from attacking
Volux. He calmed their fears, and then, calling

Heaven to witness the treachery of Bocchus, sternly
ordered Volux to leave the Roman camp.

Volux assured him, with tears, that no treachery
was intended. Jugurtha, he said, had discovered
their road, but he assured Sulla that Jugurtha
could, or would, do no harm, and dared not use
violence while he, Volux, was present to bear
witness to it. He urged Sulla to march straight
through Jugurtha's camp. He offered himself as
hostage for his good faith. He would leave his
men behind, or send them forward, and accompany
Sulla alone.

It required much less intelligence than Sulla
possessed—perhaps much less than Volux possessed
—to see that the situation was much more dangerous
than the prince admitted. As a hostage, Volux
was of little practical value. If Jugurtha could
make away with Sulla, Bocchus would never be
able to clear himself in Roman eyes, and would be
hopelessly committed to Jugurtha. If Sulla killed
his hostage, it would prevent nothing, avenge
nothing, but only part Bocchus more finally from
the Romans. The case was one in which Jugurtha
stood to win everything, without involving himself
in a single additional liability. . . . But Volux was
right. Bluff, bold and unhesitating, was the only
safe course. Sulla made up his mind.

Accompanied by Volux, he rode straight through
Jugurtha's camp. No movement was made : no
weapon was lifted. He rode on, and a few days
later reached the presence of Bocchus. If ever
Fortune befriended Sulla, she had befriended him
then. Nor can the wildest guess tell us why Jugurtha, with every crime on his soul and his foe at his
sword's point, did not strike. . . . The answer

of Sulla would be easy. It was Fortune. What else ?

One danger was over ; the second began.

King Bocchus had every reason for concealing his intentions, but he concealed them so well that even Sulla could not be sure of them. The agents of Jugurtha were active at the court. Sulla had come to negotiate for the surrender of Jugurtha. What if Jugurtha were successful in negotiating for the surrender of Sulla ? The quaestor took no risks. He assumed that the danger existed, and he took steps to deal with it.

Bocchus sent to Sulla to assure him that all was well. He invited Sulla to name a day for their conference. The understanding between them was (he said) unaltered ; but Sulla must not mind the presence of Jugurtha's envoys, who were permitted for reasons of prudence. Sulla was non-committal. He accepted the official conference, but told the king that the real business was for his private ear alone.

The official conference accordingly took place. Sulla informed the king that he had come to enquire whether he had decided on peace, or intended to continue the war. It was agreed that the king should deliver his reply in ten days' time ; and Sulla retired from the official conference. Late that night Bocchus sent for him, and the secret conference took place. Even then Bocchus spoke with curious guardedness. He was grateful and cordial to Sulla personally. He repeated his old assertions—that he had never been animated by hostility to Rome, but had merely sought to protect his own frontiers. He now suggested that the Senate would be satisfied with his complete with-

drawal from all alliance with Jugurtha, and with the
cession of the disputed frontier territory ; but if
Sulla had any other specific demand to urge, he
would give it his best consideration.

Whatever the king had determined to do, he had
evidently determined to do it only under some show
of compulsion. Sulla accepted the condition without knowing whether it were genuine or diplomatic.
After returning proper thanks for the personal
references, he warned the king plainly that Rome
was too great a power in the world to trouble about
trifles ; what Rome wanted was something different,
namely, the surrender of Jugurtha, which was
within his power to compass. This, indeed, would
be an act worthy of the friendship of Rome. . . .
And the reward would be the treaty he wanted,
and the transfer of a portion of Numidia. . . .
Bocchus continued to hesitate. . . . Kinship, the
law of hospitality, public opinion : all these troubled
him. Sulla pressed his point, and at last the king
gave way. He would do all that Sulla wanted ;
but, if it were to be done, there must be a pretence
of making Jugurtha a party to the official treaty,
or the bird would fly away before it could be caught.
Sulla consented to this.

Sulla probably never met a more dexterous
intriguer than Bocchus. How well the king realised
some elements in the case which were hidden from
Sulla can be seen from the reply of Jugurtha when
he was asked for his views on the contemplated
treaty with Rome. He replied that he would consent
to any terms, but he pointed out that the action of
Roman generals was sometimes repudiated by the
Senate, and he suggested a guarantee. Let Bocchus
hand Sulla over to him, and they would have a

guarantee which the Senate would not lightly disregard. . . . This communication no doubt gave
great pleasure to Bocchus. Jugurtha knew much,
but not all. Jugurtha was a crafty diplomatist ;
but Sulla was a craftier diplomatist than he ; and
the craftiest diplomatist of all was Bocchus, King
of Mauretania. Bocchus agreed to Jugurtha's suggestion ; and even then Sulla could not be certain
where the diplomacy ended and the reality began,
nor which was which. But he never wavered.

The conference was arranged. Bocchus, Sulla
and Jugurtha were to meet. Bocchus kept every
one in doubt to the very last moment. If his
indecision was imaginary, it was at least magnificently
acted. He spent much time in brooding alone.
But on the night before the meeting he sent for
Sulla. The last details were settled, and early the
next morning the two kings and the quaestor met
together. . . . Jugurtha's escort was cut down to
the last man, and he himself was delivered into the
hands of Sulla.

The war was at an end.

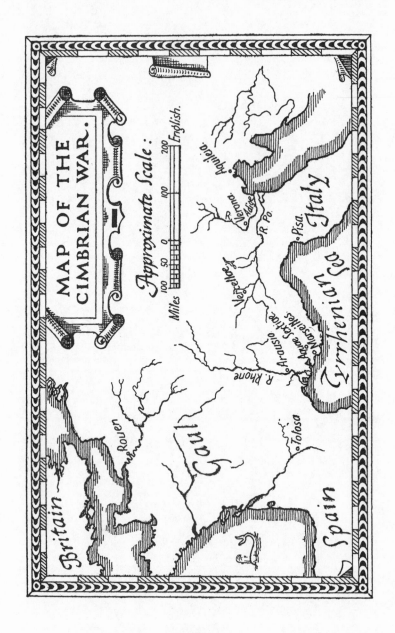

MAP OF THE CIMBRIAN WAR.

Approximate Scale:

Miles 100 50 0 100 200 English.

Britain

Rouen

Gaul

Spain

Verona
R. Adige
Aquileia
R. Po
Pisa
Italy
Tyrrhenian Sea

Vercellae
Arausio
Aquae Sextiae
Marseilles
R. Rhone
Tolosa

CHAPTER V

THE TRIUMPH OF MARIUS

I

SO far, so good. From the party point of view
the controversy was a drawn battle. If Fortune had stayed her hand at this point, there might
be no more tale to tell; but when does Fortune
stay her hand? Men might have settled down to a
prolonged dispute concerning the merits of the case,
the virtues of the respective policies, and the amount
of credit to be apportioned to Marius and to Sulla :
but before the African war was completely wound
up, it was suddenly revealed as merely the training ground on which Rome had found her men and
prepared for the real contest. For now Jugurtha
sank into insignificance before the terror of the
north.

The invaders of Gaul had lain beyond the official
Roman frontiers, an ominous, unremoved threat.
Information about them began to filter through.
There were two principal nations among them (they
were far too vast to be called tribes), the Cimbri and
the Teutones, besides a certain number of Celts who
had joined them. They were not themselves Celts,
but came from the far north. Ptolemy the
geographer marks them as from Jutland and
Schleswig-Holstein, neighbours of the Angles and
the Langobardi : and two small tribes of the same

name certainly existed there in later years. The
Cimbri and Teutones were not only more numerous,
but had a discipline and order, an equipment,
leadership and general sense of organisation, which
speak of a much higher social level than had been
reached by the poor and backward frontier tribes of
Germans along the Rhine. And it is fairly certain
that the scanty social achievements of the latter were
a very misleading index to the degree of civilisation
reached by the Baltic peoples to whom the Cimbri
and Teutones belonged.

The Cimbri and Teutones spent two years in
prospecting Gaul, and were either dissatisfied with
the result or gathered intelligence which led them to
think that they could do better for themselves. The
difference of language, and the utter strangeness of
each party to the other, probably made the information they managed to obtain about the Romans as
vague and scanty as the information which the
Romans acquired about them. But towards the end
of the year 105 B.C., the king of the Cimbri, Boiorix,
set his great hosts in motion again, and their movements made it clear that their destination was
Italy.

In the meantime, the course of political events in
Rome was indirectly affecting the military prospect
in Gaul. Marius had owed his consulship, two
years before, largely to the good impression he had
made upon the great Roman financiers and merchants. Through Marius, therefore, the old
coalition between the *equites* and the *Populares* was
revived : a truly alarming outlook for the oligarchy,
which made every effort to gain the consular elections for 106 B.C.—and succeeded in doing so. As
soon as Marius was safely in Africa, pursuing the

elusive Jugurtha, the new consuls, G. Atilius
Serranus and Quintus Servilius Caepio, set to work
to punish the renegades. The *lex Servilia* of Caepio
took away from the *equites* the control of the judicial
courts which Gaius Gracchus had given them, and
restored it to the senatorial order. The great
financiers did not take this meekly. They had
the power of striking back ; and they used the
power.

Caepio took his proconsular year in Gaul : this
very year when the Cimbri and Teutones began
their new movement against Italy. He did not have
the free hand and untrammelled governorship he
may have hoped for. So serious was the situation
considered, that the consul for the year, Gnaeus
Mallius Maximus, was sent to take up the command
in chief. Caepio was relegated to the position of
commander of the second Roman army—very much,
it would appear, to his disappointment.

What followed was a scandal which far surpassed
in magnitude anything that had gone before. A
detached corps under M. Aurelius Scaurus was first
defeated, and he himself captured and executed.
The consul at once sent word to Caepio to join him
with the second Roman army. Caepio was in a
thoroughly perverse mood. When engaged, some
little time before, in punitive measures against those
suspected of too great tolerance for the Cimbri, he
had plundered a wealthy temple at Tolosa. The
treasure subsequently disappeared in a somewhat
unsatisfactory way ; it was alleged to have been
stolen by Ligurian bandits, but was thought to have
found a final resting-place nearer Caepio's strong-
room than he admitted. This treasure became
notorious. Caepio was believed to lie under a curse.

He certainly acted in a very strange manner. He joined Maximus as ordered, but refused to occupy the same camp or to act in unison. . . . Maximus, in these difficult circumstances, prudently negotiated with the Cimbri. Caepio, by this time quite crazy, at once hurled his army upon them, because—it was said—he thought Maximus wanted to keep all the credit in his own hands. . . . The defeat which ensued was the most tremendous military disaster the Romans had suffered since Cannae, one hundred and eleven years before. The enraged Cimbri annihilated the army of Caepio, and then, pressing on in the heat of victory, overthrew the army of Maximus and wiped it out. The Romans fought with the Rhone in their rear. There was no room for retreat ; practically none even for flight. Eighty thousand soldiers and forty thousand camp-followers fell. The famous Quintus Sertorius, wounded, and having had his horse killed under him, only escaped by the athletic feat of swimming the Rhone in full armour, shield and all.

The frontier was broken through. Panic spread through Italy. The news which arrived was terrifying enough to justify it. It became known at last that the numbers of the Cimbri and Teutones surpassed even the first reports ; they could put into the field three hundred thousand fighting men alone— and fighting men of the most formidable description, who stopped at nothing. Every Italian-born person capable of bearing arms was sworn in to remain in Italy during the crisis. So great was the terror in Rome that the name of Caepio became a byword.

The political reactions of the great defeat at Arausio were tremendous. As an election cry, the scandal could not have been bettered ; and the *equites* had interests at stake which ensured that their influence should be thrown whole-heartedly into the scale in favour of the *Populares*. The general outcry found voice in the demand for Marius. He was the man wanted. No oligarchic candidate stood the slightest chance against him. With enthusiastic defiance of the law and of constitutional custom, Marius, absent in Africa, was nominated and elected. The *Populares* secured both consulships, together with a long list of other successes.

The scandal of the wretched Caepio's conduct in Gaul was an excuse for the ferocity with which he was hounded, rather than a cause of it. The cause lay in the *lex Servilia*. He was made the scapegoat of the political party he represented. He was— illegally and unconstitutionally—deprived of his proconsular rank, and his property confiscated by decree of the Assembly of the People. During the year that followed he was expelled from the Senate by a second and equally illegal decree. Not content with this, the *Populares*, headed by the tribune Gaius Norbanus and L. Appuleius Saturninus the quaestor, obtained an extraordinary commission of enquiry. Caepio was arrested ; he and Maximus, with others, were condemned. Caepio saved his life only by breaking prison and escaping to Smyrna, whence he never returned. . . . His judges were jurymen of the *equites* ; for C. Servilius Glaucia had drafted and passed the necessary law to remove the control of the courts once more from the Senators to the *equites*. . . . Caepio may have deserved his fate. But the fate of Caepio was only that of an owl nailed to a barn-door as a warning and a threat. . . . Ten years later, his party attempted to rehabilitate—or at least to avenge him. They did not succeed.

II

Marius was elected consul two months after the battle of Arausio ; and he was, as we have seen, at this very moment free to return. He lost no time, but shipped his armies back to Rome at the beginning of January, 104 B.C. His arrival was the occasion of wild enthusiasm. The news that met him was, as far as it went, reassuring. For some reason that has never been discovered, the Cimbri and Teutones had changed their plans, given up their march upon Italy, and taken the Pyrenaean passes for Spain. There was breathing time.

Before taking in hand the urgent measures of defence called for by the situation, Marius first celebrated in state his official triumph for the African campaigns. Jugurtha was led in chains through the crowded streets of Rome, and when the processions and the sacrifices were over, he was pushed into the dreaded Tullianum, the ancient Well-house of the Capitol, and there he was left to die. . . . As far as any human being ever deserves such a fate, he deserved it. There were few crimes he had not committed, and we know of no good deed he had ever performed.

Political feeling, instead of being allayed, was embittered. On the very verge of making good its repute the oligarchy was discredited afresh. Nothing overt could be done against the rough darling of the people ; but there are more ways than one of conducting hostilities. The *Optimates* were full of the deplorable incident which attended the triumph of Marius : he had walked into the Senate in his triumphal robes—and his critics were divided as to whether this were the ignorant blunder of a low-bred

clown, or the offensive pride of an ambitious upstart.
Sulla, drifting pleasantly back to the dinner parties
and aristocratic clubs of Rome, found himself
famous. It was generally agreed that to him, and not
to Marius, was due the successful ending of the
African war. Sulla had not the least objection to
receiving the full credit of his exploit. He had no
false modesty ; he knew as well as any one could
tell him that he had succeeded in precisely those
ways, and exactly those matters, in which Marius was
least successful—in cool dealing with infinitely complicated situations, in urbane persuasion of difficult
and undecided people. He enjoyed his new popularity, and commemorated it by having a ring made,
which he constantly wore, with a little design of
Bocchus delivering Jugurtha into his hands.[1]
  These things were repeated to Marius, who,
naturally enough, was not particularly pleased. He
recognised the enmity that was embodied in the
applause given to Sulla. It is only by means of a
powerful religious discipline (which no Roman of
that age possessed) that any man can rise above the
normal human prides and jealousies. Marius knew
that, without him, Sulla would never have been in
a position to achieve the capture of Jugurtha : yet
with the sensitiveness that so often goes with external
roughness of character, he was vexed that men whom
he considered corrupt and worthless should be
eager to give the credit elsewhere. He had nothing

[1] It is suggested with great probability that the design on
Sulla's ring is reproduced on the coin issued by Faustus Cornelius
Sulla in 62 B.C. (illustrated on Plate II, facing p. 86), and that
the design of the gold plaque (see *post*, p. 157) was identical.
Grueber : *Coins of the Roman Republic in the British Museum*,
Vol. I, p. 471.

against Sulla personally, to whom, as an able officer, he offered employment in the coming campaigns. Sulla accepted.

III

It was now the task of every patriotic man to raise and train an adequate army against the Cimbri and Teutones. Throughout the year the work went on. When Marius had left again for Africa, after his first consulship, his old colleague on the staff of Metellus—Publius Rutilius Rufus—had taken in hand and developed the general indications Marius had transmitted for the training of the new army. Rutilius had arranged a complete scheme of drill based on the methods of the gladiatorial gymnasiums : on which scheme the whole of the new forces now recruited were trained. Hitherto, Roman armies had possessed no particular advantages over others, save those implied by superiority of *moral*. Rutilius invented—or developed—a mode of fighting which brought the advantages of *moral* and discipline to their full fruition. He shortened the Roman sword, and turned it into an exclusively stabbing instrument,[1] utterly different from the long double-edged sword of the Celts and Germans, which descended, only slightly modified, to the mediaeval knight. This step was nearly as great a revolution as was created by the supersession of the muzzle-loading musket by the breech-loading rifle in modern times. It is important to realise that Sulla was from the first connected with all these changes, and was trained in the new military school of Marius.

The popularity of Marius with the army continued

---

[1] Marius may have picked up the idea in Spain. See Livy, xxii, 46.

to increase. His competence, his perfect understanding of the ordinary man, his grim justice and
stern familiarity, made him the most trusted general
in the Roman world. He was re-elected consul for
the ensuing year without difficulty, in the teeth of
the oligarchy. The election was as unconstitutional
as the last, but it was impossible to prevent it. In the
meantime, the Cimbri and Teutones, disappointed
with Spain, came pouring back over the Pyrenees,
and reoccupied Gaul. Marius moved his main
forces up into Gaul, to watch them. He was in no
hurry ; time was on his side. Every month made
the military machine a better instrument, more perfectly under his control. He was laying the foundation of a new reputation for the Roman army—that
reputation for discipline, organisation, hard work
and engineering skill which afterwards distinguished
it, and by which we best know it.

The Cimbri and Teutones, up in the north, were
evolving fresh plans. Before they moved, the third
consulship of Marius expired. Leaving a deputy in
command, he returned to Rome to consult his
friends. He seems to have had some feeling that
his unconstitutional consulships were perhaps not
altogether desirable ; but his respect for conventions
was overruled. The wire-pullers of the *Populares*
were not only convinced of his importance as a
political weapon against the oligarchy, but clear as
to his necessity as a commander. The tribune
Saturninus told Marius publicly that he would be a
traitor to refuse the supreme command at such a
juncture, and Marius, obediently giving way, was
elected to a fourth consulship with Quintus Lutatius
Catulus as colleague, a man who was acceptable to
both political parties.

Sulla's quaestorship had, of course, long expired.
During all these years he held no magisterial office,
but worked as a military legate, a soldier pure and
simple. It was clear to him that he could not hope
for much more from Marius, who looked upon him
with some suspicion, limited his opportunities, and
gave him no great scope to repeat such dangerous
exploits as the capture of Jugurtha. His political
affiliations made it much wiser to seek a post under
some other commander. Even if political sympathies had played no part in the matter, there were
temperamental divergencies which made such a
course expedient. It is hardly likely that the subtle,
cultured and loose-living Sulla could see eye to eye
with the almost illiterate, puritanical man of the
people. Catulus was the obvious resource, and the
right one. Catulus was on all grounds delighted to
welcome Sulla. A wise, yet a lazy man, he was only
too ready to turn over all his important work to his
new assistant, and Sulla settled down with energy in
the post of what we should now call Quartermaster-
General to the second consul. He was therefore in
Italy during the Gallic campaign of Marius, carrying
out the reduction of the wild Alpine tribes, and
watching the north-eastern passes. Some miscalcu-
lation over the question of supplies having brought
about a shortage, Sulla took over the problem, and
not only organised an adequate service for Catulus,
but for Marius too. With his cynical acuteness, he
realised very well that this method of heaping coals
of fire on the head of Marius was his pleasantest
method of revenge. It irritated Marius profoundly
that he, the greatest of organisers, should be caught
napping by his old subordinate.

IV

The Cimbri and Teutones divided their forces. The storm was now at hand. Starting from their new base in northern Gaul, near modern Rouen, the Cimbri re-crossed the Rhine and aimed at the eastern passes of the Alps, while the Teutones marched south for the western entrance to Italy. Marius occupied a strong position on their route, and dug himself in.

The Teutones arrived, a terrifying sight to the Roman troops. Their immense numbers, their impressive appearance and strange language were intimidating. Marius remained in his encampments, and strictly forbade any sort of forwardness. A few days rather changed the feelings of the troops, as they grew accustomed to the sight of the enemy ; but Marius sustained his prohibition. A three-days assault on the Roman camp was repulsed ; and being unable either to force the entrenchments or to persuade Marius to a battle in the open, the Teutones resolved to leave him in their rear. They were six days in defiling their enormous host past the Roman camp ; whereupon Marius followed, never losing sight of them, but digging in every night. He followed them to Aquae Sextiae, where there was a difficulty about water. The Romans drove the Teutones from the only available water supply. The skirmish developed into a partial action. The Teutones were finally forced over the river with heavy loss, and pursued as far as their laager, whence the Romans were repelled, and withdrew.

They spent an anxious night, greatly impressed by the strange wailing and lamentations from the laager ; and even the iron Marius was apprehensive of a night attack. Nothing, however, happened ; and throughout the next day the Teutones remained immobile, changing their dispositions and re-arranging their battle line. Marius seized the opportunity to detach a flanking force which took up a concealed position on the hills. After another night's rest he was ready for the general action, convinced that no better opening would arrive.

It was an easy matter to draw the Teutones, who wished for nothing better than to come to hand-strokes. They charged up-hill with fury. Marius ordered the ranks to be locked, and reliance to be placed on the new sword. He himself took a position in the ranks, where he had once begun his career. The assault was with difficulty stopped ; the Teutones were thrown back and forced down the hill before a wall of swordsmen. At the very moment when they paused to recover themselves they were in turn attacked by the flanking force. It was the critical moment. The moral prestige of the enemy, their repute and their numbers, their unbroken success hitherto in shattering the firmest array, had all along been exercising a nervous terrorism over the Roman troops. Now, as if a spring had been touched, the process was reversed. The Teutones fell into confusion ; their very numbers made recovery impossible ; they could scarcely even flee.[1] A hundred thousand were either slain

---

[1] The short sword allowed a greater number of troops to be brought into action on any given front. A Celtic or German fighting man, then as later, needed a good deal of room around himself. He would find two, three, or more short swordsmen facing him. Once the Teutones were jammed, they could no longer use their weapons, whereas the short sword was the ideal instrument for use in a very crowded fight. . . . We shall

on the field or captured there : and the sack of the
laager, which followed, put into the hands of the
delighted legionaries an immense booty, the fruit of
years of successful plundering.

It is said that the Massiliots built fences of the
huge bones of those who fell that day, and that there
were never such crops as those that afterwards grew
on the fertilised fields of Aquae Sextiae.

V

The danger was not yet over. Marius was offer-
ing the sacrifices of thanksgiving on the field of
battle, when the official news reached him of his fifth
election as consul ; and shortly afterwards he received the military despatches which explained it.
The Cimbri had been more successful than their
allies. They had forced the passes of the Alps in
a way which illustrates the moral terrorism they
exercised. They were magnificent athletes, after a
fashion wholly unlike the gymnasium training of the
southern races. They outflanked the Roman out-
posts by daring feats of crag-climbing, toboganning
down the snow slopes on their broad round shields.
The troops of Catulus were pushed back, lost their
heads, and were soon on the run, in one of those
unreasoning panics which are so difficult to stop.
Catulus [1] did his best, but was obliged to go with
them. He succeeded in reorganising a corps to hold

find the Cimbri at Vercellae partly anticipating these considerations, by throwing out wings ; and Marius anticipating their
anticipation by immediately striking at those wings.

[1] Here we should probably read " Sulla." The story, that
Catulus, unable to lead his men against the enemy, led the
retreat rather than not lead them at all, is not especially like
Catulus, but is very much like Sulla.

the Adige ; but the Cimbri built a great causeway across the river, and outflanked him ; his retreat was followed by the spread of the Cimbri over the plain of the Po. The corps which Catulus had left to defend the Adige fell into their hands after a stern struggle. The Cimbri appreciated the quality of the defence ; and generously dismissed the survivors after swearing them not to take up arms again.

Precisely what share Sulla had in these events we do not know : but it is not unreasonable to surmise that there was depression of spirits at the general head-quarters of Catulus, and a corresponding sense of critical satisfaction at those of Marius.

Marius returned to Rome to take up office. He refused any formal triumph for his victory at Aquae Sextiae, realising that it was too soon to rejoice. The Cimbri, however, made no organised advance, spending the winter in recuperating after their long march from Gaul. It is probable also that they were waiting word from the Teutones—messages that now would never come.

After making all the necessary arrangements, Marius in spring left Rome to join Catulus, while his own troops took the road from Gaul. The forces which confronted the Cimbri were composed of practically the whole of the new armies which Marius had raised and trained. The negotiations with the Cimbri were interesting. They demanded land for themselves and their brethren. Asked who these brethren were, they answered, the Teutones. When told that these brethren " already had lands which they should possess for ever " their resentment showed that they had some suspicion of a truth which they were very unwilling to acknowledge. They threatened that the Teutones should answer for themselves when they came. Marius retorted by producing the captive kings of the Teutones, in chains. The Cimbri were in no two minds about fighting.

The indispensable necessity was to find some means of stopping the onslaught of those formidable storm-troops, and giving the short sword opportunity for its deadly work. Hitherto, the Roman javelin had been of a pattern fairly common to all nations, the head fixed to the shaft by two metal pins. Marius had one of the metal pins withdrawn, and replaced by a wooden peg. The object of this was that the wooden peg should snap with the shock as the javelin entered the shield of an opponent, when, pivoting on the iron pin, the shaft would form a drag hopelessly encumbering, even enforcing the abandonment of the shield altogether. It is true that this expedient could only be used at the first contact of the lines of battle ; but this was the only time when its use was called for. The repulse of the first charge was the crucial necessity.

One of the principal authorities for what followed is Sulla himself, who was present throughout.

Boiorix, the Cimbrian king, invited Marius to name the time and place of battle. Marius answered that Romans never consulted their enemies when to fight : but he named the plain near Vercellae, and the time, three days hence : an arrangement which was strictly observed. Marius must have had some ground for confidence as to the result.

Catulus commanded the centre of the Roman army, over twenty thousand strong. Marius placed his own men—thirty-two thousand altogether—on the wings, expecting that the real struggle would take place there.[1]

The Celtic horsemen of the Cimbri, helmed and crested like mediaeval knights, opened the battle by deploying their ranks with the object of enveloping the Roman forces—a movement which their superior numbers made a feasible plan. The idea was to drive the whole mass of the Romans upon the Cimbrian infantry in the centre. Had the operation succeeded, it would have prevented the new Roman tactical system from establishing any superiority to that of the enemy, would have caused the battle to be fought upon much more level terms, and might have ended by catching the army of Marius in a trap from which there was no escape. It took a little time, however, and while the Celts were galloping into their new positions, Marius charged. The onslaught of the cavalry was therefore never really made at all ; caught at pause, and in some disarray, they were hurled back on the rear of their own infantry. The flight of a great body of cavalry can be nearly as destructive as its charge. In dense clouds of dust, through which the soldiers of Marius came on in pursuit, they burst in upon the Cimbrian

[1] It is to this time, not to the Gallic campaign of the previous year, that we may best attribute the exploit of Quintus Sertorius, who, after learning some of the language, entered the enemy's camp disguised as a Celt, and gathered much important information. The dispositions of Marius indicate that he expected certain tactical manœuvres on the part of the Cimbri : and these were probably connected with the extension of the cavalry wings to envelop the Roman flanks. This fits in very well with the mission of Sertorius, and is consistent with Sulla's own statement that Marius expected the armies to make contact on the wings. (Plutarch : *Marius*, xxv ; *Sertorius*, iii.)

infantry : and at the same time Catulus, in the centre, launched his attack.

It was August : and it was Italy. A burning sun was pouring its rays through the dust clouds, full in the faces of the Cimbrians. They were big men, but they were of the Baltic stock, built for cold and snow, not for sun and dust. Choked, blinded, running with sweat, outflanked, their rear broken, they met the attack of the short sword wielded by men trained to a nicety, and native to the climate. Sulla records with pride that not one of his men was distressed ; and we may grant a proper credence to the man who, probably, was the staff-officer responsible for their condition. . . . Marius, in the dust, missed contact with his objective, and was groping about to find where the Cimbrian centre lay ; so that it was the men of Catulus, guided by the astute brain of Sulla, who burst the locked ranks and set the flight going. What followed was memorable, and its horror still reaches us effectively through the pages of Plutarch, copying Sulla, who saw it.

The Cimbrian centre, the flower of their fighting men—the front ranks chained belt to belt—was slaughtered until the rear could loosen the pack by its flight. As the legionaries emerged into the clearer ground, they saw the laager, and the despairing women, dressed in mourning, slaying those who fled, and themselves and their children also. One hanged herself in their sight from the pole of a wagon, with her children tied dangling at her heels. They stampeded the draught oxen, and threw themselves under their feet. Yet, despite those who took their own lives, above sixty thousand prisoners fell into the hands of the Romans, and more than that number lay on the field.

The troops of Marius were the men who stormed
the laager, and the booty fell to them ; but Catulus
and his men claimed the true spoils of war. An
angry dispute arose even on the field of battle. The
Parmanese, who were present, were called in as
witnesses. The men of Catulus led them among the
slain, showing them the official marks on the javelins.
Thirty ensigns, and numbers of trumpets and similar
spoil were piled in the camp of Catulus.

VI

Sulla was always unfair to Marius. His account
of the battle slurs over the crucial achievement at the
beginning, which decided the fate of the day. But
Sulla had taken the utmost pains to restore the *moral*
of his army, and he was intensely anxious that it
should do well ; he could not resist the temptation
to belittle the part played by Marius, and to magnify
the quite sufficiently important and honourable part
played by his own men. He is not to be blamed for
his ambition ; but popular opinion, in giving the
whole praise to Marius, was not far off the mark.
The command in chief was his ; the responsibility,
the methods, the organisation were all his ; and the
battle of Vercellae could never have been fought at
all save for the previous victory of Aquae Sextiae.

Marius was now at the supreme height of his fame,
hailed as the third founder of Rome, his name
coupled with those of the gods in religious offerings
and libations. He took it well. Had he been
deprived of any jot of his due fame, he might have
been as unfair and as bitter as any man ; that once
fully granted, he could be not only fair but generous.
Disregarding the wishes of his partisans, he associated
Catulus in his triumph.

But Sulla, at least, must have known that whoever said "Catulus" really said "Sulla." It was his turn to miss the honours he deserved. So Catulus, that lazy versifier and art-collector, acquired one treasure that must have been the last he ever expected to collect—a Triumphal Car. It ought by rights to have been inscribed : "A present from Lucius Cornelius Sulla."

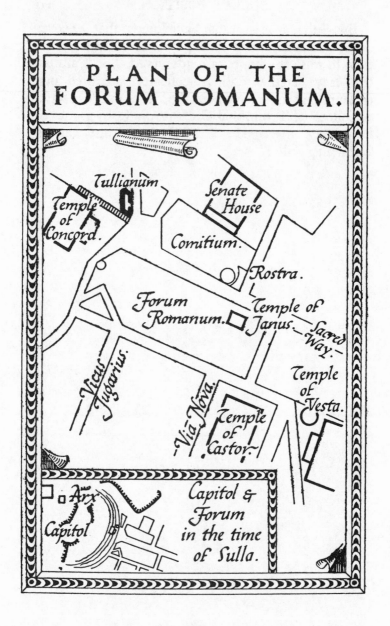

PLAN OF THE
FORUM ROMANUM.

Tullianum

Temple of Concord.

Senate House

Comitium.

Rostra.

Forum Romanum.

Temple of Janus.

Sacred Way.

Temple of Vesta.

Vicus Jugarius.

Via Nova.

Temple of Castor.

Arx

Capitol

Capitol & Forum in the time of Sulla.

CHAPTER VI

THE POLITICAL STRUGGLE

I

THE end of the war brought forward a number of problems familiar to the modern statesman. There was the question of the demobilisation of the army ; and this was a matter which raised issues for which the Roman politician was totally unprepared. Marius and his officers had probably foreseen and discussed the event. The Roman soldier of the old type, after a war, returned to his farm or his business —what was left of it. The whole weakness of that old system lay in the fact that very often little was left of it : the negligence of the oligarchy to guarantee or secure the property of the small farmer was a main reason for the decay of the class from which the armies of Rome were chiefly drawn. Still, the farm or business had been there in the majority of cases. . . . The new army, raised on military grounds alone, was composed of men of whom many (perhaps the overwhelming majority) were in the strict sense proletarians—men without property. What was to be done with the legionaries who had overcome Jugurtha and defeated the Cimbrian terror ?

The oligarchy, of course, intended to do nothing at all ; but the matter was not to be dismissed so lightly, for a variety of reasons. Marius was not the man to ignore the claims of those whom he had

organised and led. And then, too, the *Populares*
were in a position different far from that of the
Gracchan days. Their clients were not the mob
which had cheered Tiberius and Gaius Gracchus,
and deserted them when the pull came, but men
trained and hardened to war, knitted together by
common memories and a common craftsmanship in
the new military art. . . . Peremptorily to send
such an army back to its street corners was a dangerous proposition. An army has a way of becoming
a society or fraternity, which can act in peace time as
well as in war. These men were the men who had
saved the State. The oligarchs now held their
property in virtue of the protection which the army
had extended to it. What was more to the benefit
of the State than that these men should be settled
on the land, and the destruction of the small-farmer
class stayed ?

More than this, the *Populares*, as a party, were by
this time systematically organised. The nemesis
which attends proscription and repression had
arrived : the *Populares* had slowly grown again, but
not to the Gracchan model. The new popular
leaders, thrown up to the control by the natural
working of the party machine, were men whose
closest parallel is the less reputable type of American
party-boss. They were fierce demagogues, sur-
rounded by their bodyguards of bruisers and
" slugs," living and basing their power on the Corn
Dole. The oligarch who let loose his gladiators on
the street would find it already occupied by men
native to it.

The theory that systems do not matter, and that
any system will work well in the hands of good men
is true only in a somewhat limited and qualified

sense. There are some systems which naturally take the control out of the hands of good men. There are even some which necessarily put it into the hands of bad ones. The system which had grown up in Rome since the days of Tiberius Gracchus had a good deal of this quality about it. No one could work it in a completely honest manner. In the days of Marius, practically no one tried to do so—save, possibly, Marius. The embarrassing factor for the *Populares* was that Marius was essentially an honest man. It remained to be seen how far such a man could survive in the world of Roman party-politics.

II

Only when driven through by the solid phalanx of these popular leaders had the demands of Marius the slightest chance of success. The clubs of the oligarchy were already in a ferment of activity. The issues at stake for them were immense, and united in one camp men who took divergent views of political questions. Gaius Gracchus had threatened the State with a perpetual magistracy. Gaius Marius threatened it with a military tyranny ; at any rate, with the end of the system of legal, constitutional government which was the whole difference between civilisation and barbarism. There were men perfectly serious in this conviction ; there were others who, in the heat of political agitation, believed that they believed it ; there were undoubtedly some who entertained a good deal of scepticism about the points at immediate issue, but had their own hand to play for results not immediately in question, among whom it is fairly certain that Sulla must be numbered.

Sulla (as will be obvious enough at a later stage of

this story, when we get the details in fuller measure)
had no especial objection to the military policy represented by Marius. He was perfectly ready to take
over the methods of Marius when it suited his own
policy. We need not imagine, therefore, that Sulla
was seriously alarmed over the mere programme
which the *Populares* put forward ; his concern would
be with considerations still remote from practical
politics. But he would be ready enough, for good
reasons, to throw his whole energy into the task of
preventing Marius himself and his allies, as persons,
from securing political supremacy in the State.

He had more important reasons for opposing
Marius than mere dislike. They can be illustrated
by evidence which is in all probability his own. The
criticisms which have come down to us respecting the
way in which Marius conducted this electoral campaign fall into two classes. One is a criticism of his
external conduct. It consists in the allegation that
Marius spent vast sums in bribery ; and this rests
upon the testimony of Publius Rutilius Rufus, an
austere and upright man who also disliked Marius.
We may well believe that Marius spent lavishly on
his campaign. The customs of Roman electioneering (whatever the law might be) were not as austere
as Rutilius ; and the *Populares* were little likely to
split hairs over the use of the funds provided by their
powerful ally. But the second class of criticism
touches, not so much upon what Marius did, as upon
what he was. It consists of an acute analysis of
Marius's character by a somewhat cynical observer
who had a gift for psychology. This observer was
almost certainly Sulla himself. The analysis so
closely accords with the kind of " third degree " to
which Marius was consistently subjected during the

election and after it, that it may well be a memorandum by the man who superintended the process. It explains both the methods by which Marius was successfully sidetracked, and the reasons why the observer should be opposed to him.

Marius (says Sulla) lowered the dignity of the consulship by treating it as a favour bestowed by the people—instead, that is, of an office to which they raised a man for his qualities [1] : and he falsified his own character by trying to be amiable and popular, for which nature had never designed him. He was so anxious to be appreciated that it made him politically a weakling ; he could not preserve his balance before a public audience as he could before the enemy in the field : he was easily upset by the most ordinary praise or criticism. He was essentially a soldier, who had no faculty for pushing his own interests in the surroundings of civil life. He had no political principle (Sulla thought)—he accepted whatsoever ideas were approved by the people, and imagined that they must therefore be right. . . . Sulla's final caustic judgment was that Marius considered anything politically right if it redounded to his own praise and fame.

There is bias in this ; but it is a bias without malevolence. The picture is convincing in its portrait of the stern but sensitive old disciplinarian, who was lost without the support of the army regulations, and who made himself absurd by a *bonhomie* unnatural to him. There is even a suggestion that Sulla saw the pathos of it. If he did, he ruled it out

[1] Sulla may have been thinking of Aemilius Paulus, who, when elected consul, instead of returning thanks, simply remarked that he supposed they considered him the best man for the post. This was the principle Sulla had in mind.

of his mind as a feeling which it was not permissible to entertain.

Throughout the fierce contest which was waged Sulla was conspicuous by his absence. His friends and allies crowded the stage ; he alone does not appear in the limelight. But that he took a very important, if unobtrusive, part in the proceedings there can be little doubt. Almost the first person to be pushed to the front was that elegant and polished figure-head, Catulus. He was deposited before the political footlights as the true saviour of his country, the real victor of Vercellae, the decisive battle (it was alleged) of the war. The speakers of the *Optimates* were put up to push Catulus and his men for all they were worth. . . . Even Catulus himself, in the excitement of the moment, began to entertain the pleasing but improbable hypothesis that he was perhaps a second Camillus, whose justifiable laurels were being stolen from him by the wicked Marius.

The acerbity, violence, and depth of feeling evoked is a testimony to the discernment of the astute psychologist who now began to play off the foibles of Marius against their possessor. That the man was Sulla it is impossible to doubt. His qualification as election-agent for the *Optimates* was that he had already been responsible for the tactical triumph of having split the new army as a political force before it could bring its weight to bear. The dispute on the field of Vercellae was no meaningless wrangle. It meant that the new armies were not to be a *bloc* solid for Marius. Catulus was never anything more than a decorative military and political dummy carried about by the enterprising Sulla.

The candidate put forward by the *Optimates* to

stand against Marius for the consulship was no less
a person than Metellus Numidicus himself. Metellus
was well chosen ; he had a personal quarrel with
Marius, and, moreover, he had that particular sort of
probity and intelligence which is not imaginative nor
profound, nor especially wide in scope ; he would
work with sincere belief in the transcendent importance of the stake at issue ; his very strength was
based on the seriousness with which he took trifles.
He was the precise man who would have been the
choice of a more subtle, more sceptical mind which
saw more truly the relative values of things and men.
Whether Sulla could have made himself very angry
over the programme of the *Populares* is doubtful ;
but it was certain that Metellus would take it very
gravely indeed.

Such a man as Metellus was in addition the precise
sort of man who would wither within him the heart
of such a man as Marius. He had all the dry, formal
virtues which are horrible in the eyes of an illiterate
man of strong natural genius.

Marius was rapidly goaded to fury between the
propaganda on behalf of Catulus, and the pro-
pinquity of the obnoxious Metellus—a fury strangled
and frustrated by his constant sense that he was not at
home in these city surroundings. Although he could
talk to the man in the street, and turn a fierce and
memorable phrase, he could not present a coherent
and rational case to the educated portion of the electorate, the bankers and capitalists whose votes would
be the determining factor in the contest. He was (as
Sulla had perceived) sensitive to praise and criticism
to an extent ridiculous by comparison with his secure
fame and powerful character. There was some fatal
flaw in his composition. He was capable of facing

the Cimbri and Teutones, and of wresting victory
whence no other man could wrest it ; but he could
not learn confidence in himself, nor acquire the
intellectual skill on which such confidence is securely
founded in civil life.

III

From the point of view of the *Populares*, this was
by-play. Pushed on by their united forces, Marius
was rushed into his sixth consulship. L. Valerius
Flaccus, a nonentity, secured the second place :
Metellus was defeated. L. Appuleius Saturninus
obtained a tribuneship ; his principal ally, G.
Servilius Glaucia, the praetorship ; so that the
party was well equipped with office. It entered upon
its year of power pursued still by an intelligence bent
upon its downfall.

It fell accordingly to Saturninus to introduce the
programme of legislation into the Assembly of the
People. His programme was bold—the most complete and carefully-thought-out scheme since Gaius
Gracchus. Saturninus was what we should call an
abler parliamentary hand. He constructed his series
of proposals in a way far more dexterous than that of
his predecessor.

Taking advantage of the fact that Marius had
enrolled his armies not only without troubling about
questions of property qualification, but without
particular heed to domicile—having included both
Roman and Italian citizens indiscriminately—he
proposed to settle the discharged soldiers upon land
first in Africa, and then in the other provinces outside Italy : by which he could reckon upon a first
practical step towards placing the ordinary Italian
upon a level with the Roman citizen. The army

service itself was to qualify the applicant for the grant—not the citizenship. It is usual to describe these proposals as "revolutionary": they were assuredly extensive : but that Saturninus approached the problem as a statesman, not merely as a party politician, is clear from the subsequent course of events. His scheme might have saved Italy from two disastrous civil wars which ended in even greater concessions than he proposed to make.

Marius was to superintend the settlement.

Saturninus included in his legislation several other measures dictated by political necessities. He conciliated the *equites* by extending their juridical powers still further, and he increased the Corn Dole. Thus all the electors who had voted for the *Populares* got something.

The position of the party, impregnable as it seemed, was from this point onwards slowly undermined. The attack was against the nerves of Marius, its weakest point. Marius found the task of leading the Senate much more arduous than that of addressing the man in the street. He suffered just what a sensitive and uneducated man would suffer at the hands of a hostile audience of higher social standing, intent upon paralysing the action of his natural intelligence. In the task of reconciling the oligarchy to the new proposals he offended both parties and was suspected by each of insincerity. His soldiers came up to the polling in their thousands. Saturninus and Glaucia were thoroughly in their element in shepherding their own supporters to the poll. The legislation was pushed through with success in the teeth of resistance. The culminating point arrived when it left the Forum and was carried up to the Senate House.

Saturninus was aware of one of the difficulties that would await him. The contention that the entire series of consulships which Marius had held since his return from Africa—the second to the sixth—was illegal, and therefore void, was not to be disregarded. He had provided against it by attaching to his legislative measures one further provision—that the senators should individually take an oath to accept and observe the new laws : in effect, an act of oblivion and indemnity to cover any illegality in the past. The senators had no power to reject the new laws ; but they had the power to declare them invalid ; and they still had the power to refuse to take the oath. It was over this mental tangle that Marius finally lost his footing and fell.

There were violent differences of opinion. Some of the senators were utterly against taking the oath. Marius, unable to formulate in a convincing shape the arguments in favour of taking it, was apologetic. He agreed that if the laws were invalid, the Senate ought not to swear to observe them ; while if they were valid, it was perhaps insulting to ask the Senate to swear to obey the law. Some hand—probably Sulla's own—has described the impression created by Marius in his attempt to be reasonable and conciliatory. Metellus Numidicus, in holy horror and righteous indignation, vowed that he would refuse to take the oath, and Marius was understood to endorse his views. When the time came, however, Marius did take the oath, " in so far as the laws were valid " —a ridiculous qualification which may well have stupefied Saturninus. The other senators followed the lead of the consul. Metellus, however, stood by his refusal, and after solemn and dramatic scenes

was placed under interdict and went into exile with
copy-book maxims upon his righteous lips—a perfect
picture of the Roman prig—amid excited accusations
that the episode was a sinister plot on the part of the
Machiavellian Marius. Sulla, in the background,
must have enjoyed this little political comedy. The
views of Saturninus have not come down to us.
They were, we may imagine, very strong.

The contempt which Marius—who did not repeat
copy-book maxims, but created them—felt for
Metellus might well change to bitterness when he
saw how admirably the episode went down with the
Roman public. The Catonic pose was as sound a
resort in Roman politics as the appeal to the Noncon-
formist Conscience is in British. Other influences
added their weight. It had been shown by figures
in the Senate that the proposals of Saturninus
respecting the Corn Dole were more than the
treasury could bear. Worse than this, there were
distinct signs of a reconciliation between the Senate
and the *equites*. The bankers and capitalists began
to lose confidence in Marius : and no bait could be
thought of by which to hold their interest. Their
control of the courts could hardly be extended
further. It grew clearer and clearer that the
Optimates were awaiting a swing of the pendulum
which would place in their hands the power to
invalidate the laws of Saturninus, and to call him to
account.

The leaders of the *Populares* decided that Marius
must go. He was not only useless but dangerous as
an ally. Their only chance lay in regaining office
for the following year. It was arranged that
Glaucia should stand for the consulship, and
Saturninus for re-election as tribune. Glaucia was

not legally eligible for the office for another two years, but something had to be risked. There was always the possibility of another act of indemnity. With the courts in the hands of the *equites*, and the *equites* hostile, the leaders of the *Populares* were facing the alternatives of exile or death after a political supremacy of five years. The moral temperature of Rome rose to fever heat as the fateful elections approached. One of the candidates for the *Optimates* was Gaius Memmius. If Memmius could be put out of the way on the eve of the polling, it might be difficult for them to replace him at short notice. Glaucia saw to the job. The excitement now burst all bounds. The street skirmishes of the bruisers and slugs on both sides developed into a pitched battle in the Forum. The *Populares*, beaten by the defection of the *equites*, retreated upon the Senate House, and entrenched themselves there. They were pursued; the roof was torn off, and Saturninus himself was killed by a tile.

Marius was still consul. Called upon by both sides, he intervened with such military force as he could muster. His attempt to act fairly and impartially was once more his undoing. He compelled the surrender of those in the Senate House by cutting off the water supply, but he undertook to protect their lives. When they did surrender, they were torn out of his hands and slain. Glaucia was unofficially executed two days later.

If ever man were discredited, Marius was now that man. Nobody wanted him; nobody respected him; and if Marius were still Marius he must have been agonisingly conscious of his fall. The laws of Saturninus were invalidated; Metellus was recalled, and the land settlements that had already been founded were allowed to peter out as they would. The triumph of the *Optimates* seemed complete.

And so it was, but for one factor. The astute psychologist, having played steadily and successfully for his own hand, stopped short at that point. He had no further interest in the struggle. The victory remained wholly negative. The non-Roman element in the army was convinced that it confronted a hostile government, willing to use Italians to save its property, but unwilling to give them in return either the rights of citizens or the land-pensions they had earned by their deeds. The discontent of the Italians was the stray thread which the oligarchy neglected to catch and enclose in the otherwise unbroken circle of its success, and this proved to be the deadly negligence which rendered the success vain : for the feeling of the Italians was to count presently, when opportunity came.

One more point must be observed. The method by which the success had been won had thrown power, not so much back into the hands of the oligarchy, as into those of the men whose immediate action had brought it about—the great bankers and capitalists. Not only Marius, but the astute psychologist himself had—for the time being, at least—fallen into the pit he had dug.

IV

Marius did not care to remain in Rome after his failure as consul. He was still too powerful for his life to be touched ; it was not forgotten that after all he was the man who had saved the State ; and the astute psychologist was perhaps convinced that he was thoroughly harmless as a politician. To witness the triumphant return of the virtuous

Metellus (doubtless repeating some more copy-book maxims) was intolerable to the old man. He had had enough. He had not the self-confidence to stand for the one remaining office open to him—the censorship—grimly remarking that he did not want to show what he thought of his fellow-citizens. He left for a prolonged tour in the east, on the excuse that he had vowed a pilgrimage to Cybele.

He had probably intended from the first to make this tour, though he may reasonably have expected to do so with a proconsular command : for as the most famous, and in many respects the greatest soldier of his age, he had a particular interest in it. He wanted to examine on the spot the military condition of the eastern provinces of Rome.

It is impossible now to trace the information on which he acted ; but it cannot be doubted that a good deal of relevant news, and perhaps more than mere news, had come to the capital, especially when we consider the events which followed a few years later. The wave of unrest which had upset Africa and Italy was likely enough to trouble other parts of the Roman dominion. Marius, as the professional watchdog of the State, was on the alert. He held personal conferences with Mithradates, the King of Pontus. We, realising who and what Mithradates was, can see the proceedings of Marius to have been useful and significant. He was ahead of all his contemporaries in appreciating the possibilities of Mithradates. But Marius was too much feared for the oligarchy to allow him any further opportunities of displaying his military genius. The storm was allowed to gather—to burst, a few years afterwards, as an appalling cataclysm.

When Marius returned, he seems to have been

full of a new project—a command in the east. He must have realised only too well that if he got it, it would not come from the oligarchy. The *Optimates* made that fatal mistake which is so natural to timid men : they dared not take the bold course of conciliating him by the gift of the command, and they forced him back among their enemies. Sulla might have enlightened them, but he was silent. Marius took a house near the Forum, where he could keep in touch with public affairs ; and he complained bitterly because very few people came to see him. The astute psychologist, who was watching with interest, has explained to us why : namely, that apart from his military genius, Marius was not a particularly interesting man.

Other considerations entered into the matter. An eastern war was not like an African or a Cimbrian war : it was not all kicks and no halfpence. It had possibilities which afterwards made Lucius Lucullus more famous as a millionaire than as a general, and yet Lucullus was a great general. Accordingly the question stood over.

V

During the next three uneventful years, the agitation which afterwards bore fruit in the Italian demand for the franchise must have penetrated throughout Italy. There was a variety of means by which it could be carried on. The old framework of leagues and alliances between the cities which had once been independent City States still subsisted, long divested of political meaning, but maintained as more or less social and religious institutions. It was not difficult for the Italians to use the machinery as a method of secret political propaganda. The

Optimates were aware of the agitation, but could do nothing to stop it. They might have dissolved the leagues ; but it is of very little use to pronounce the public dissolution of bodies which could easily continue their operations privately, in a way making them even harder to trace ; and equally, it is waste of time to trouble about the methods of an agitation which, when hunted out of one, will always turn to others. The oligarchy took a stronger course. Quintus Mucius Scaevola, the famous jurist, held the consulship in 95 B.C. with Lucius Crassus, the almost equally famous orator. Through Scaevola, the oligarchy made an attempt to close the constitution on the franchise agitation. The Licinian-Mucian law prohibited non-Romans from laying claim to the Roman franchise. But the Roman constitution, having grown by the accumulation of statute law, was a difficult one to close. Whatever could be made illegal could as easily be made legal, and the growing public opinion of non-Roman Italy was not diverted.

It was round Quintus Scaevola, one of the truly great men of his time, that the first omens of the coming trouble centred themselves. Concurrently with the Italian franchise agitation, a second serious agitation was going on in Rome itself. The conviction was growing—at least, among a certain group —that the equestrian courts [1] used their judicial powers for the purpose of determining the policy of provincial governors, who were of the senatorial

---

[1] In this year, Gaius Norbanus was brought to trial for his action against Caepio in 104 B.C. If this trial were part of a demonstration against the equestrian courts, and an effort to rehabilitate the author of the *lex Servilia* of 106 B.C., the case is more comprehensible than if it were merely an attempt to

order. The charge can be brutally formulated in this shape, that the local governor whose policy played into the hands of the Roman bankers and merchants was secure after his term of office, while he who took a more impartial view of his duties was practically certain to be accused of some offence cognisable by the equestrian courts, and as certain to be condemned : a process which practically meant the control of provincial government in the interests of the Roman capitalists, who had no responsibility to either Senate or people.

It is extremely probable that the charge was true. It affected the views of the more intelligent of the *Optimates* in several ways. The threat in the east might pass off without war—or, at any rate, without a dangerous war—if the eastern provinces could be kept contented and happy. The real danger from Mithradates lay in that Asia was rapidly becoming a hotbed of discontent which might at any time culminate by welcoming any invader, any change of master, as a refuge from the oppression of the great Roman corporations to whom Gaius Gracchus had handed over the collection of the taxes. The struggle against Mithradates thus began in Rome itself. If it failed, if Asia fell into the hands of Mithradates, then there might once more be no alternative but resort to Marius. Hence a real effort was needed to recover control of the courts.

But this involved important political questions. The *equites* swayed the political balance in Rome.

whitewash the man responsible for the defeat of Arausio. Caepio was not to be forgiven so easily, and Norbanus was acquitted, though his action in 104 B.C. had been at least of very doubtful legality. Lucius Crassus (significantly enough) had been one of Caepio's prime helpers in passing the *lex Servilia*.

We have seen that their alliance with the oligarchy had overthrown Saturninus and Glaucia. The prosecution of such an effort as far as the necessary legislative action would mean some fresh change in the situation. The oligarchy was not anxious to invoke any such change. To share the spoil by compromising with the moneyed interest, in return for political security, seemed to the majority the safest course. In this they were, of course, wrong. To compromise in this manner was no more than to stave off the consequences without averting them. The oligarchy was confronting one of those problems so complicated that nothing but honesty, that last bitter resort of man, can solve them. To compromise with the moneyed men might keep it in power ; but then it had to fear the awful results of misgovernment and oppression, for the information that came to Rome was the complaint of angry and desperate men.

To the group who took up the question of the equestrian courts belonged several of the most eminent men of the day : Scaevola, Publius Rutilius Rufus, Marcus Livius Drusus, Marcus Aemilius Scaurus,[1] who was in some respects the most influential of all ; and Sulla himself.

After the year of office which saw his attempt to close the constitution on the franchise agitation, Scaevola took the bold course of accepting Asia as his proconsular province. With him went Publius

[1] Scaurus, though by his name an Aemilius, and therefore a high aristocrat, was a self-made man whose father had been a charcoal-burner. He rose to wealth and power by his own efforts, and became the leading man of the oligarchy. His youthful poverty may explain his chief weakness, namely, that he could never refuse money.

Rutilius Rufus. With the support of Scaevola, Rutilius took a strong line against the agents of the financial corporations. Abuses were rigorously repressed ; justice was done with severest impartiality. Instead of men privately in league with their oppressors, the Asiatics found above them men who could be relied on to carry out the law without fear or favour. If Scaevola could have been followed by a succession of governors as wise and courageous as himself, Asia might have been rescued from the trough into which it was slipping. His year over, he and Rutilius returned to fight their battle on the real field of war—the judicial courts of Rome.

Sulla—the least wealthy or important member of the group—was all this time struggling to get into a position to help its operations. He put up for election as praetor, but he was defeated. He gives the semi-humorous explanation that the electors, knowing his friendship with King Bocchus, wanted him to be aedile instead, and have control of the wild-beast shows. The next year, however, he got in, and was praetor during the impeachment and trial of Rutilius, in which office he was no doubt able to exert his influence to assist his ally. All the legal knowledge of Scaevola was at his disposal. No praetor can ever have had a better adviser ; for Scaevola was the greatest jurist of his age, and the founder of scientific jurisprudence. When, in after years, as Dictator, Sulla put forward a number of epoch-making ideas concerning the reorganisation of the judicial system and the division of legal procedure, which could never have occurred to a mere soldier or a mere man of fashion, we may bear in mind that he held a great judicial office during his praetorship, in close friendly association with a man

whose private conversation must have been a foun-
tain of ideas on such subjects.

All the knowledge and influence that could be
brought to bear in favour of Rutilius—legal or
political—was of no avail. After a long struggle he
was condemned for malversation and sent into exile.
Scaevola was too powerful to be touched. The
Senate passed a resolution approving of the actions
of Scaevola, and ordering his methods and principles
to be regarded as a guide for the conduct of future
governors.

Of these " future governors " the first was Sulla,
who obtained Cilicia as a pro-praetorian governorship. He may possibly have travelled in company
with Rutilius, who retired first to Mitylene and then
to Smyrna, where he settled down to write historical
works, and an autobiography which we would give
much to possess. That Rutilius should pass the rest
of his life honoured and admired in the province he
was alleged to have misgoverned is sufficient answer
to the court which condemned him. He never
returned to Rome. Sulla, in later years, sent to
recall him ; but he would not come.

VI

Sulla's praetorship marks an important stage in his
progress. From this point onwards he steadily rose,
and never looked back. When he embarked for
Cilicia, he was still under the shadow of Marius.
Neither he nor any other Roman of his time had as
yet broken away from the ascendency of the old
man's genius. They all of them still followed where
he went. They might wreck his work, disappoint
his hopes, steal his credit, and adopt his plans ; but
it was still his work, his hopes, his credit and his

plans that formed the main staple of Roman imperial policy. But Sulla was growing. He was not the kind of man who merely frustrates without creating. He was entering upon a path whose direction reveals his intentions. To use all he had learnt from Marius for the purpose of strengthening and restoring aristocracy was the plan he had in mind. Without possessing the peculiar form of genius Marius possessed, he had the range of faculties which enabled him to employ its results for his own purposes. He had studied the new military system, and learnt to work it ; he had used his praetorship to equip himself with a knowledge, not perhaps of law, but of the way in which law should be administered in the public interest ; his task now was to lay hold of some experience of governing a civilised State and, incidentally, to measure the new danger that was growing up on the eastern frontier. . . . When we smile at the oddity of the various posts a Roman had to fill during his career upward, it is well to remember that they formed, taken all together, an ideal education for the rare hundredth man who could gather the benefit of all the experience they afforded. Sulla was this hundredth man.

If Fortune liked Sulla, it was possibly because Sulla made the most of Fortune, who, like a woman, loves to be appreciated.

It was part of Sulla's good fortune to arrive in his eastern province at a particularly interesting time. The Hellenisation of Asia by Alexander and his successors had slowly faded ; the submerged native powers were beginning to revive ; and when Sulla took up office, the first stage of the reaction was already in progress.

Asia Minor has been very little altered by thirty centuries of history. The modern " Turk," who is supposed, and alleged by anthropologists, to be of comparatively recent Central Asiatic origin, differs little, if at all, from the aboriginal breed. Mithradates VI, King of Pontus, the source of the trouble threatening the Asiatic provinces of Rome, was a man of the familiar type which has its parallels to-day. He was the incarnation of the Asiatic revival : a romantic figure, whose personal qualities (he was a big, handsome, strong and clever man) were still further magnified by an adventurous youth. Like the finest type of Turk, he had wonderful gifts as an individual, and entirely lacked moral responsibility, the sense of the State, the sense of duty to God and man. His idea of government was to have more and more people to govern. That government had a purpose ; that it was an art and a science were conceptions beyond his horizon. The familiar result was foredoomed. With his energy and ability he began to lay the foundations of an immense kingdom ; foundations based chiefly on ruthless crime. The City State was dying in Asia as it was dying in Europe ; but in Asia what replaced it was this ivy-like growth, inferior in nature even to the primitive governments of earlier times—a parasitic, destructive growth of politics grown wild, doomed to destroy what it fed on, and then to die itself. . . . Sulla, regarding it, could have but one thought : this military tyranny was the kind of government to which the policy of Marius led : this was government by the hired soldier.

It is hardly likely that the condemnation of Rutilius had passed unnoticed by Mithradates. He knew that he had nothing to fear : the eastern provinces of Rome, ripe for revolt under the hand of the financial corporations, would in due course fall willingly into his hands. He interfered with Cappadocia and Paphlagonia, claiming the latter as his own in virtue of an alleged testamentary grant made in favour of his father ; and after murdering Ariarethes, the King of Cappadocia, and his young son, he governed the country through a local tool named Gordius. Ariarethes was a brother-in-law of Mithradates, but this was perhaps unimportant to a man who either murdered or kept in captivity his mother, three sons, three daughters, and a brother.

Sulla was very much in the position of some of the earlier British governors in India. He had no Roman army with which to enforce any policy ; he had no money, save the ordinary revenues of his province. He knew, of course, what problems he had to face, and what he was authorised to achieve : but he had yet to find out how and by what means he could achieve it. It was therefore in the most advantageous circumstances possible that he began his career as an independent commander. To practise the art of creating his own means and methods was a valuable addition to his education. Fortunately, he had been prepared in a good school— that of Gaius Marius.

The Asiatic were the richest of the Roman provinces. Sulla organised the local resources in men and money, and after a vigorous campaign drove Gordius out of Cappadocia, saw that a native king (one Ariobarzanes) was duly chosen and set up, and compelled Mithradates to acknowledge the independence of Paphlagonia. He did more than this. He got into personal touch with the powerful new forces of which Mithradates was but one example. Pene-

trating as far as the Euphrates, he met in conference
the king of Greater Armenia, and the Parthian
ambassador. A great power, of which the Romans
were destined to know more, was growing up in
Parthia. Sulla was the first Roman official to
establish contact with it.

This conference was famous. Sulla had much to
conceal. The comparative unimportance of his
office, and the somewhat dubious nature of his
military resources, had to be glossed over by a good
deal of vigorous bluff. Fortunately, again, Sulla
was admirably trained for such a necessity. He
showed all the self-confidence of the aristocrat, and
all the sense of dramatic appropriateness which
belongs to a good actor ; and he bluffed with an
easy and insolent hauteur which was much criticised
and admired at home. When the chairs were set for
the conference, Sulla promptly took the middle one,
as the most important person present : and it is said
that this cost the Parthian ambassador his life on his
return to his master.

His countrymen were not the only persons who
criticised and admired. One of the Chaldaeans in
the Parthian's retinue studied Sulla intently, and
remarked that it was impossible that he should not
become the greatest of men ; the marvel was that he
should not yet have proved it.

It is certain that, if nothing else were attained,
Sulla's vigorous measures, following upon the wise
administration of Scaevola, kept Mithradates in
check until other methods, and the state of politics in
Rome, made war too tempting to be resisted. For
now Sulla himself in turn had to return home to
answer for the crime of having maintained the credit
of Roman government. His friends prepared the

way for him. King Bocchus was communicated with, and undertook to celebrate the occasion by dedicating in the temple of Capitoline Jupiter a gold plaque decorated with a relief of himself handing Jugurtha over to Sulla. The wrath of Marius was great. He attempted to have the invidious plaque removed ; but the *Optimates* with one accord came to Sulla's rescue. This famous plaque was intended to remind the Roman public—as usual, at Marius's expense—that Sulla deserved well of his country. The expected impeachment was handed in by Gaius Marcius Censorinus,[1] one of the leaders of the *equites*.

Sulla would probably have put up an even more vigorous fight than Rutilius, but it was not called for. The impeachment was first suspended, and then dropped ; for a redoubtable protagonist had stepped upon the scene, and the curtain went up for one of the main acts of the drama.

VII

Marcus Livius Drusus, the son of the man who had been chiefly instrumental in destroying the hold of Gaius Gracchus upon the electorate, was very wealthy, highly cultivated, and of that lofty, almost insolent courage [2] which great wealth and high

[1] Sulla's enemies treated him with respect. Censorinus was no common person, but a highly respectable member of a very old family, numbering among his ancestors the first plebeian censor, the first plebeian dictator, and the only man who ever held the censorship twice. He was among the prisoners massacred after the battle by the Colline Gate. See Ch. XI, p. 257.

[2] Some anecdotes of the foibles of Drusus have survived. His famous reference to " *Our* Commonwealth " seems to have tickled his contemporaries : while when the Senate requested his presence he replied : " Let it come to me ! "—and it did !

culture are apt to breed in those who are not destroyed by them. Since the oligarchy paltered and hesitated, and no one else seemed in a position to take up the case of the equestrian courts at the source—the Assembly—he came forward as a candidate for the tribuneship on the eve of Sulla's return from Asia, and was elected. Some one had to " bell the cat," and Drusus proposed to do it.

He had the support of those of the group who were available in Rome—notably of Lucius Crassus, whose power as a speaker would be invaluable, and of Marcus Scaurus, the most influential of the senators. Scaevola is not mentioned ; he could perhaps not overtly support the course Drusus proposed to take, in view of the Licinian-Mucian law, though Crassus had no such scruples : Sulla was absent, and Rutilius in exile.

The oligarchy was lukewarm. Various considerations distracted it. It dared not endorse the action of Drusus too cordially, lest the great financial interests should again go over to the *Populares*. Drusus was prepared to make the compromises necessary in order to form a *bloc* of electors in favour of his proposals. He undertook to increase the Corn Dole, to provide land-settlements in Italy, and to grant Italians the franchise. . . . He was, in fact, mobilising the whole mass of other interests against the *equites*.

It is one of the most engaging ironies of history that now, after all that had happened, a programme such as this should come from the heart of the oligarchy itself. The spot of strategic weakness in the scheme was that Drusus rather outran public opinion in his proposal to grant the franchise to the Italians ; and he was bound to come into collision

with the Licinian-Mucian law. Moreover, owing
to considerations of political tactics, he could not
prudently stress the principal object of his legislation,
so that his contemporaries were left in some doubt as
to which of the various items in the scheme was the
chief one. Was Drusus making more or less in-
sincere concessions to other sections in order to
pass his law regarding the equestrian courts ?—or
was the attack on the *equites* itself a concession
designed to gain over the oligarchy for some other
purpose ?

Drusus was successful in passing all the items of
his programme, with the exception of that concerning
the franchise, which he kept back for the present.
When the courts were safely out of the hands of
the *equites*, he would run a much better chance of
escaping impeachment under the provisions of
the Licinian-Mucian law. The *equites*, now fighting
for their privileges, exerted all their power. The
Consul Lucius Philippus led the opposition, and
though Drusus used his tribunician power to im-
prison Philippus, the latter called upon the Senate
to reject the proposals. It refused ; and Philippus
warned it that he might seek another Senate.
Confronted with this monstrous threat of revolution, the Senate wavered. Then Lucius Crassus
died suddenly, in ominous circumstances, and
hesitation grew into apprehension. Finally, the
proposals of Drusus respecting the Italian franchise
became known. So great was the outcry, so
thoroughly were even his supporters intimidated,
that the Senate gave way, and declared the laws of
Drusus to be void. Drusus himself was struck down
by an assassin shortly afterwards : the slayer
escaped ; the crime was not investigated too closely ;

and the moneyed men remained masters of the situation.

VIII

Thus ended the great attempt to keep the power of money under political control. Had it succeeded, it might have changed the course of history : but it had failed.

The *equites* may only have intended to destroy the schemes of Drusus as far as they themselves were affected ; but if so, they worked more wildly than they knew, for now the first thunderbolt fell, the first of a series which was not to end until Sulla stood the supreme master of Rome.

Revolt broke out at Asculum, where all the Roman citizens were murdered. It spread rapidly throughout Italy : the Marsians and the Samnites rose, and Rome was in a death grapple, not now with Carthaginians or Cimbri, but with the very men who had defeated the Carthaginians and Cimbri.[1] The Samnites were the most dangerous of all. They were the people who, beyond all others, had once been the real rivals of the Romans, and had shown precisely the same powers and qualities. With the Samnites in the field it was diamond cut diamond ; and in this emergency all Rome rose, with equal unanimity, for the defence.

[1] " No Triumph," said the proverb, " without Marsians or against Marsians." (Appian : B.C. I, vi, 46.)

THE SOCIAL WAR
B.C. 89-90.

Umbria

Picenum

Etruria

Adriatic Sea

W   N   E

S

Marsi

□ Corfinium. (Italia)

□ Rome.

□ Aesernia.

Latium

□ Bovianum.

Teanum.

Samnium

Apulia

Capua.

Acerrae.

Neapolis

Nola.

□ Venusia.

Pompeii.

Campania

Lucania

Tyrrhenian Sea.

Rough Scale.

M 20 I 40 L 60 E 80 S

CHAPTER VII

THE MILITARY STRUGGLE IN ITALY

I

THE insurgents sent to Rome, notifying that they would lay down their arms if the franchise were granted them. The Senate, unable to grasp the real causes or the real magnitude of the catastrophe, could only answer instinctively with a refusal. It was the first maxim of Roman policy that Rome never negotiated with enemies who bore arms. Thought, reflection, understanding must come later, as the truth penetrated into men's minds. Those who had favoured the grant of the franchise, those who had opposed it, and those who had been neutral, all alike prepared for resistance.

The Italian army was a typical revolutionary army—that is to say, it was a patchwork of elements with the same interests and ideals, but different concrete objects to attain. The Samnite was out to smash Rome ; the men of Marius's army to avenge their lost pensions ; others—the most part—demanded the protective privileges given by Roman citizenship—equality before the law. From yet another aspect, the war was a revolt of the small farmer of central and southern Italy against the landlordism which had already reduced northern Italy to serfdom, and against the moneyed men who held the financial strings, and had overthrown and murdered Drusus. 'The Roman army, deprived of the flower of the allies, was perhaps the worst which the Romans had ever put into the field—a mixture of sound old soldiers with the rabble of the slums, Cis-Alpine Gauls who were all but foreigners, slightly touched as yet with Roman tradition; Numidian cavalry, and Greek seamen. This fact reveals, suddenly and clearly, that Rome herself was undergoing a change of character. She was no longer the definite, independent City State ; she was, in fact if not in name, the capital of Italy ; the war was, in fact if not in name, the revolt of nationals against a national government. There were then no names for these things. Theory lagged so far behind fact that the Roman still conceived the war to be a foreign war of the Roman State against its allies. He had not yet grasped the idea that the walls of Rome were the coasts of Italy.

The principle really involved was illustrated by the proceedings of the Italians. They did not act merely as independent City States allied against an independent City State. They chose Corfinium as a capital, named it " Italia," and organised a general government. That they planned it exactly on the Roman model is not a matter for surprise. No better was known. The essential point is that they did realise the conception of the political union of Italy, Rome or no Rome. The Italians had discovered the nation, as distinct from the City State.

Hence, on the Roman side the war was fought partly by men who had no policy at all except to maintain certain privileges ; partly by sincere men who were still applying obsolete theories to a world of facts that had changed. As soon as these latter realised their position, there was certain to be dissension.

II

The *equites*, having plunged Rome into this war, endeavoured to justify themselves by carrying it through. For a while a reign of terror prevailed. At the instance of Quintus Varius Hybrida a special commission was appointed to investigate the alleged treasonable relation between Drusus and the Italians. As a result of its sittings, a considerable number of important persons were exiled. Marcus Aemilius Scaurus—safe, if any man were safe—needed all his influence to avoid being numbered among them. Sulla, who—either through his absence, or through prudence, or, like Scaevola, on principle—had not been connected with the actions of Drusus, escaped the enquiries of the commission. The old group was practically broken up. Only Scaevola and Sulla remained—one in the secluded but influential background of the seniors, the other, in the prime of his energies and abilities, in the field.[1]

War raged in Italy for two years. Two Roman armies were organised : one, under the consul Publius Rutilius Lupus in central Italy ; the other, under the consul Lucius Julius Caesar, in Campania. Sulla took a command under Caesar. The war

[1] The Commission took evidence to prove that Drusus was the head of a vast secret organisation of Italians. The allegation is utterly improbable. That Drusus was in touch with the heads of the Italian organisation is probable. Sulla, for the reasons given on p. 82 *ante*, may not have shared the views of Drusus on the franchise, but have been interested chiefly in the attempt of the group to wrest the judicial courts from the *equites* and to preserve the control of the political government over the provinces. No court could proceed against him on account of such views.

opened disastrously. Caesar sent on an advanced
corps into Samnium, followed with his main force,
and was repulsed with heavy loss. Aesernia, the
chief Roman stronghold in Samnium, was in consequence isolated. Sulla distinguished himself by
throwing help into the besieged town, but it was
forced to surrender. The Samnites, under Papius
Mutilus, entered Campania, and effected a junction
with the army which had expelled the Romans from
Lucania. With the exception of the city of Nuceria,
all Italy south of Vesuvius was lost to the Romans,
who held little more than the coast and military road
from Rome to Naples. A second defeat drove
Caesar right back upon Teanum. He reorganised
and advanced afresh to Acerrae, which was his
furthest south.

While the southern army was faring thus badly,
the campaign in central Italy, on which Caesar's
lines of communication entirely depended, barely
held its own, and there only owing to the presence
of a hated figure. The consul Lupus had Marius
as one of his corps-commanders. Detaching
Gnaeus Pompeius Strabo to operate in Picenum, and
bar the road north, Lupus proposed to advance on
Italia. Marius cautioned him that the army needed
much more training before it was capable of serious
military operations ; but his advice was rejected
with contempt. The result proved that Marius still
knew his business. A corps under Perpenna came
badly to grief. Lupus removed Perpenna, and
incorporated the remnant of the defeated troops
with the corps of Marius. Proceeding with his
plan, he was himself taken by surprise crossing a
river, and fell with eight thousand men. Marius
effected a crossing elsewhere, extricated the army,

and forced the enemy to withdraw. The Italians gained no more successes while he controlled operations.

The Senate, however, could not allow the old man to remain sole commander. Quintus Caepio was sent, for political reasons, to act as colleague. Caepio did not last long. He fell into an ambush, and was slain with most of the force he led. Marius once more took over the command, and once more the tale of enemy successes abruptly stopped. He knew how to handle the brittle and treacherous stuff he commanded.[1] He proceeded with great caution, relying on entrenchments and defensive tactics. It was during these slow operations that he uttered one of his best sayings. " If you are a great general, Marius," called out the Marsian commander, Quintus Silo, " come out and fight a battle." . . . " If *you* are one," returned Marius, briefly, " make me do it." When at last Silo succeeded in making him do it, Marius destroyed his army. The occasion was characteristic of the time. The commander of the southern army nearest at hand was requested to co-operate, and that commander was Sulla. Marius drove Silo's troops upon Sulla, and Sulla intercepted them, and promptly took the credit. Marius and Sulla were the only two generals on the Roman side who emerged from the first year of the war with honour.

III

Under the stress of disaster, a shifting of opinion was taking place in Rome. The landholding

[1] In " dressing down " these troops after a disgraceful episode in which both sides had run away, Marius said : " I do not know which are the worst—you, who could not face their backs, or they, who could not face yours."

senatorial class was suffering more than the men of
money, for Italy was being devastated, and all work
on the land was at a standstill, while the provinces
were unaffected. The corn dole was greatly reduced, ostensibly as a measure of economy, but
partly, no doubt, to drive the idle class of loafers
into the ranks. There was a general suffering in
which the moneyed men came off by far the
best.

The danger to their power lay in the alliance
between certain elements of the *Optimates* and the
Populares which Drusus had created. That *bloc* still
subsisted, and in the critical state of public affairs
it began to regain its influence. To many men it
became clear that the war was the kind of war in
which every one loses and no one wins—a brutal,
bruising, bungling, destructive war, which might go
on as long as there was a Roman left to pound a
Samnite, and a Samnite to pound a Roman. After
all, why not give the Italians the franchise ?

The opposition to the extension of the franchise
was a coalition of all kinds of men with all kinds of
motives. The able-bodied loafers of the Forum
and the wealthy bankers were standing frankly for
their private interests ; the typical oligarch was, of
course, on principle opposed to change. But there
was a considerable residuum of all parties who had a
more reasonable basis for opposition. The extension
of the franchise meant a fundamental revolution in
the character of the State, without any clear prospect
of a new form of State to justify it. Rome owed
its political value to its solidity and coherence.
Where was the sense—where even was the sanity—
of dissipating this coherence without adequate cause
among a million men ? All men knew what a City

State was. But what was this monstrosity which would result from an extension of the franchise ? It was the change in the feelings of this residuum that decided the future. They saw the whole structure of the Roman State, which had successfully resisted Hannibal, being shaken down by intestine strife. The will to survive was powerful in the Roman. Better anything than this destruction. The change of feeling spread. Rome refused to go down fighting ; rather than go down at all she would compromise, and make this amazing leap in the dark. The same faith which had once made the triumph of the plebeians possible now made the triumph of the Italians possible.

It may have been no more than a coincidence that it was Sulla's commander-in-chief, the consul Lucius Caesar, who, returning to Rome late in the year, took the first bold step by initiating a law to give the franchise to all Italians who had remained loyal. The Varian commission was dissolved, and a new commission appointed, in which all classes were represented. It acted with vigour. The leaders of the *equites* were at once involved. Quintus Varius, the author of the original commission, was now openly charged with responsibility for the murder of Drusus, and himself sent into exile. It became obvious, however, that the Julian law was insufficient to meet the emergency. A fresh law was soon brought forward by two tribunes, granting the franchise to all Italians who surrendered within sixty days.

How easily a policy of concession might have avoided the whole trouble is clear from the results of even these halting and imperfect compromises. The new law had serious restrictions in it, affecting the electoral influence of the new voters—as we should say, it " gerrymandered the constituencies." Yet it so weakened the Italians that the second year of the war was marked by an increasing tale of effective Roman successes.

If the agency of Lucius Caesar, Sulla's commander-in-chief, be a mere coincidence, there can be no doubt as to certain arrangements which were made at the same time. A general re-shuffle of the commands took place. Marius, who had held the main ground for Rome during the disastrous early days of the war, was superseded on the ground of age and health. To prove them wrong, the angry and disappointed old man at once set to work, appearing regularly in the Campus Martius at the athletic exercises : at which, though he had put on weight, he was still expert. Lucius Porcius Cato was given the consulship and the command which Marius had vacated, while his colleague, Gnaeus Pompeius Strabo, remained in Picenum. Sulla was sent south to take over Caesar's Campanian army. Fortune was playing steadily into his hands.

These arrangements, made simultaneously, were obviously parts of a connected design. Campania was not only strategically and politically important, it also was the favourite and fashionable resort of the most influential families of the oligarchy, who would not have sent thither any man save one in whom they had confidence. It was practically a promise of the consulship. It was also on the main road to Brundusium, the port of departure for the east. The government was fully aware of the danger of the situation in Asia, where the corporations, set free from all interference during the supremacy of the *equites*, had rapidly created a condition of affairs

leading straight to war. Taken in connection with
the recall of Marius, the appointment meant that
Sulla could expect, if he made good, the highest
promotion, and a command in Asia.

If politics be a child's game, in which the apple
must be shared with scrupulous equality among the
players, then Marius had been badly treated. But
all the good reasons favoured the appointment of
Sulla. The east needed not merely a soldier, but a
statesman. Sulla was already acquainted with Asia ;
his views were in harmony with those prevailing in the
bloc ; it would probably be necessary to send a man
who bore the highest credentials ; and Sulla had the
necessary familiarity with the Greek language and
with Greek culture. The difficulty about Marius
was not only the political one, but his ignorance of
Greek and his incapacity as a statesman. He perhaps did not know enough even to realise the nature
of the objections.

IV

The Italians opened the second year of the war by
attempting to carry the struggle north into Etruria.
For a while the stress centred round Strabo, who, in
a great battle—one of the greatest of the war—held
his ground. Cato rapidly followed his predecessors
in that command which hitherto no one but Marius
had succeeded in surviving. He fell in battle,
whereupon Strabo took over his army and proved
himself competent to control the entire field of war
in central Italy.

Sulla was thus set free to act. He first operated
in southern Campania, recovering the small towns
of the Sorrentine peninsula—Stabiae, Herculaneum,
and Pompeii. The siege of Pompeii absorbed some

time, and the Samnites undertook its relief. Two serious efforts were made to raise the siege. They were resisted ; and in the second battle the Samnite general, Lucius Cluentius, himself fell.

Sulla, like Marius, had had trouble with his army. A section of it had mutinied and beaten their commander, a man of praetorian rank, to death. Sulla's attitude to the episode rather shocked his contemporaries. He took no punitive action, but hoped, in return, that his troops would fight the better by way of apology for this breach of discipline. The astute psychologist obtained his hope. The army appreciated him. On the fall of Cluentius the troops paid their commander the compliment of presenting him with the grass wreath which was the mark of honour bestowed on a soldier who had distinguished himself in securing the safety of his comrades. Sulla received many distinctions during his lifetime, but none that did him more credit as a man and a soldier.

It was particularly urgent for Sulla to get his army into fighting shape. Any severity or leniency that helped to this end seemed to justify itself by expedience. He was playing for enormous stakes. The whole future of Rome, the whole future of civilisation, toppling to irremediable downfall, rested to some considerable extent upon him, his intelligence, his tact—above all, his Fortune. He emerged from this war with his faith in Fortune confirmed. To this was due the inconsistency which his critics saw in him—the incalculable mingling of the lenient and the severe. He was too prudent to strain at the very tenuous thread of discipline. The example of Strabo was before him. Strabo had licked his own army into order, but remained as one

of the most hated men in Roman history. This
was of no use to Sulla, who needed to be not only
obeyed, but admired and loved.

The fall of Cluentius at Pompeii was the signal for
a change in the conduct of the war. The Samnites
had been attracted in force into southern Campania,
and the defeat inflicted on them would detain them
with reorganisation. Sulla's army was in a good
mood. He marched past the cities of Campania
which were still in the possession of the enemy, and
struck right into the heart of Samnium itself.

The raid was successful. He got astride of the
great highway, the Via Appia, that ran to
Brundusium, took Aeclanum, the principal town on
that portion of the route, and received the submission
of the Hirpinian lands around it. Pushing north, he
met Papius Mutilus, beat him in a pitched battle,
and penetrated to Bovianum itself, the Samnite
capital, which surrendered to him. At the end of the
season, when operations had to be suspended, the
struggle had been transformed. Strabo was busy
in reducing the whole of Central Italy ; the praetor
Cosconius, by the reduction of Apulia, was further
opening up the way to Brundusium. The war was
going definitely against the Italians.

Their defeat, now certain, did not alter the political
results for which they had begun their revolt. If, in
a military sense, Rome was once more to be victor,
and if her political supremacy was still to be maintained, none the less the franchise had been granted :
no matter in how grudging and imperfect a shape.
Once the principle was established, it could only be
a matter of time before its terms were enlarged and
liberalised. Such was the upshot of the Social War

The most vast events come secretly. Neither the

Italian nor the Roman, those who had fought for the franchise, nor those who had opposed it, knew that one of the transcendent revolutions of history had been accomplished. The City State was dead ; the Nation was born. It took long to get the corpse of the old form of State removed and buried ; longer to get the new form to walk and talk of itself ; but the change had been made.

v

Calamity was heaped upon calamity in those disastrous days, for into this cauldron of trouble dropped an appalling catastrophe. Mithradates had acted as soon as the Social War began ; his allies were inspired to place themselves afresh upon the thrones of Bithynia and Cappadocia, and drive out the Roman nominees. A commission was sent from Rome to see the matter put right. The commission, appointed under the regime of the *equites*, acted with a recklessness almost beyond belief. King Nicomedes of Bithynia was urged by it to make war upon Mithradates, being promised Roman support in the task ; and as he had promised the commissioners a large recognition for his restoration, and, in addition, owed money to Roman financiers who were pressing him for repayment, he was obliged to fall in with their wishes. Mithradates conducted his own side of the case with admirable skill ; he was to play the part of the injured innocent person, wickedly set-upon, and turning at last to bay in desperate self-defence. His envoys were carefully instructed in their part, which they carried out well, while he himself completed the most elaborate preparations for war. That his designs were far-reaching might be guessed from the fleet he assembled : over three

hundred ships, for the command of which he had at
last to send to Phoenicia and Egypt to find officers.
His diplomacy reached in every direction. Syria,
Egypt and Armenia were approached to secure their
friendly neutrality. The commission (perhaps
encouraged by the injured innocence of the plea)
refused him satisfaction for the hostile acts of
Nicomedes.

This was what Mithradates wanted. He promptly
seized Cappadocia afresh, and addressed a further
protest to the commissioners, demanding satisfaction, and appealing to Rome ; but his tone was
now stronger. The commission, considering his
message " insolent," once more expelled him from
Cappadocia and dismissed his ambassador.

They at once, without communicating with Rome,
prepared for war, and assembled their forces along
the frontiers. They had a small Roman force, and
the same sort of local levy that Sulla had employed,
besides the Bithynian army of King Nicomedes, and
a fleet which held the straits of Byzantium. The
army which Mithradates set in motion was over a
quarter of a million strong. Its first operations
resulted in a disastrous defeat of Nicomedes ;
Manius Aquilius, the chief commissioner, was forced
to flee to Pergamus ; the fleet at Byzantium, when
it heard the news, scattered ; the whole of Asia
Minor fell into the hands of Mithradates with
scarcely a serious battle. Only Rhodes held out.

The cities received Mithradates with an
enthusiasm that was remembered against them.
The Roman government—whatever it might have
done had it been consulted before—had now no
choice, so declared war. The financial case was
desperate. It was necessary to sell the sites on and

near the Capitol, which had never been built on since the foundation of Rome. This expedient raised nine thousand pounds of bullion gold for the treasury. Hardly had these decisions been taken, when news followed only to be compared in moral effect with the news of the Indian Mutiny. Mithradates had issued secret orders for a general massacre of every person of Italian birth throughout Asia. On the disastrous day, the most frightful scenes were witnessed. Men and women were torn from the sacred sanctuaries of the gods and butchered. At Tralles, the citizens, afraid to do the work themselves, hired a Paphlagonian ruffian named Theophilus, who herded his victims (with, let us hope, unconscious irony) into the temple of Concord, and there murdered them all, chopping off the hands of those who clung to the sacred images and refused to let go. The utmost care was taken to render the massacre complete. Rewards were offered for information leading to the apprehension of any Italian-born person ; strict penalties were fixed against those who should conceal the living or bury the dead. Freedom was offered to slaves who betrayed their masters ; and to debtors who slew an Italian creditor, discharge of one-half of their debt. The number of those who were slain is variously estimated. From eighty thousand to a hundred and fifty thousand Italians of all classes are asserted to have been massacred. Against everything, Rhodes still flew a defiant flag, strong in its great walls and fighting fleet.

Asia thus lost, Greece itself threatened—such was the news which fell upon a prostrate Italy and a Rome in chaos.

VI

The Social War, like all such wars, was as damaging as it was scandalous. It produced a general slackening of *moral* throughout Italy, a widespread injury to all the peaceful pursuits by which the prosperity of men is secured. How far civilisation really does depend on mere law and order we only realise in times of anarchy. The whole civilisation of the Italian peninsula emerged from the Social War much the worse for wear. Acute distress was widespread ; and the loudest cry of all was against the moneyed class which had caused the war. Borrowing had been a universal necessity. The creditors now, in many cases, foreclosed on debtors who rushed to the praetor to apply for time to realise their assets. The praetor, acting on the strict letter of the law, remitted the cases to the courts to be dealt with under the old obsolete acts governing interest. He was murdered by the infuriated creditors, headed by a public officer, the tribune Lucius Cassius. A general agitation began for the cancelling of all debts.

The *equites*, alarmed by these ominous signs, made a bid for safety by driving a wedge between the *Optimates* and the *Populares*. The tribune P. Sulpicius Rufus [1] brought forward three proposals. The first was that all senators who were in debt above £82 should be removed from the Senate. The

[1] Publius Sulpicius Rufus was a much admired orator and a man of ability. He took a leading part in impeaching Gaius Norbanus in 95 B.C. for his action against Caepio nine years earlier. (See f.n. p. 148 *ante*.) It is, therefore, to be deduced that Sulpicius was of the *Optimates*. Now, Sulpicius was 6,000,000 sesterces in debt when he died. He certainly did not owe this sum to men who themselves were borrowing ; he owed it to

second was the recall of all the exiles banished by
the Varian commission. The third was the equality
of Italians and Romans in respect of the franchise.
This clever and sinister triad of proposals showed
signs of succeeding in its object. The third measure
conciliated the *Populares* and the Italians ; the first,
they regarded with complacent indifference ; while
the second might possibly neutralise those of the
Optimates who had belonged to Sulla's group. The
first would, however, destroy the Senate as then
constituted, for there can have been few large land-
lords who had not borrowed during the war. The
Senate was, in fact, the strategic point to assail.[1]

Sulpicius was furnished with a first-class gang of
armed volunteers to protect him, and to carry out the
propaganda for his measures. He called it by the
humorous but significant name of his Anti-Senate.

The Senate answered by securing the election of
Sulla and Quintus Pompeius Rufus as consuls for
the year. Sulla was the one man they felt they could
rely upon in emergency, and when he walked into the
Senate House, with his blue eyes, purple complexion,
and shock of golden hair, they must have felt nearer
safety. Sulla had, by his work, deserved his
reward. No other man emerged from the Social

men who were lending, and who had lent it probably later than
95 B.C.

The idea that Sulpicius was bought by Marius is unlikely.
Mommsen spends three pages (Vol. III, pp. 531 ff.) in
speculating over the motives of Sulpicius. His own account
proves that Sulpicius was commissioned by the *equites* to hold
the street and smash the Senate in their interests.

[1] The great bankers were themselves heavily involved in the
financial consequences of the troubles in Asia. To hold their
own, they needed all their assets ; and to retain their political
power, they needed to cripple the Senate.

War with a reputation equal to his. His friends thought him the greatest of commanders. His foes (who knew no commander greater than Marius) admitted that he was certainly the most fortunate. Sulla welcomed the admission, played with it, and turned it into something between a jest and a faith. It is in the Social War that we first hear in earnest of his Fortune. How far it may have begun as a jest, we do not know ; but it rapidly became something more serious. What power had brought him upon the scene at this critical juncture ? Not calculation. No human foresight could have worked out the reckoning.

And now his prudence and foresight were justified. He left his army intact in Campania, and returned to Rome.

More than the consulship awaited him. He was brought forward into the front rank of his party. He was quite ready. He dissolved his marriage with his wife Coelia, on the ground of her barrenness. There was nothing remarkable in that. But when, shortly afterwards—too shortly afterwards, some people thought—it appeared that a fresh marriage had been arranged for him, with Caecilia Metella, daughter of Metellus Dalmaticus, then the Sulpicians sneered, and even some of his own party disapproved. It gave opportunity for lampoons and verses—a chance not missed. Sulla is not likely to have failed to hear of them : and if any of them contained any reference to his personal appearance, he is not likely to have forgotten them.

Practically no information has survived about Metella, but Sulla evidently had a regard for her which was much more than the respect a man pays to the partner of a political alliance. There was some factor which seems to have made him protectively jealous on her behalf, and almost grateful to her. There is only one thing which, at a guess, would explain both attitudes on his part. It is his appearance. Metella was a high-born woman. She may have been the one person who never betrayed that she noticed anything unusual about Sulla : and to a sensitive man this would have deserved any silent acknowledgment he could give.

In all that follows, it must be borne in mind that the question at issue was not that of a popular revolt against an oppressive oligarchy, but that of rescuing the State from an attempt on the part of the *equites* to regain power. Sulla had no intention of repudiating the policy of his party. He had come to the rescue of the *bloc* which had supported Drusus.

He at once challenged Sulpicius by the first and most obvious " call " he had at his disposal. He and Pompeius Rufus officially suspended all assemblies on the legal ground of Religious Observances. Sulpicius, quite ready, replied by letting loose his slugs. Pompeius Rufus bolted, but Sulla held his ground. It was afterwards asserted that Sulla took refuge from an indignant People in the house of Marius, who nobly protected him against their wrath. Sulla emphatically denied this account. According to his own much more probable version, he was seized by the slugs and forcibly carried to Marius's house near by, where an ultimatum was presented to him. He was to raise the embargo, or take the consequences. Sulla had plenty of other cards to play ; it was not yet necessary to die a martyr's death. He took the expedient course of raising the embargo. He left Rome and returned to his army, prepared for business.

Why he had not been killed is a curious question.

He was not yet at the height of his fame, and they may not have realised his importance : or they may have feared to go too far. A consul still retained a prestige comparable with the sacredness of the royal rank. It may be true that Marius intervened. Possibly it was Fortune.

Sulpicius saw the necessity of yet bolder measures. To gain a stronger backing against a military consul, he offered Marius the command in the east. The old man jumped eagerly at the bait ; the fish was hooked ; and the *equites* had plunged Rome afresh into a war worse even than the Social War.

VII

Two tribunes were despatched to Sulla's camp at Nola to demand that the army should be handed over to them. Sulla declined. He had not done all that he had done merely to surrender meekly at the first demand. Right was upon his side ; and more, might, he suspected, was there also. He was never a great orator, but now he addressed his troops with the first public speech we find recorded of him. They were enthusiastically in his favour, willing to go wheresoever he went : they broke out into mutiny at the idea of leaving him, and killed the tribunes. This was war in earnest : for a tribune's life was sacred with awful and irrevocable sacredness. Reprisals were at once made against Sulla's friends in Rome, and the first turmoil of the coming civil war distracted the city : the parties sorted themselves out, some men fleeing to Sulla, some away from him. The Senate, terrified by its own champion, sent messengers of praetorian rank to stop him. The troops wished to kill these, too. Sulla intervened, and got the envoys off with torn clothes and damaged dignity. The agitation in Rome now became frantic. Sulla was at hand !

Six complete legions, numbering thirty-five thousand men, moved out of camp at Nola and began a forced march upon Rome. Sulla was still undecided in his own mind, not sure what he was actually going to do. To introduce armed force into Rome was an almost unheard-of thing. Exactly how far was his action bluff ? No one knew ; he did not know himself. But one night he had a dream, in which he thought the Earth-Mother put thunderbolts into his hands and bade him smite his enemies, who all disappeared when he did so. He arose refreshed and convinced. He now knew what he had to do, and he intended to do it.

At Pictae he was met by a deputation begging for delay, and assuring him that the Senate would take up his cause. Sulla halted, and sent out to measure ground for a camp, saying that he would do as they wished. The deputation hurried joyfully back, and Sulla resumed his march. He sent on an advanced guard under Lucius Basilus and Gaius Mummius, to secure the gate and walls on the Esquiline Hill side of the city, where the street led straight down by the shortest way to the Forum and the heart of the city ; and followed rapidly on their heels.

Basilus seized the gate ; but street-fighting in a classical city was complicated by the flat roofs of the houses, and he was forced back, when he sought to advance, by a bombardment of tiles. Sulla was not far behind ; and on his arrival he instantly gave the word to fire the houses. He himself led the operation, torch in hand, while the archers shot fire-darts upon the roofs. Everything now had to give way to the military necessity ; and friends and foes alike saw their property involved in the flame and smoke which drove the tile-fighters off the roofs. Panic became general. Marius had called upon all the help he could muster, but he had missed his moment. An offer of freedom to all the slaves who joined him produced, it is said, three recruits.[1] Before long it was every man for himself. Sulpicius fled one way, Marius another; and the adventures of Marius are a whole romance in themselves. He was too much beloved to be caught; but Sulpicius was betrayed by a slave, whom Sulla first made free, in accordance with the reward offered, and then threw over the Tarpeian Rock on general principles, to discourage the practice of betraying one's master. Twelve of the allies of Sulpicius were proscribed with him. The head of Sulpicius was set up publicly in the Forum. Sulla was master of Rome.

VIII

Sulla's armed entry into Rome is one of the most astonishing deeds in history in its promptitude, its vigour, and its unexpectedness. It was unpremeditated in the sense that it was not part of a plan, but arose naturally out of a chain of events. The manner of it was especially startling. If Sulla had not personally committed himself by taking the initiative, even the most war-hardened troops might have wavered at the astounding order to fire Rome itself! Historians have not sufficiently underlined the magnitude of the audacity, nor its probable moral effect. He had committed the first of those actions which revealed to the world that he was a

[1] This sounds like one of Sulla's own jokes. He was fond of understating figures.

man who would blench at nothing—not even at shocking its moral susceptibilities.

But although he had come in a fashion such as not even Marius had dreamed of adopting, he did not come as a revolutionary, a despot, or a militarist. He, the legal consul, had been assaulted and intimidated; the son of Quintus Pompeius Rufus, who had married his daughter, had been killed by the men of Sulpicius. An attempt had been made to use constitutional forms, backed by illegal violence, in a way fatal to the State. Here, if ever, was an occasion when men must choose between mere adherence to convention and bold initiative. Sulla did not intend the *equites* to return to power by the bludgeon. He replied to the " slug " and the bludgeon by the soldier and the sword.

Unlike some men, he knew precisely what he was going to do. After his term of office as consul, he was going to take up the proconsular command against Mithradates. The first thing, therefore, was to settle affairs in Rome, permanently if possible, but at any rate temporarily; and matters could then await his return.

Sulla's measures were unexpected in their nature and in their realistic adaptation to the circumstances of the day. No consul for many a year previous had shown the originality and the turn for political action which he suddenly revealed. His measures may be divided into three classes, levelled impartially at the three classes of the State. Against the Senate, he filled its numbers with three hundred new men who might possibly have a little more brains and courage than their predecessors. Against the bankers and capitalists he cut down the amount of interest they could legally enforce. Against the electors who had

swallowed the bait of Sulpicius so easily, he altered
their voting arrangements back to the ancient Servian
methods, giving a preponderant vote to the higher
qualifications. On the other hand, legislative proposals were first to be laid before, and passed by the
Senate, before they could be submitted to the
Assembly for adoption. Sulla did not think it
worth while to raise fresh trouble by attacking the
equestrian courts. He left that problem alone.
Finally, he made arrangements for land-colonisation.
Every class lost something and each gained something in this remarkable programme, so neatly dove-
tailing the conservative and the radical.

No one was particularly pleased. When the
elections came round, the people rejected the
candidates who stood for office with his support,
and carefully elected the candidates least acceptable
to him. Sulla expressed his pleasure. He loved to
see the People in dignified exercise of its inherent
sovereignty. At least, he assured them that these
were his feelings ; whereupon he and they bowed
themselves out of further discussion.

With respect to the ordinary administration of the
State, he had not been idle. The Samnites had made
a great effort to recover their hold over Samnium.
They recaptured Bovianum, but were defeated with
heavy loss by Sulla's lieutenant, Marcus Aemilius
Scaurus the younger. Quintus Metellus Pius, the
able son of Metellus Numidicus, had cleared the
road to Brundusium by the recapture of the great
fortress of Venusia. In central Italy, Strabo was
putting out the last embers of revolt. As soon as
the Campanian cities were reduced, the war would
be extinguished. Sulla thought matters sufficiently
advanced for him to leave Italy.

One of his last actions was to cause both the new consuls, Lucius Cornelius Cinna and Gnaeus Octavius, to take a solemn oath to maintain the new arrangements. Cinna—another Cornelius—was an able officer, but otherwise little known. Octavius was interested in spiritualism and prophetic mediums. The story—which takes dramatic interest in view of later events—is that Cinna ascended the Capitoline Hill, carrying a stone in his hand and, casting the stone, swore solemnly that he should be cast out of the city as that stone if he proved false. . . . This was the best that Sulla could do. He removed Strabo from the command in central Italy, and gave it to his kinsman Quintus Pompeius Rufus : and was ready to leave for the east.

Every one was waiting with polite impatience till he should be gone.

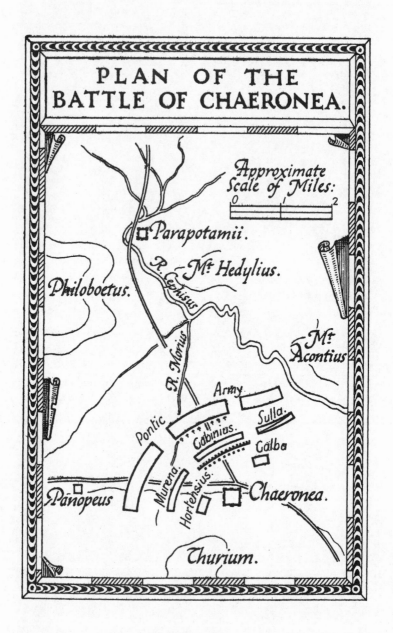

PLAN OF THE BATTLE OF CHAERONEA.

Approximate Scale of Miles:
0   2

Parapotamii.

R. Cephisus

Mt Hedylius.

Philoboetus.

R. Morius

Mt Acontius.

Army

Pontic

Gabinius.

Sulla.

Galba

Murena.

Hortensius.

Panopeus

Chaeronea.

Thurium.

CHAPTER VIII

SULLA IN GREECE

I

SULLA landed at Dyrrachium in the spring of the year 87 B.C. How little he anticipated what was to occur at home we can see by the fact that he left Metella and her children, the twins Faustus and Fausta, behind him. He put aside all thought save for the matter in hand. He was preparing to grapple with a gigantic task, in which all his abilities would be needed, and much help from his friend Fortune. He left nothing to Fortune that he could do himself, and Fortune played up nobly.

His chief staff officer, Lucius Licinius Lucullus, who had been his right-hand man during the Social War, had preceded him to report on the situation. Lucullus found that a very able commander, Bruttius Sura, lieutenant to the governor of Macedonia, had taken up the defence of Greece. Asia was entirely in the hands of Mithradates, whose armies, under his trusted general Archelaus, had already begun the occupation of European soil. Archelaus had complete command of the sea, as well as possession of all the Ionic islands. Making Athens his base, he had set up there an adherent of the king, a certain Aristion, as ruler, had secured the alliance of the Achaean cities, and of the Lacedaemonians, and was pouring troops through this open gateway.

Euboea was in the hands of Metrophanes. In Macedonia and Thessaly Ariarethes, a son of Mithradates, was reducing the country with a powerful
army. Hitherto the operations of Archelaus had
been confined to the coastal districts. Sura had
successfully held the roads that led from Athens
over the mountains into the heart of Thessaly.

Lucullus seems to have been very pleased with
Bruttius Sura, and to have reported in high com-
mendation of his actions ; but he pointed out that
the legal commander was now in the field, whereupon
Sura handed over the command and returned to
Macedonia. Sulla advanced southward and eastward, picking up such supplies and reinforcements
as he could on the way. He meant to do something
much more than merely hold his own ; he meant to
strike direct at Athens, the enemy base.

There can seldom have been a general as great as
Sulla, who had for his chief of staff another general
as great as Lucullus. It says much for both men that
from beginning to end their official relations and
personal friendship were unclouded and unbroken.
They had much in common, both socially and in
personal tastes, though Lucullus shunned politics.
Both men were connected with the family of the
Metelli. The mother of Lucullus had been a sister
of Metellus Dalmaticus and Metellus Numidicus.
Lucullus was perhaps the finer gentleman, but the
dominating intelligence was Sulla's. It was Lucullus
to whom he afterwards dedicated his memoirs, and
whom he made the guardian of his children. To
have by him, during all these difficult days, a second
brain, as acute and courageous as his own, and
absolutely loyal, was one of those strokes of Fortune
which Sulla thoroughly appreciated.

II

On his arrival at Chaeronea, Sulla received the delegates of all the cities of Greece, save Athens. He severely visited those which had shown disaffection. Having made it clear that there was no slackening of Roman control over the provinces, he advanced into Attica and began the siege.

The port of Piraeus was the first objective. Once that fell, it would be impossible to reprovision the city, isolated from the sea. Camps were established at Eleusis and Megara, the cordon was drawn, and in this perilous position Sulla tested Fortune as he had not tested her yet.

The operations were vast ; the expense great. Ten thousand mules were at daily work about the trenches. Engines were built, saps driven ; labourers had to be maintained, money found. When timber ran out, Sulla ruthlessly cut down the sacred groves, and the trees of the Lyceum and the Academy. He was not going to be stopped now by any consideration whatever. To apply to the government at home for money would have been merely absurd. For one thing, it had none ; for another, it would not have granted any had it possessed it. Sulla sent to all the rich temples of Greece, which were as wealthy with devotional offerings as the greatest of mediaeval cathedrals. Epidaurus and Olympia had to disgorge their treasures. He wrote in person to the Amphictyons at Delphi, the richest of all. The more serious he was, the more sardonic his words grew. He invited them to let him take care of their wealth, as he would look after it better than they could ; and if he needed to use any, he would replace it. The Amphictyons were embarrassed. It was

perfectly reasonable that Greece should pay for her
defence from an Asiatic king much more likely to
plunder her temples without return than any Roman ;
but that the curators of a world-famous temple,
themselves no more than trustees for posterity,
should strip their altars is a proposal to be reflected
over.

Caphis, a Phocian, was the apologetic messenger
who carried the letter to Delphi, and was commissioned to receive the treasure by weight. He
sympathised with the committee of Amphictyons,
and was full of excuses for himself. The committee
tentatively suggested that they had heard the sound
of a harp in the inner sanctuary. Caphis promptly
sent an express messenger back to Sulla with this
grave news. Sulla as promptly sent back another
express, to say that he was surprised that Caphis did
not know that music was a sign of joy, not of sorrow ;
he was to go forward, and gratefully accept what the
god so graciously offered !

After this there was no alternative. The temple
was stripped of treasures that went back to the
earliest and most famous days of Greece. The great
silver tun was too large to go on any carriage, so
was cut up for transport. Lucius Lucullus superintended the coining of the precious metals in
Peloponnesus ; and his money long remained current
on account of its excellence. Sulla triumphantly
demanded whether Fortune was not unmistakably
with the man for whom even the gods emptied their
treasuries.

The siege went on, however, without sen-
sational success. Piraeus, which was defended by
Archelaus in person, seemed impregnable. Sulla,
on the other hand, defeated every counter-move

aimed against him. Mithradates threw in by sea a
fresh army, which made a desperate sally. It was
so successfully repressed, in the nick of time, that
Archelaus himself was shut out, and had to be drawn
up the walls by means of ropes. Sulla steadily prevented the re-provisioning of Athens. Every known
resource of engineering was employed. A fresh
Pontic army, under Mithradates' son Arcathias,
entered Macedonia, cut Sulla's communications and
advanced southward. Fortune intervened. Arcathias died at Tisaeus, and for the time being the
army came no further. Still Piraeus could not be
forced by Sulla, nor relieved by Mithradates. The
siege dragged on, after all, into a blockade.

Sulla turned his attention to Athens itself.
Aristion, in spite of the sufferings of the beleaguered
city, which did not touch either his heart or his
intelligence, grew more and more confident as time
went on. He took a daily constitutional upon the
wall, during which he was mad enough to make
jocular remarks about Sulla, and still worse, about
Metella. The whole of Sulla's strength was con-
centrated on the siege ; it only needed this to con-
centrate the whole of his weaknesses too. He did
not respond to Aristion's jests ; he waited savagely,
biding the time.

News began to come in thick and fast from Rome ;
news so disturbing that it must have given him
many moments of secret irresolution and per-
plexity. His camp began to fill with refugees of the
Optimates, with whom came Metella herself, with
the news that his houses had been burned and his
property seized. Still he held on. Though all
assaults on Piraeus had failed so far, the Athenians
were starving. Corn was at famine prices ; people

were stewing feverfew and boiling down old shoes
and oil-bags for food. The most influential men in
the city were in favour of surrender. After much
difficulty, they induced Aristion to make overtures.

Sulla received the delegates, but on finding that
instead of seriously entertaining his terms, they only
made antiquarian speeches about the ancient might
and glory of Athens, he abruptly dismissed them
with : " My good fellows, put up your speeches
and be gone. I was sent to Athens, not to take
lessons, but to reduce rebels to obedience." And
they went.

Fortune had given Sulla many inducements to
doubt her ; but he had remained steady, and she
now returned smiling upon him. One of his spies
reported that some elderly men, talking together in
the Ceramicus, had criticised Aristion for not properly securing the approaches at the Heptachalcum.
Sulla seized the hint. He himself went by night to
examine the place, and finding it accessible, as the
old men had declared, lost not a moment. Work
was instantly put in hand : saps were driven, and
the wall mined, while troops were moved up in
readiness.

Nine hundred feet of the wall were brought down
between the Sacred and the Piraeic Gates, on the
south-west side of the city. The fall was brought
about at night ; the ground was cleared and levelled
sufficiently for access ; and at midnight, with torches
flaring and trumpets and horns blowing, the storming
detachments entered the breach, and Athens was
given over to the appalling horrors of a midnight
sack.

The storming of Athens was historic. This was
Sulla's answer to Aristion ; and he had much the best

of the exchanges. The blood that was shed in the market-place is said to have flowed down through the Ceramicus, past the gate, till it entered the suburbs beyond the wall. Many killed themselves under the terror of that nightmare. It was only when two of his Greek friends, Midias and Calliphon, absolutely knelt at his feet, and all the Roman senators present added their entreaties, that he consented to call off his war-dogs. Then he relaxed. Perhaps his sense of the dramatic was satisfied. Recollecting what city this was, and who had once been its citizens, he said : " I forgive the few for the many, the living for the dead." The emperor Nero must often have regretted that he had neither the opportunity nor the ability to take Athens.

Aristion had taken refuge in the Acropolis, where he held out until forced to surrender by want of water. Having received the full force of Sulla's retort, he had now to suffer an even more stinging repartee from Sulla's friend Fortune : for at the very moment when he walked down from his impregnable refuge to the hands of the Roman officer who received him, the rain came, and the Acropolis was plentifully replenished with water.

III

The fall of Athens came none too soon. The relief force was at hand. Sulla broke camp at the earliest moment. He kept his word to the Athenians. He restored the full freedom of the city, and all its possessions, for the sake of those mighty dead who yet made it a sacred spot, and still make it so to-day.

It was imperatively necessary to move. He made a last determined attack on Piraeus, so prolonged and hard pressed that Archelaus abandoned the

walls and retired to the citadel, against which, having
no ships, Sulla could do nothing. Sulla had already
despatched Lucius Lucullus to raise a naval force
by some means or other. It was impossible to
maintain an army longer in Attica, as long as the
Piraeus was closed. The army of Arcathias, now
under Taxiles, a hundred thousand strong, was on
the march from Thessaly. Sulla had to meet it, and
he had also to effect a junction with Hortensius, who
was bringing reinforcements from Macedonia. For
these reasons he was anxious to be away. The
problem was solved by Archelaus himself, who
voluntarily evacuated Piraeus, and went north to
join Taxiles and take command of the united forces.
Sulla burned Piraeus, including the magnificent
arsenal with its marble columns, and the shipyards.
Since he could not yet occupy it, the only course was
to make it useless to Archelaus. He then followed
northwards, where he was within reach of supplies,
though in ground more favourable for the enemy
cavalry.

Meanwhile Lucullus, with three small Greek ships
and three Rhodian galleys, was on his way south
through seas scoured both by the warships of
Mithradates and by corsairs. He touched at Crete,
where he gained the authorities over to Sulla's side,
and then he successfully ran the blockade to Cyrene
on the African shore. He was always popular,
wherever he went. Opinion was divided in Cyrene :
but Lucullus persevered until he induced the
principal citizens to take a more favourable view.
He lost most of his vessels to a pirate fleet, but
gained Alexandria, where he made a stately entry.

King Ptolemy was full of cordiality and compliments. Lucullus was received in state by the royal

fleet, invited to the palace as a personal guest, and
loaded with presents such as were usually given to
men of much higher rank. He refused these gifts,
and accepted nothing but necessary supplies. He
likewise declined invitations to visit the archaeological
wonders of Egypt, on the ground that these things
were for men of leisure and curiosity, not for one who
had left his commander in the trenches. But in spite
of his cordiality, the king would not lend any ships.
The situation was too delicate, and the future much
too uncertain, for him to side frankly with either
party. He nevertheless saw the little squadron of
Lucullus convoyed as far as Cyprus by the Egyptian
war-fleet, and on parting pressed upon Lucullus a
magnificent cameo portrait of himself, cut in emerald.
Lucullus did not see his way to refuse so personal a
gift without giving offence.

Either the king's emerald was lucky, or Sulla's
Fortune began to carry across the sea ; for from this
moment onwards Lucullus was successful in finding
ships. A general reaction against the government
of Mithradates and his deputies was everywhere in
progress. Lucullus, with his charming person and
persuasive speech, was welcomed in a score of
places, with greater or less publicity, as a deliverer.
Mithradates, with the lordly indifference of the
Asiatic despot, had adopted what he understood to
be a democratic policy, which would engage the
people in his favour. Slaves were freed, land distributed to the poor, and a general moratorium
announced : of which the chief result was frantic
agitation amongst the commercial classes of Greek
Asia and the islands. The appearance of Lucullus
with the Sullan programme, and reassurances, at once
engaged the influence of these men in his favour.

It is probable that he gathered a good deal of useful
information which in due time he reported to Sulla.
He can hardly have failed to become a much wiser
man regarding the inner causes of political revolutions, and the means by which they can be avoided.

IV

While Lucullus was away on his mission, the
crucial battles had been fought. Sulla's advance
into Boeotia brought him into a position from which
he could comfortably watch the roads leading from
Thessaly. There were not many points to guard.
The march of a great army would come by Thermo-
pylae and Elatea ; and Taxiles had no particular
object in taking a less convenient route merely in
order to avoid the same Roman army he was anxious
to fight and to wipe off the face of the earth. Sulla
effected his junction with Hortensius, who was
guided over the mountains by Greeks perfectly
acquainted with the paths, and the united forces
occupied a hill called Philoboetus, a spur of Mount
Parnassus commanding the Elatean plain and the
valley of the Cephisus, where supplies were secure,
and wood and water in abundance. Sulla admired
the advantages of the position. The army of
Taxiles must come down from the north through
the defile, and turn at an angle along the main
valley where it narrowed, towards Chaeronea and
Orchomenos.

When it came, it would cut off all retreat, and
bottle him securely into southern Greece, with no
escape but by fighting.

It came at last : an impressive sight. It seemed
overwhelming in numbers, and its array was rich
with all those gorgeous military equipments which

overawe simple souls, but not a cynical and experienced man of the world, like Sulla. It encamped down in the valley, whence its commanders could take a general view of the Roman army. Its forage parties were soon spread far and wide, looting and burning on a generous scale, while the troops of Sulla kept to their positions on the hill. Sulla by no means relished an inactivity so damaging to the country, and so bitter a reflection upon his ability to protect it ; but he had no alternative. The neighbouring temples came in for a full share of enemy interest. During the next few days the most encouraging declarations of prospective success poured in upon Sulla from the oracles of all the gods of the country-side. The oracle of Lebadea, which received a particularly attentive visit from the enemy, was emphatic in its assurances that Sulla should be victorious. Other interesting predictions and indications were related afterwards. Sulla received them all with satisfaction, and was sufficiently appreciative of divine help to see that all such communications were made public.

With the forces which Archelaus had brought up by sea to join Taxiles, the united host far outnumbered the Roman army, which was less than seventeen thousand strong : and even if the Macedonian and Greek allies were included, the disparity was still over three to one. Archelaus had wished to pursue a policy of attrition—the wisest course ; but Taxiles brought positive orders to fight. In the circumstances Archelaus hardly ventured to press his own view too far. A battle was determined upon.

Sulla was perfectly willing, in his own time, and at his own place. His confidence in himself

and Fortune was not affected by the disparity of
numbers. But the army saw the prospect in a
different light. The oracles notwithstanding, to
give battle to an enemy five times the Roman
numbers, and more than three times that of the
whole army, seemed hopeless and beyond reason.
Sulla, accepting public opinion, patiently waited,
and turned the screws of discipline a little tighter.
If the men would not fight, what more profitable
than a little digging ? So the army was set to
work to dig itself in for safety, and since the task
was urgent, if they were to stand still and await
attack, it was pressed on, and slackness was severely
visited. After three days of digging trenches the
army made angry representations to its commander
when he came to inspect the work. Sulla acidly
told them that their new desire to fight was merely
a dislike of work, but if their martial ardour was
so great, they might go and occupy the hill of
Parapotamii. They consented.

The ancient city of Parapotamii, long a ruin,
lay at the very point of the angle where the host
must begin to wheel eastward, and commanded
the fords on the road to Chaeronea and Thebes.
Archelaus had already marked it for occupation.
There was now a race for it. The Sullan veterans
gained it first, an almost impregnable position from
which it was difficult to dislodge them. Sulla's
design was to withdraw upon a prepared position
where he could give battle to the greatest advantage.
His first movements seemed like a retreat. The
Chaeroneans with the Roman army implored him
not to leave their city to its fate, whereupon, as this
chimed in with his own views of the situation, he
at once sent them off with the tribune Gabinius,

and one legion, to occupy the town and prepare an entrenched position : left Murena to hold the fords till all was clear, and himself marched along the right bank of the Cephissus.

Archelaus, as soon as Murena's withdrawal opened the fords, crossed over and began to take up a position between Mount Hedylius and Mount Acontius, facing Chaeronea. He extended a flanking force to occupy Mount Thurium on his right. Sulla now linked up with Chaeronea and went himself to view the position. An entrenched line, fronted with strong stakes, had been erected, sufficient to prevent the passage of war chariots, but not that of infantry. Before it were massed the legionaries of Gabinius, and behind it the siege-engines from Athens had been set up like a battery of heavy field-guns. Murena was falling into position on the left of this, close under Thurium. Sulla's cavalry corps (which he intended, as part of the general plan, to command in person) was posted on the right, out in the plain. On the rising ground in the rear, Hortensius on the left, and Galba on the right, commanded cohorts of reserve.

Sulla inspected the men of Gabinius, and after receiving the complimentary presentation of a laurel wreath, spoke a few words of encouragement and thanks. The force on Mount Thurium was a danger which might render the fortified position untenable ; but Gabinius had already secured local volunteers, acquainted with the ground, who undertook to deal with the danger. Satisfied that they were able and trustworthy, Sulla approved, before leaving to take up his position on the right wing.

V

The first movements of the coming battle were set on foot. Cautiously outflanking the flanking party by means of the mountain paths, the Chaeroneans gained the hill-side above them. Attacked from above, the enemy were hurled down the hill-side in disastrous confusion. Some three thousand are said to have fallen there; of the remnant, some were cut off by the men of Murena, while others broke in upon the wing of Archelaus's position, seriously upsetting it.

The war-cars opened the battle in earnest by hurling themselves upon the division of Gabinius in the centre, which withdrew within the staked line. Their frustration was utter and complete, to the delight of the legionaries, who mockingly called them on with the familiar catch-cries of the Roman circus. The support which followed the cars was a corps of fifteen thousand men, slaves freed for the purpose of enrolment, who were armed and trained in the old Macedonian fashion, as a phalanx, with close packed ranks of pike-men. On open ground, the attack of the cars, with their scythe-armed wheels, followed up by such a phalanx, would have been a most formidable one; but it bore no relation whatever to the situation which Sulla had constructed for its benefit. The phalanx, like the cars, was unable to operate against the masked entrenchments. Met by the hand-to-hand grapple of short-swordsmen fighting on an entrenched line, played upon by the war-engines which hurled stones and shot bolts into the rear of its massed ranks, the phalanx could not bring its power to bear. Even so, the struggle was a stern one. The slave troops fought with the utmost valour, and kept their ranks. The legionaries had to wrestle bare-handed with the hedge of pikes, to get near enough to use the short sword.

Archelaus had not been idle. He had flung out the cavalry of his right wing to envelop the Roman left. Hortensius moved up his troops to meet the danger, but was pressed back, and was in some danger of being cut off. Sulla, who so far had not been engaged at all, came swiftly to the scene and restored the line. Archelaus, guessing by the dust what sort of movement was in progress, recalled some of his cavalry, and ordered a concentration upon the weakened right wing from which Sulla had come. To replace the troops he moved, the division of Taxiles was brought up against Murena. Sulla hesitated. . . . This operation, however (which must have taken some time for an army so numerous, and of mobility inferior to the Roman standard), resulted in giving the Pontic army a distinct " slew " towards its right. Sulla made his decision ; he pushed in all the troops he could spare with Hortensius, to support Murena, and then dashed back to his right wing. He regained it before the movement of Archelaus had matured, found it holding its own, and ordered an advance.

The cavalry charge which followed upon the weakened Pontic left was the turning-point of the battle. The host of Archelaus crumpled like a house of cards. The wing being routed, and pursued off the field, the centre was driven in by Gabinius with frightful slaughter. Sulla, as soon as he was assured that all went well, hastened back to the danger-spot—Murena. But even Murena was now advancing, and the whole Pontic army was in flight. It soon found that it was trapped. Every avenue of flight somehow led back to the Romans. Archelaus placed himself in front of the camp, and bade the desperate mob turn again to fight. It turned, but having no longer any cohesion or direction, it turned only to be slaughtered, and was driven on helplessly to the gates of the camp. At last Archelaus ordered the gates to be opened to receive the fugitives ; but it was too late. The victorious legionaries entered with the stream. The disaster was complete and irremediable.

It is said that of all that immense host, only ten thousand arrived at Chalcis. Possibly that number may have been the only force surviving as an organised body ; but in any case it was a " retreat from Moscow." Sulla reports his own losses as fourteen missing, of whom two returned towards nightfall, a remark which may be received in the sporting spirit in which it was made. He may only have counted the men who ran away.

Sulla was conscious of the improbability of what he had done ; for the trophy he erected on the field of battle, on the scene of his cavalry charge, was dedicated not only to Mars and Victory, but to Venus, the spirit of Fortune, and the lucky throw of the dice.

He held games at Thebes, to celebrate his victory. It was perhaps then, or shortly afterwards, that he received news perhaps more serious than that of the approach of Taxiles and Archelaus—Valerius Flaccus was upon the road.

But to estimate the significance of Flaccus we must go back a little.

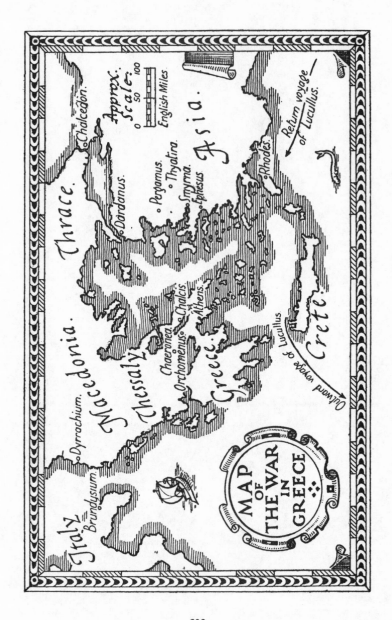

Thrace.

Chalcedon.

Approx. Scale.

0   50   100

English Miles

Asia.

Dardanus.

Pergamus.

Thyatira.

Smyrna.

Ephesus.

Return voyage of Lucullus.

Rhodes.

Macedonia.

Thessaly.

Greece.

Chaeronea.

Orchomenus.

Chalcis.

Athens.

Crete.

Outward voyage of Lucullus

Dyrrachium.

Italy.

Brundusium.

MAP
OF
THE WAR
IN
GREECE

CHAPTER IX

THE VENGEANCE OF MARIUS AND THE RETENTION OF ASIA

I

TO accomplish all that Sulla was destined to accomplish, it was strictly necessary to possess the temperament of Sulla. He never trusted more absolutely to Fortune than when he left Italy in order to carry on the war against Mithradates. That he never could have acted more wisely, we can see at this distance of time ; but it was not altogether so clear then.

The situation in Italy was as dangerous as it could very well be. The revolt of the Italians was still smouldering : the terms on which so many of them had laid down their arms had either not been carried out, or had been carried out in a way which made them ineffective. The Samnites were unappeased : the Varian exiles had not been recalled : and Sulla had added a fresh swarm of them, amongst whom was Marius himself—Marius, whose sensitiveness and austerity now added their force to the effects of his age and his genius and his popularity. He was an old man, and an embittered old man, and a terrible embittered old man, and a terrible embittered old man of genius who was worshipped by half the inhabitants of Italy.

The *equites* who had supported Sulpicius were in

a state of thorough discontent. Who was not ? The whole of Rome was in that condition in which no one is contented, no one satisfied, and every one is on the watch to make a bid for greater safety. Sulla had reduced the amount of interest they could recover from their debtors ; and although he had not revived the project of Drusus for removing the control of the courts from the *equites*, he probably intended to do so sooner or later, if only to escape impeachment when he came home. The corporations can hardly have expected the restoration of their privileges in Asia, when Sulla resettled the east. They are unlikely to have failed to inform themselves of Sulla's views on that head. In spite, therefore, of the obvious fact that Roman dominion, and with it the financial position of the great bankers, hung by the most tenuous of hairs, an effort was made to upset Sulla's settlement, restore the Gracchan constitution, and recall Marius.

The new arrangements made by Sulla before he left for the east did not permit a tribune to bring a motion directly before the Assembly in the old way hitherto customary. The intermediation of a consul was necessary. Cinna was therefore approached as the likeliest person. He was influenced by the overtures made to him, and consented to act.

He brought before the Senate two proposals : one for the re-enactment of the cancelled law of Sulpicius, allowing of the enrolment of new citizens in any of the tribes ; the other, for the recall of the exiles.

These proposals were fair enough upon the face of them, and would certainly command a majority when referred to the Assembly. If brought forward in a time of profound peace and security, they would have been wise measures of conciliation, and perhaps this is what they seemed to Cinna. But in the circumstances of the day, their meaning was something very different from this. If passed into law, they would bring to his support practically the whole of the Italians, and would also secure him the alliance of the party of Marius. The repeal of Sulla's measures and a return to the Gracchan constitution would then be easy. Marius would take over the command against Mithradates ; and the settlement he made would, naturally enough, be all in favour of the friends who had loyally supported him. Sulla would be impeached before an equestrian court. The stripping of Delphi would alone be ground enough for a condemnation.

The men who hatched this scheme must have had strangely imperfect ideas concerning the peril in which civilisation lay [1] : a peril which was cutting the ground from under their feet while they conspired for prizes they might never see. Asia had not yet been recovered. It might never be recovered. And if it were lost, then with it would go all that Rome meant, both to contemporaries and to succeeding ages.

II

Cinna's colleague Octavius, who stood firmly by Sulla's settlement, was an example of a type of man common enough in all ages, a formalist who might have made an excellent administrator, but

---

[1] There is, however, another possible explanation. The plan of campaign which Marius proposed to adopt against Mithradates may have been known, and may have seemed to the bankers to promise greater advantages. (See f.n. p. 224 *post*.)

who had no trace of the easy adaptability which allows men to see beyond the letter to the spirit. He was a severe, honourable man, who treated the Roman constitutional usages " as if they had been immutable mathematical truths." His only conception of the task Sulla had set him was to cling at any cost to the letter of the arrangements, without intelligence, and above all, without any sort of elasticity or discretion. The rigid policy of Octavius, however well-intentioned, was of itself enough to destroy Sulla's hope that things might be left alone for a time to settle and heal in peace. Octavius could not even exploit his own strength to any advantage. Between the two well-meaning physicians, the patient, who needed rest and quiet before all else, was once more turned out of bed into turmoil.

The conflict between the consuls culminated in a pitched battle in the Forum. Although he had Quintus Sertorius as an organiser, Cinna was beaten, and had to make a rush from the city, leaving ten thousand of his followers on the field. The Senate passed a decree outlawing Cinna and the leaders of the *Populares*, who presented themselves before the Italians with a good cause and overwhelming arguments. Money, arms and recruits poured in upon them : the army in Campania went over to the *Populares*, and furnished cadres for a much greater army, which Cinna proceeded to organise. A fleet was collected. A general arrived, for Marius himself landed in Etruria with a small force of exiles and of Numidian cavalry, and sent to Cinna to offer himself as a private soldier in the ranks. Cinna welcomed him, and bestowed proconsular authority upon him. If Octavius had plotted the creation of these events, he could not have brought

them about so effectively and so swiftly. All the
advantages Sulla had given him had been thrown
away. And now the forces of the *Populares* began
to march on Rome. It is impossible to describe in sufficiently damning
terms the incompetence which Octavius and the
Senate proceeded to pile upon incompetence. They
appealed to Strabo. Strabo came, pitched his camp
at the Colline Gate, and demanded the consulship
for next year. The Senate did not relish the
demand, and went elsewhere for help. It conferred
the franchise on all Italians formerly allied with
Rome. This concession, which might have done
something to stop the trouble at its source, if made
in time, produced ten thousand recruits. The
Samnites were approached, to see whether some
arrangement could not be made with them, by which
the army of Metellus Pius, then in Samnium, might
be set free. The Samnite terms were too humiliating
to swallow, so Metellus was recalled to Rome :
whereupon the Samnites promptly joined Cinna.

Rome was by this time completely invested by
land and sea. Marius had acted with vigour.
He was in no good mood. Since the day of his
exile he had never cut his hair. He had offered
Cinna to serve as a private soldier. When he
received the proconsular fasces from Cinna, he had
remarked with ominous irony that he was unworthy
of all this grandeur. He had collected about
himself a bodyguard of Illyrian Celts, Ardyaean
tribesmen as savage as himself. With forty ships—
the tale reads more like the story of a viking foray
of the ninth century than that of a Roman consular
—he blockaded Ostia, cut off the provision fleet
and captured the freights. He then hove in to

Ostia, stormed the port and barred the river : after which he marched up to the Janiculum hill on the right bank of the Tiber, where he commanded the great highway to Etruria and Gaul. What was coming from this quarter was no ordinary Roman army, but a host of fierce desperadoes unshackled by Roman tradition, led by a man who had invented one more novelty in the way of military strategy. No one before had ever thought of capturing Rome through Ostia—but the plan was not forgotten.

To add to the agony, pestilence broke out among the troops in the city, and swept away seventeen thousand persons. Those who remained were in no great heart for fighting. They requested Metellus Pius, who was in favour of compromise, to take command of them. Metellus declined the responsibility. Octavius, who refused all compromise, remained in command. Desertions became alarmingly frequent. The Senate opened negotiations with Cinna. While they were in progress, Cinna pitched his camp close up to the city gates, and the desertions from the city reached such numbers that it became clear that resistance was hopeless. The Senate surrendered unconditionally, save for the stipulation that Cinna would shed no blood. Cinna promised.

But there were more generals than Cinna in the field.

What of Marius ?

III

Like many rough and self-made men, Marius was by nature sensitive. As Sulla had noted, the most ordinary praise or criticism upset him. He could be firm as a mountain in those great things before which common men collapse ; but he was weak

where common men are strong. He had an almost
morbid craving for justice in a world inherently
unjust. He had been brooding over his own
wrongs and humiliations—as if six consulships and
innumerable honours, official and unofficial, were
not enough to set a man up in his own conceit.
His failure to gain the Mithradatic command had
been a blow ; his flight before Sulla and all the
hardships he had undergone had been the final
straw. He returned from exile with his mind distinctly unhinged. He had been worried, persecuted,
frightened, enraged, till the emotions became fixed
as an obsession. And an obsession in a man like
Gaius Marius is indeed a terrible thing. Who is
to overpower Hercules himself ?

We do' not know how far Cinna and his friends
realised the truth. In any case, Marius was not an
ally they could easily reject. Sertorius had held a
serious conference with Cinna over the question—
a conversation which shows that Sulla was not the
only man who entertained doubts concerning the
fitness of Marius for office. Sertorius strongly
dissuaded Cinna from allowing Marius to join
them. They were already victorious without
Marius ; and he knew of no one less easy to deal
with, or less to be trusted when in power. Cinna
was apologetic ; he expressed his real regret ; but
in fact he had actually invited Marius to come.
Sertorius at once answered that there was no more
to be said. He had supposed that Marius came
of his own accord ; but if he had been invited,
they were bound by their word to accept him.

Marius pointedly refused to enter Rome until his
sentence of outlawry was officially and ceremoniously
reversed. A scratch collection of electors was

hurriedly assembled in the Forum, and the necessary legislation scrambled through. Then Marius
entered. The gates were closed, and for five days
the terror reigned. Octavius was the first victim ;
but for weeks and months the sleuth-hounds were
still seeking those who lay hid from vengeance.

That Marius was insane there can be little doubt.
All his actions point to mental derangement. His
reign of terror as much exceeded anything that had
been known in Rome in the past as he exceeded
Nasica or Opimius in moral stature. But it was
strictly an individual vengeance. He appealed to
no law, held no court, heard no defence : in his
madness he revealed himself to be just what Sulla
had thought—a military tyrant, a Mithradates who
neither really understood nor really cared for the
processes of civil life. The corpse of Lucius Julius
Caesar was stabbed afresh at the tomb of Quintus
Varius, the author of the Varian Commission.
The slayer of Marcus Antonius the orator was
publicly embraced. His Ardyaei left corpses lying
about in the streets, ravished the wives and children
of those they murdered, and sacked their houses.
Only one man of eminence among the *Optimates*
stayed at his post in Rome and escaped with his
life. Even in his madness Marius had nothing
against Mucius Scaevola. . . . Catulus was allowed
to take his own life.

We know that Marius was not naturally an evil
man. His life had been stern, austere, and public-
spirited : he had been much loved, and that alone
is evidence of some inherent quality in him that was
just and merciful. But we know that he fretted
over unfairnesses and injustices ; we have not the
slightest evidence that he possessed one spark of

the cynical humour which oiled the wheels for Sulla.
He was a demented moralist determined to root-up,
destroy and stamp on all wickedness and evil disposition, which in practice meant all who had
opposed Gaius Marius. . . . To destroy injustice,
the recipe of the morally ignorant in all ages has
been to destroy the unjust man. . . . He knew of
no solacing theory of original sin. He was unable
to see himself towering giant-like among the pygmies,
his genius untouched and unaltered by their in-
gratitude and hostility. Least of all could he see
any of the reasons why the injustices had not been
at root unjust, nor the unfairnesses really unfair. . .
So he struck with all his force at the foes who had
imperilled that frailest of delicate growths—the
huge and immortal reputation of Gaius Marius.

There was no nervous specialist to certify him
as insane. No one had the power to restrain him.
The *Populares* were themselves alarmed at the
terrific thing they had evoked, which at any moment
might strike at them. They approached him with
increasing apprehension. So the terror went on :
and the giant set his foot on the bleeding bodies of
those whose chief hold on the remembrance of
posterity is that they were his victims.

Marius had, among his obsessions, the conviction
that he was destined to have seven consulships :
which certain omens and predictions had foretold.
The anxious *Populares* put him up for his seventh
consulship in the ensuing year. He lasted just so
long ; he had been drinking heavily and moodily
against insomnia ; and a few days later he died
raving in delirium, fighting his battles over again
on his sick-bed, and leaving others to face the awful
reactions of the deeds he had done.

So died Gaius Marius, seven times consul, twice triumphator, the creator of the new Roman armies, the saviour of his country, the beloved commander. He died of insufficient conviction of his own importance.

Quintus Sertorius acted swiftly on the death of Marius. The Ardyaei, stained with every enormity known to human crime, were rounded up and slaughtered by his Celtic troops.

The vital statistics of contemporary Rome would make interesting reading, if we had them.

IV

We may now review the situation. The *Populares* were at long last in absolute possession of the field, save for Sulla, far away in Greece, without money or resources, fighting, with his back to the wall, against the perpetually reinforced hosts of Mithradates. . . . They had captured the machine ; the control of policies, of armies, of government, was entirely in their hands. They had nothing more to fight for : their victory was complete.

And now they had to pass the grand test. What were they going to do with their victory ? It is doubtless important to gain victories—though some men are able to dispense with them—but it is of far greater importance to be able to use a victory when it is gained. For the only use of victory is the opportunity it gives to exercise freely the creative power of the human mind. A fruitless victory is so much energy wasted.

The three years which followed illustrate a characteristic which often, perhaps usually, marks popular revolutions : they proved that the revolt of the *Populares* was not a bid for a new creative effort, but a revolt for certain particular reforms. There was nothing to prevent them from introducing any millennial ideals they might possess, and of making the Roman world, if they desired, a political paradise. But having extended the franchise to the Italians, the *Populares* could positively think of nothing else, except to cancel Sulla's laws, and return to the old system, and to organise an army to fight Mithradates. . . . This was surely a very small mouse for so very great a mountain to produce. When we look back upon the blood shed, the damage done, and the hatred engendered, we may well stand astonished at the amount of energy one party had expended to prevent, and another had expended to achieve, such results. Perhaps nothing illustrates better than such an instance the core of truth in the creed of the cynics, who think the folly and evil of humanity larger than its wisdom or its goodness.

V

It was the refugees from this revolution who filled Sulla's camp outside Athens with their presence and their reminiscences. They cannot have been soothing company. They fled to him as to a man recognised as a strong refuge in times of trouble. Sulla did not hurry and did not worry—overtly, at least ; he lost no time, but he pursued his way uninterrupted, finishing his work to the end as he went along, and trusting to Fortune.

Most of the provinces adhered to the *Optimates*, Africa fell early into the hands of the *Populares*, and the east was to be their next objective. Although Sulla had been, of course, deprived of his command, and placed beyond the pale of the law, he had grown so to dominate the situation and the thoughts of men that there could be no settlement till he was dealt with. In addition to this, Mithradates also had to be dealt with, if any Rome were to be left to govern.

The new government undertook the task with interesting light-heartedness. After the death of Marius, L. Valerius Flaccus, his old consular colleague back in the days of Saturninus and Glaucia, had been elected to fill his vacant place. Sertorius, the only member of the party capable of handling a great campaign, was entirely passed over. A large army was organised and despatched under the command of Flaccus, who, being no soldier, was given as chief of staff a certain Fimbria. Flaccus crossed over the narrow seas and set out on the march through Macedonia.

Sulla was still in no hurry ; the quickest way was to wait, and Sulla was always excellent at waiting. Mithradates still commanded the sea, although the fleet of Lucullus was busily at work, and growing. Flaccus approached through Thessaly driving the Mithradatans out before him ; and Sulla moved north through the passes, pitching his camp just beyond the mountain barrier. There Flaccus found him. For some time the two armies lay almost in contact, neither commander making any move.

A great deal can be done by waiting. The process revealed a number of surprising reactions. The troops of Flaccus began to desert. The magnetism of Sulla was acting. The trickle became a steady stream ; and Flaccus broke camp. To have remained longer would have meant the absorption of his entire army by Sulla.

Besides, a great deal can be arranged in silence. Sulla had a considerable number of factors to

take into account in his calculations. He must
already have known that another army of Mithradates was on the way by sea ; Lucullus would have
kept him informed on that score. To waste time
and men in fighting Flaccus would have been
inexcusable in a man so acute and so public-spirited
as Sulla always showed himself to be. Flaccus
may very well have seen matters in the same light ;
nothing was to be gained for any genuine purpose
by fighting, with the inevitable result of the crippled
survivor having to turn at last to encounter the
hosts of the Pontic king. The two Roman commanders therefore silently distributed their tasks.
Flaccus marched north again, round through Thrace
to Byzantium, crossed the straits and arrived in
Chalcedon, on the northern flank of Mithradates'
dominions. Sulla retired back through the mountain passes, and moved a few miles eastward past
Chaeronea towards Orchomenos. . . . Domestic
differences could be settled afterwards.

Sulla chose Orchomenos because he was no longer
threatened from Thessaly and the passes. The new
army would land at Chalcis : and Orchomenos lies
very conveniently on the edge of a vast lake or
marsh, the Lake Copais, fed by the Cephissus and
the mountain streams. The position formed a
natural entrenchment which only needed a little
finishing in order to be defensible by a small force
against a large one. Sulla was not wandering about
Greece in an aimless way. He knew with formidable
precision just what he was doing.

Athens would have been the best base for the
use of a Mithradatan army ; but Sulla had carefully
made it his task to acquire Athens. All things
considered, Chalcis was practically the only other

landing-place possible. Any other to the south
would have been a blind alley ; any other to the
north would have placed the new-comers between
Sulla and Flaccus, with the certainty of having
their communications cut as they advanced into a
difficult country. Chalcis was a port perfectly
adapted for the landing of a large army ; and
Orchomenos was beautifully designed by Fortune
to enable Sulla to fight that large army. Orchomenos,
therefore, was the district where he dug himself
in with all the resources of Roman engineering.

VI

When Dorylaus and his army arrived, eighty
thousand strong, to join Archelaus, it was with the
most express orders to fight. Mithradates frankly
disbelieved that his last army could have been
defeated at Chaeronea without incompetence or
treason among its commanders, and Dorylaus seems
to have taken the same view : a view which he
considerably modified after his first taste of Sulla's
methods. Archelaus occupied Boeotia, and took
every measure calculated to draw Sulla into a battle.

Sulla was still in no hurry. He went on driving
his network of ditches, and drove them as near as
he could to the camp of the Pontic army. But he
was not merely digging himself in : he was digging
Archelaus in also, and shaping the ditches to a
definite strategical end. The ditches were dykes,
the flooding of which would pen in the Pontic
army, and limit the cavalry operations which were
its main reliance.

When this fact dawned upon the perception of
Archelaus he at once gave the word to attack the
ditches. The workmen were driven out, and the

covering troops, moving up to their support, were broken by formidable charges of cavalry, and for a moment the line seemed to be giving way. Sulla rode to the spot, leaped from his charger, and seizing an eagle rushed through the broken ranks with it, calling upon the fliers to follow him : " and when they ask you where you left your commander —remember *Orchomenos* ! " The line was rallied and reformed ; two fresh cohorts were thrown in from the right wing, and the advance of the cavalry was checked.

Sulla reorganised and rested his troops before proceeding. Then he moved up to continue the work on the dykes. Archelaus replied by hurling his cavalry once more upon the accessible Roman front. It was met and driven back in confusion with great slaughter ; and now the legionaries followed, and drove before them the archers who sought to protect the retirement of the horse. Throughout the course of the battle, the floods must have been creeping over the adjacent country. The Pontic army was penned into its camp, where it passed a miserable and disheartening night. The dykes were still pushed on.

On the second day of the battle of Orchomenos, Archelaus made a determined effort to break the ingenious toils which were closing upon him. The whole remaining force of the Pontic army was thrown upon the Romans along the causeways yet open. What began as a sally ended in a complete rout, for the legionaries pressed so closely upon their flying foes that in the struggle they took the camp by storm. The fall of men was so great that Plutarch records with interest that weapons and armour could still, in his own day, two hundred years after the battle, be fished out of the mud of the marshes. Archelaus hid for two days in the fen, until he could escape in a small boat to Chalcis.

VII

The deed was done ! The battle of Orchomenos, lasting over two days, was one of the world's decisive battles. It determined that Roman dominion was to survive, Roman tradition to be unbroken, and that her evolution was to be continued till it gave rise to the civilisation of modern Europe. Never again would Lucius Cornelius Sulla need to assume an ingratiating smile to any man ! The bar was crossed, the crisis surmounted : Fortune had crowned him. This was the hour of supreme triumph for Sulla, unalloyed by any regret or remorse. . . . Fortune can do great things. Fortune had done this. Ditches or no ditches, surely no mere human power could have done it !

In the meantime, the army of Flaccus had had its own adventures. Although elected by the vote of Roman citizens, Flaccus, whether through his vices or his virtues, was an unpopular man with his troops. He became involved in a growing quarrel with Fimbria, who was on all grounds much more acceptable to them. It is possible that Flaccus was, as alleged by the historians, a rascal intent on feathering his own nest ; and it is equally possible that he may have been a Catonic idealist sternly refusing to connive at the rapacity of a corrupt soldiery.[1] Whether he were one or the other, the act of the electors could only present their troops with a commander who was a misfit. The trouble

[1] It is significant that Flaccus distinguished his consulship by bringing in a measure for the cancellation of debts.

culminated by Flaccus taking refuge in a house, whence, waiting for night, he escaped by climbing a wall and fleeing to Chalcedon, and then to Nicomedia. Fimbria found him there, hidden in a well ; and although Flaccus was a consular, and commander-in-chief, he hauled him out, cut off his head, threw it into the sea, left his body unburied, and appointed himself general.

These highly unconstitutional proceedings at any rate gave the army an acceptable and able head. Fimbria advanced into Asia. The newly acquired dominion of Mithradates being founded, as such things are, merely upon a superficial military conquest without political root, was collapsing as rapidly as it had extended. The great mercantile communities of Smyrna, Ephesus and Sardes were in revolt against his policies, and were not pacified by the execution, at his order, of the whole Senate of Adramyttium. He deported the population of Chios to cure it of disloyalty, but he could not stop the rot that set in. The suspected Celtic chiefs of Galatia were invited to a conference, and shared the fate of the Senate of Adramyttium. A few, however, got away, and raised the tribesmen. The oriental ways of Mithradates proved incapable of achieving his aims. Defeated by Fimbria, he was obliged to leave Pergamus and take refuge in the island of Mitylene. He would not even have gained that refuge but for the hesitation of Lucullus, who was unwilling to grant Fimbria the political advantage of making the master-stroke. Had the king been victorious in Europe, the tale might have been widely different, but two magnificent armies had disappeared into Boeotia, never to return. Mithradates temporised. He recognised his most important foe—the man who, with a handful of troops, had dispersed his vast dreams of empire. It was Sulla.[1]

A merchant of Delos brought the first private enquiries. Sulla consented to meet Archelaus and to talk matters over. They met at Delium, " where the temple of Apollo stands," on the sea-front near Tanagra, southward of Chalcis.

Archelaus opened the conversation by reminding Sulla that Mithradates had been a friend of his father. The rapacity of the Roman corporations had been the real cause of this war, but the king was ready to make peace if he could gain, as he hoped, fair terms from such a very different kind of man as his old friend's son.

Sulla had every practical reason for jumping at the proposal ; but he kept an unrelenting front. He replied that if Mithradates had been wronged, he should have taken peaceful and diplomatic means of obtaining redress—not the course of

[1] The following suggestions do not quite deserve to be called speculative. They have natural and inherent likelihood, even if evidence to support them be lacking. It is extremely improbable that Marius never mentioned to his friends the plan of campaign he intended to adopt against Mithradates. It is even probable that he would vehemently criticise Sulla's strategy, and lay down the lines on which he himself would proceed. The course of action taken by Flaccus and Fimbria would then represent the outline of Marius's plan—namely, to enter Asia Minor across the straits and strike towards the Pontic homeland of Mithradates. This might automatically have brought about the evacuation of Greece and western Asia Minor by Mithradates. It is only fair to recollect that even under Fimbria the plan was by no means a failure. We cannot exactly estimate the degree to which the campaigns of Fimbria and Sulla exercised mutual influence. The conception of Sulla's campaign in Greece deserves discussion from a military point of view. Finlay thought that, economically, Greece never recovered from it.

murdering and torturing Roman citizeɳs in Asia.
Sulla said that he considered the actions of Mithradates to show deliberate hostility rather than the
indignation of a wronged man. As for that friendship with his father, *that*, said Sulla, had only been
remembered after he himself had defeated two
Pontic armies. It was a weakness to make peace
at all. The war ought, by rights, to be firmly
carried on and driven home.

Archelaus answered by advising Sulla to abandon
the idea of conquering Asia. The state of affairs
in Rome, he suggested, urgently demanded Sulla's
presence. The king was willing to assist him with
money and ships and men. . . . Sulla's irony came
out in his prompt interposition. He recommended
Archelaus to pay no further heed to Mithradates,
but to grasp the crown himself, surrender the
fleet, and become an ally of Rome. He reminded
Archelaus of the way in which the king treated
his friends, and of the consistent loyalty with which
the Romans had treated theirs. . . . Archelaus
was somewhat shocked. He would never think of
treason to his master. Sulla came down upon
him with force. " So you, Archelaus, a Cappadocian and a servant (or ' friend ' if you prefer the
word) of a barbarian king, would not, for such a
great reward, be guilty of a dishonourable action :
and yet you talk to *me*, Lucius Cornelius Sulla, a
Roman commander, of treason !—as if you were
not the man who fled from Chaeronea with few
left out of a hundred and twenty thousand men,
and who hid two days in the marshes at
Orchomenos."

Archelaus changed his tone and came to the
point. Would Sulla make reasonable terms with

Mithradates ? Sulla replied that he would. The articles of agreement which he drafted provided that Mithradates should evacuate Paphlagonia and the Roman province of Asia, restore Bithynia and Cappadocia to their lawful rulers, and pay an indemnity of three thousand talents, besides delivering up seventy fully equipped ships of war, and restoring the Chians to their city. On these terms he would confirm Mithradates in his other possessions, and declare him an ally of the Romans.

These terms were such as a victor dictates to a vanquished enemy ; but Archelaus (not the first man nor the last to succumb to Sulla's dominating magnetism) provisionally accepted them on the king's behalf until a personal meeting could be arranged. The king at first refused to countenance the terms. Sulla prepared to visit Asia, to see the negotiations through. He also wished to be a little closer to Fimbria, whose nearer acquaintance it was now time to cultivate. As Archelaus, in execution of the terms, removed the Pontic troops from Europe, no obstacle stood in the way.

He set out by land, through Thessaly, Macedonia and Thrace, taking Archelaus with him. It was noticed that he treated Archelaus with great consideration. The Cappadocian general was taken seriously ill at Larissa : whereupon Sulla stopped his march and treated him " as if he had been one of his own officers, or his colleague in command." Suspicions were revived. The battle of Chaeronea was something which Archelaus had difficulty in living down. It was also observed that, with the exception of Aristion (who was not on good terms with Archelaus), all the friends of Mithradates who fell into Sulla's hands were released. Sulla

gave Archelaus a considerable landed estate in
Euboea, and the status of Friend and Ally of the
Roman People. Men scented some secret understanding. Sulla dealt with these criticisms in his
memoirs : to what effect, we are not told. But
Sulla had every reason to be civil to Archelaus,
whose influence might yet mean very much ;
Archelaus would feel much more free to act as
he thought best, if he knew that he had a safe refuge
in the event of his master's anger ; and, besides,
Sulla could be carelessly generous when the mood
came to him.

Envoys arrived, who had authority to accept the
terms Sulla had transmitted through Archelaus,
with the exception of the cession of Paphlagonia,
which the king could not part with ; as to the
ships of war, there was some mistake, as they knew
of no such clause. They also hinted at better
terms that might be obtained from Fimbria. Sulla
was not to be bluffed. He could himself do very
well in that line. He took a very angry and bluster-
ing tone. " What !—hold back Paphlagonia ? And
deny the clause about the ships ? I expected to
see Mithradates at my feet, to thank me for leaving
him even that right hand which destroyed so many
Romans. He will sing another tune when I come
into Asia ! In the meantime, let him take his ease
in Pergamus, directing a war he has never seen."

The envoys were intimidated. Archelaus intervened, and begged Sulla to leave the negotiations
to him. Receiving Sulla's consent, he left to visit
the king, while Sulla settled affairs in Macedonia.
Archelaus returned to Philippi with the king's
unqualified agreement to the terms. He seems to
have been successful in persuading Mithradates

that Sulla was both a more formidable opponent
and a more profitable friend than Fimbria : in
which without doubt he judged rightly. Mithradates requested a personal interview.

VIII

The fleet of Lucullus, which had won two considerable sea-battles off the Trojan coast, was joined
by a fleet that Sulla had equipped in the Thessalian
ports, and the united squadrons, sailing up to the
Hellespont, met the army after its long march
round by Thrace. The interview with Mithradates
took place at Dardanus, on the Asiatic side of the
straits. It was interesting, because it illustrated
two opposite forms of bluff, one of which will
always successfully browbeat the other. Two
hundred ships, twenty thousand infantry, six thousand cavalry, and an array of war cars, were the
trifling escort intended to convey to the world the
pomp and power of Mithradates. With arrogant
insolence Sulla arrived with four cohorts, two hundred horse, his own genius, and the moral power
of the Roman name. He at once put Mithradates
in his place. As they met, and the king extended
his hand, Sulla imperiously demanded whether he
were willing to ratify the terms of peace. The
king was at first too astonished to answer, but
remained silently reckoning up the man before him.
" How is this ? " demanded Sulla harshly. " I
think the petitioner speaks first, and the conqueror
listens in silence." Mithradates therefore began,
and explained his view of the war. It had been
partly an inevitable fatality ; some sort of war was
bound to happen, and no one was really at fault ;
and partly the Romans had only themselves to

blame. He developed the argument which turned up in one form or another in all discussions of the subject. It was the venality and corruption of the Roman officials and corporations which were the real cause of the war. Sulla openly derided this point of view. He had heard (he said) that Mithradates was a man who never lacked plausible reasons to justify a bad case—and now he could see that it was so. He took the case point by point, and reminded Mithradates of all the indisputable facts which showed that the king had had hostile intentions independent of any offence of the Roman officials. Of these latter Sulla said significantly little, and nothing at all in palliation of their conduct : but he insisted that they were excuses, not reasons, for the war, and that peaceful means of redress had always been open. He again detailed in particular the barbarous acts committed by the orders of Mithradates, reminded him that he was in an impossible military position, and demanded afresh whether the treaty arranged with Archelaus were to be ratified. Mithradates meekly said that it was. Sulla therefore at once embraced the king, and gave him the kiss of peace and friendship.

Mithradates, having handed over the agreed number of ships, sailed home to Pontus, and the first Mithradatic war was ended. He was to be heard of again, but Sulla had other things to occupy his mind. Sufficient to the day was the evil thereof.

IX

Enthusiasts are always more royalist than the king. The army, which, being Roman and not Pontic, had ideas of its own, was somewhat scan-

dalised and critical at letting King Mithradates off
so easily as this. It was all in favour of " hanging
the Kaiser." Sulla had no objection to explanation.
He quieted the enthusiasts by a public address,
pointing out that such compromises were necessary
and expedient, since any attempt to enforce harsher
terms might simply have resulted in Mithradates
transferring the negotiations to Fimbria. An alliance between Fimbria and the king would have
been too powerful for Sulla. Now, however,
Fimbria was isolated, and it was time to pay a
friendly visit to his army.

Fimbria was encamped at Thyatira. Proceeding
thither, Sulla pitched camp not far off, and began
to dig in. He sent to require that Fimbria should
deliver up his command, since it was held on an
illegal and unauthorised tenure. Fimbria, who
evidently thought this demand a good joke, replied
that Sulla's own command was now illegal. Sulla
did not see the joke. His official commission had
been perfectly in order from the start, and he had
never admitted the validity of the order superseding
him : whereas no possible argument, from any
point of view, could make out Fimbria's commission
to be legal.

For all his popularity, Fimbria apparently had
not the peculiar power over men which Sulla
possessed in such plenitude. He could not—at
any rate, he did not—prevent his men from meeting
and talking with the Sullans. It became clear that
they could not be relied upon. Before long, some
of them were helping Sulla's men to dig the trenches,
and did not trouble to come back. Fimbria called
an assembly.

He urged his men to stand by him. Many let

him know plainly that they would not fight fellow-citizens. He rent his garments in desperation, and spoke to the disaffected personally ; but it was without effect : the desertions continued. Fimbria canvassed the officers, and managed to get some support. Calling another assembly, he asked these officers to take an oath to remain with him : but now they too hesitated, and suggested that every one should be called upon to take the oath. He made a personal appeal to those who were under special obligations to him. The first he named, a close friend, refused to take the oath. Fimbria drew his sword, and was prevented from killing him only by the intervention of those around. It was evident that the whole army was breaking up under the magnetism of Sulla.

The only possible resort was to wipe out the cause. Fimbria persuaded a slave, by money rewards and the promise of freedom, to undertake the perilous gamble of going to Sulla as a " deserter," and assassinating him. Fortune stood on guard over Sulla, for even here Fimbria bungled in choosing his man. The man began to lose his nerve at the last critical moment, attracted attention, was arrested, and confessed. The indignation of the Sullans was deep and outspoken.

Fimbria finally went to the Sullan camp himself and asked for an interview. To his disappointment, Sulla sent an officer in his stead ; but after what had just occurred, it can hardly be surprising that Sulla declined a personal meeting with a desperate and none too scrupulous man. He was, however, moderate in the terms he offered Fimbria. In spite of all that was known to have happened in Rome, and all that was known against Fimbria

personally,[1] Sulla offered him permission to leave
Asia by sea, and go whither he would. He answered
gloomily that he knew of a better way. Leaving
the camp, he went to Pergamus, entered the temple
of Asclepios, and there stabbed himself. His ill
luck pursued him. The wound was not mortal :
so at his master's command his servant drove the
weapon home. Sulla handed the body over to
Fimbria's freedmen for burial, remarking acidly
that he would not imitate the conduct of Marius
and Cinna. The army of Fimbria was incorporated
with the Sullan. This was the end of Fimbria,
and of the popular expedition to the east.

Thus far the victory of Sulla over the *Populares*
had been extraordinarily complete and entirely
bloodless, save for the suicide of Fimbria. He
had done better than wipe out an army ; he had
absorbed one !

X

Sulla spent the winter in Asia : his men in
rest, and he himself in work. The disaster had been
enormous, and it was little use to hope that the
settlement could be other than a grievous one.
The measures of Mithradates were cancelled ; his
more important adherents, and those who had been
responsible for the massacres, were proceeded
against and executed. The financial side of affairs
was particularly important. Sulla had been living
from hand to mouth during all these months since
he left Rome. His own private income, together
with that of his officers, had been entirely cut off.
Sulla did not propose to sacrifice the greater in the
interest of the less, nor Rome (on which everything

[1] He had attempted to kill old Scaevola during the funeral of
Marius.

else depended) to the comfort of a province which had imperilled the very foundations of Roman dominion. His financial measures, therefore, were terribly severe. The hitherto unpaid revenues of the last five years were assessed, and ordered to be collected : and a special war levy of twenty thousand talents was laid upon the country. It was impossible to pay such sums : the cities were compelled to borrow heavily. The Roman bankers advanced the loans [1] : and by this huge operation Sulla's return to Rome was financed, and the great bankers given such a stake in its success that their whole influence was likely to be thrown into the scale to maintain the value of the security he represented to them. So far from committing himself to any political alliance with them, Sulla had committed them to his cause by the powerful bonds of business interest.

There was no alternative. Sulla was not responsible for the situation in which he found himself. Least of all had he been responsible for the train of events which had originally caused the Mithradatic war. And he may have reflected that it was better for Asia, in the long run, to pay these sums for the maintenance of political control, than to fall into the hands of the financial corporations without any political control to hold them in check. It was a bad business in any case.

There was discrimination. Those cities which had remained loyal to Rome received special recognition, and those which had suffered with exceptional severity were given compensation. Sulla studied on the spot the whole problem of the Asiatic adminis-

[1] With paid and unpaid interest, the loans swelled in fourteen years to sixfold the original amount. Asia, nevertheless, continued to be one of the most prosperous of the Roman provinces.

tration. He took away with him some intelligent conceptions as to the origin of the trouble and its best remedy, which were destined to bear ample fruit in days to come.

Sulla's period of office as proconsul had of course long ago expired ; he had moreover been formally deprived of command, and he possessed no authority of his own to appoint a successor.[1] He therefore merely left Murena, with Fimbria's two legions, to act as his deputy, and to see the new arrangements carried out. Lucius Lucullus also remained, in part, probably, at his own wish, to superintend the naval and the financial side of affairs, both of which needed the attention of an able man. Lucullus was never at any time a keen party man, while no one was better qualified to deal with finance. He was one of those uncommon men who are always popular, always trusted, and always trustworthy ; but if he had merely walked to and fro in the street, he would somehow have made a fortune out of it. He had a natural magnetism for money. Sulla had no objection to an arrangement which had much to recommend it. Piracy was swarming in the Greek seas, and needed to be dealt with.

While settling Asia, Sulla drafted a letter to the Senate at Rome, which constituted his political *pronunciamento*. He reported his proceedings in Greece and Asia, and informed the Senate that he was about to return to Italy. He promised to respect the rights of the new Italian citizens admitted to the franchise, and to confine his punishment

---

[1] The legal position was that Sulla's command continued in force until his successor took it over. But, so far, Flaccus was the only person who could have claimed to exercise this right, and he was dead : in addition to which Sulla denied his claim.

to the leaders of the revolution. With the rank
and file he had no quarrel. To his supersession he
made no reference whatever.

In some cases there is practically no distinction
observable between the product of a generous
instinct and that of a subtle diplomacy. It is very
difficult to judge under which of these categories
to place Sulla's motives in framing the terms of
this letter, unless we frankly admit that the heart
and the head, properly exercised, lead to the same
results. It was exactly what any man would have
written, who was inspired by resolute principle
and honest public spirit ; but it was also a shattering
blow for the *Populares*. If we compare the actions
of Octavius with those of Sulla now, we obtain a
perfect contrast between stupidity and intelligence.
Sulla's messenger was not allowed to enter Rome.
The publication of the letter might have broken
up the Cinnan coalition.

Still Quintus Sertorius was not sent. Cinna
determined to cross the seas himself. He got no
further than Ancona. The troops, on learning their
proposed destination, mutinied, and Cinna was
killed. His colleague in the consulship, Gnaeus
Papirius Carbo, gave up all further thought of
carrying the war overseas, and took up his post at
Ariminum. Moderate men, terrified at the prospect,
strove to effect a reconciliation between the parties,
but it seemed impossible to bridge the gulf. Ener-
getic preparations were made. A hundred thousand
men were held under arms in Italy, and every step
was taken to be ready against the emergency of
Sulla's return. Lucius Scipio and Gaius Norbanus,
two moderate men not involved in the Marian
proscription, were elected consuls for the year.

SULLA'S CAMPAIGNS
IN B.C. 83-82.

R. Adice

Placentia.
R. Po

Ravenna

Ariminum

N

W   E

S

Clusium.

Spoletium.

*Adriatic
Sea.*

Rome
Praeneste.

Capua.
Verusia. *Brundusium.*
Tarentum.

*Tyrrhenian
Sea.*

Scale
of miles.
0 20 40 60 80 100

Sicily

CHAPTER X

SULLA COMES HOME

I

SULLA left Ephesus early in the year, and after a passage of three days landed at Piraeus. He spent a little time in Athens, which he could not expect to revisit. He was initiated into the mysteries—then still a privilege not to be despised, even if it no longer possessed its former importance ; and he acquired the library of Apellicon the Teian, which contained the unique revised copies of Aristotle's works. This was an achievement of some significance in the history of literature. From the versions which Sulla then obtained sprang all the later complete editions of Aristotle.

The strain of the last few years was telling upon him. At Athens he was attacked by the first symptoms of gout. He was in no hurry, and went to Aedepsus in Euboea, to take a course of the hot waters, and a rest cure. For a while he put aside all business, and " amused himself with actors." No record remains of the dramatic pieces he selected for his entertainment. . . . On the beach at Aedepsus he was humbly presented with two magnificent fish by some native fishermen. He was delighted, and enquired their town. They were men of Haliae in Boeotia. He had a long memory for some things. Haliae was one of the

towns he had broken up and dispersed after the
battle of Orchomenos, for disaffection. So there
were men of Haliae still remaining. The trembling
fishermen admitted it. Sulla dryly bade them
cheer up and go in peace, as they had engaged the
services of no insignificant intercessors. On the
strength of this, the former inhabitants of Haliae
felt that they had authority to reassemble and
refound their city.

At length he took the road again, and marching
through Thessaly and Macedonia crossed the mountains to Dyrrachium. The *Populares* were now
showing the curious paralysis which before had
marked the Senate, and probably for the same reason
—the influence of the great financiers was against
them. Not only was Dyrrachium open to Sulla,
but Brundusium (which stood to it as Dover to
Calais) was not reliably held. The omens at first
were unfavourable. At Apollonia, not far from
Dyrrachium, a satyr was caught, alleged to be
exactly like the satyrs depicted by painters and
sculptors. It was brought before Sulla, and questioned through several interpreters ; but whatever,
or whoever, the uncouth object might be, it, or he,
could speak no known language, and answered only
by noises "something between the neighing of a horse
and the bleating of a goat." Sulla, in consternation,
ordered the disastrous object to be destroyed.

Whether it were the satyr, or the general situation
of affairs, Sulla felt that every possible step should
be taken to assist Fortune. He had about forty
thousand men—all old and trained soldiers, entirely
devoted to him. But to invade Italy was very
different from invading Asia. Among the peculiar
virtues of Sulla was a thorough understanding that

political conditions are more important than military, and are precedent to the latter. He never fell into the superficial error of supposing that military operations could create or destroy the circumstances that are formed by public opinion and the subtle forces which unite or dissever men. He knew that political considerations could melt armies, or bank up against him powers with which he could never hope to struggle. As Hannibal dissolved the Alps with vinegar, Sulla prepared his way by dissolving political opinion in Italy.

It was his aim to convince the Italians and the mass of ordinary men that they had nothing to fear from him. He issued a promise of unconditional amnesty to all who severed their connection with the revolutionary government ; and he solemnly undertook to confirm and protect the new Italian citizens in their hard-won franchise. Every man in his army severally made oath not to take his discharge (as was his right in strict law) on entering Italy ; not voluntarily to do any injury to Italy ; to maintain the Italian franchise, and to recognise Italian citizens as friends and equals. The army, of its own accord, offered to lodge bonds of good behaviour with its commander, each man depositing a certain sum of money which could be forfeited in the event of desertion or misconduct. Sulla thanked his men warmly, but refused this practical mark of loyalty. He was satisfied with their word.

The omens were now favourable. He transported his army over to Brundusium in twelve hundred vessels, and the great port opened her gates to him. All Apulia, the heel of Italy (and in this case her Achilles heel), came into his hands without a blow being struck.

Sulla was, in the sight of all human prudence, gambling with fortune : but his throw of the dice was firm and decisive, and, as usual, the lucky throw came up. From Brundusium he took the Appian road by Tarentum and Venusia, crossed the corner of Samnium, and entered Campania once more. At Capua, for the first time, he came into contact with the enemy. The army of the consul Gaius Norbanus was at Capua ; that of the other consul, Lucius Scipio, was on the way from Rome, and had not yet arrived. This was indeed Fortune ! Sulla attacked Norbanus at once, crushed him, and blockaded the remnant of his army in Capua and Neapolis.

There must have been a fatal lack of central direction in the strategy of the *Populares*. Besides the direct military injury, the defeat of Norbanus damaged their prestige beyond repair, and set free all the waiting disaffection which only needed reassurance in order to reveal itself.

II

The weakness of some kinds of policy was at this point illustrated by the accessions which came to him. All the proscriptions of Marius had failed to wipe out certain crucial persons who were destined to play important parts in the future : failed, for the simple reason that it was impossible even to identify them. Young Marcus Licinius Crassus joined Sulla probably at Dyrrachium ; and promptly upon the victory at Capua, Strabo's son, Gnaeus Pompeius, a young man as charming and popular as his father had been hateful and hated, came down from Picenum with strong reinforce-ments. Gaius Julius Caesar, a youth of nineteen,

with oiled hair and fashionable clothes, the nephew
of Gaius Marius and the son-in-law of Cinna, was
in Rome, and stayed there. Sulla had returned to
an Italy where the first triumvirate, that later on
ushered in the empire, was already on the threshold
of manhood. Crassus fought and Pompeius fought ;
Caesar merely looked on. Like Sulla, he could
bide his time.

Every one who came into contact with Pompeius
fell under his spell. He had not only great physical
beauty, but first-rate ability, and, to crown all, he
had a perfectly genuine humility and unselfishness
which carried away the ordinary sensual man.
Sulla, like every one else, had disliked and distrusted
Strabo ; Pompeius (as every one else did) he loved.
The news had already arrived that Pompeius had
raised a small army in Picenum, masked Carbo
from the military road that gave access to Sulla's
flank, and securely organised the district. He
came in person to report and join up.

When they met, and Sulla dismounted, to find
three whole legions and the vision of Pompeius,
the wise man of the world returned their formal
greeting of " Imperator ! " by the same glorious
name—that dream, ambition and envy of all Romans.
Indeed, here at last was his ideal, the Perfect
Aristocrat ! It was as if Fortune had greeted his
return to Italy by granting him the sight of the
human embodiment of all he wanted. . . . And
Pompeius was faultless : he blushed, was pleased,
but did not take it seriously. . . . There was
hope for Rome. . . . Many years later his head
was thrown at the feet of Julius Caesar, and even that
man of steel and crystal recoiled from it, remember-
ing what once it had been. . . . But the Perfect

Aristocrat had many a year of success and fame to come to him before that day. To Sulla, he became the pattern to point to, when blunderers and fools went wrong. And if ever we ask ourselves what mysterious ideal it was which Sulla was pursuing through the labyrinth of war and statecraft, the best answer we can give is—Pompeius. To Pompeius he invariably rose and uncovered. Of such noble material are the illusions of men sometimes made !

III

Sulla advanced rapidly northwards with his new reinforcements. Scipio had not got beyond Teanum. Sulla parlied. Now, as before, he had no intention of wasting by the use of force the men whom he could gain by persuasion. Scipio listened to Sulla's proposals for negotiation and accommodation, which were precisely what all moderate men most wanted.

Sulla was holding the door open, as he had all along held it. How long he could continue to hold it open, with his camp full of the refugees and their memories, was a different matter ; but he was still holding it open, and he did not betray any man who passed through. The negotiations with Scipio were somewhat prolonged, and while they went on the armies fraternised. By degrees Scipio's legionaries began to go over to Sulla. Scipio, still unable to make up his mind, in alarm denounced the armistice. Sulla indignantly maintained that an agreement had actually been concluded. Whether it had been concluded or not, Scipio's army heard with profound disapproval that the consul had broken off a promising negotiation for peace. It went over to Sulla in a body. The consul, having (unlike Fimbria) a clear conscience, did not commit suicide. He held his ground, and was arrested in his own tent by Sulla's order. He was removed in custody.

Many commanders have won battles. Sulla's two bloodless victories over Fimbria and Scipio are his own peculiar glory.

The desertion of Scipio's army brought the campaign to an end for that year. Sulla, who had led a forlorn hope over the sea from Dyrrachium to Brundusium, was in possession of half Italy, and safely entrenched in a position to renew the war upon favourable terms.

IV

He made no secret of his intentions. Events were marching firmly under his hand, and he could feel them to be going well. The immediate effort of the Popular leaders was to raise more troops. Yet what they really needed was leadership, not men. The moderate leaders had proved useless. The party chiefs accordingly came forward openly to take command. Gaius Marius the younger (an adopted son of old Marius) and Gnaeus Papirius Carbo were elected consuls for the year, and at once set to work. Quintus Sertorius went into Etruria to raise fresh legions. Sulla was perfectly aware of all the steps they were taking, as can be seen by the plan of campaign he drew up for the new operations.

Three armies were to be organised. One was to advance northward from Picenum along the Adriatic, towards Cis-Alpine Gaul ; and Metellus Pius was to be its nominal commander. Sulla, however,

wished Pompeius to have a practically equal standing
with Metellus. . . . Pompeius hesitated to accept
such a post, in view of the greater rank and age of
his prospective colleague, so Sulla consulted Metellus,
who at once, pleased at the consideration shown
him by a young man, cordially agreed that Pompeius
should come to him on the terms arranged, and
personally wrote to invite him. Pompeius therefore
started for Picenum.

Crassus, a natural genius who could organise
anything, and had the good sense to leave purely
military matters to his professional subordinates,
was sent into Central Italy. With native caution
he asked for an escort. Sulla answered : " I give
you for escort your father, your brother and your
friends and kindred whose unjust murder I am
avenging." Crassus accepted the rebuke, and penetrating into the Marsian land eastward of Rome,
raised there a force destined to play an important
part in the coming struggle.

When, therefore, the campaign opened, two of
Sulla's three armies were commanded by the later
colleagues of Julius Caesar in the famous " first
triumvirate." Facts of this kind are important to
remember.

V

During the struggle against Mithradates Sulla
had been playing a close intricate game of war in
which there were but few moves, and those for the
most part short ones. Circumstances were now
entirely changed, and with the change came an
alteration in his methods. His two Italian campaigns were wars of long moves and rapid marches
—a strategy boldly designed, depending much

upon the accurate conjunction of widely separated armies.

The campaign began by the advance of Metellus northward from Picenum along the great military road which skirted the eastern coast. The fleet accompanied him, and entering Ravenna isolated on that side the important junction of Ariminum, whence the road turned in a north-westerly direction straight across Italy to Placentia on the Po. He sent Marcus Lucullus forward to seize Placentia. By this means Metellus acquired a powerful position in Carbo's rear, where he could watch all the roads leading into or out of northern Italy. The task of Pompeius was to prevent this long and somewhat tenuous line from being cut by a blow from Carbo : for which purpose he advanced inland, joined up with Crassus, and drove Carbo's lieutenant into Spoletium. All these operations were not, by themselves, safe ; if they had stood alone, there was every likelihood that Carbo's counter-blow would bring down the frail scheme like a house of cards, after which Carbo would only need to wipe out the scattered Sullan forces in detail. Sulla had reserved for himself the movements which were to give meaning and strength to those of Metellus, Crassus, and Pompeius.

His own advance, on the western side of the peninsula, was along the Via Latina, through the heart of that mountainous country which was the true homeland of Rome. Near Signia, some thirty miles from the city, he came into touch with the army of the younger Marius. With all the caution of his adoptive father, Marius retreated upon a favourable situation at Sacriportus, and made ready for battle. The march was a difficult and dangerous

one ; the country is one of those in which all the
advantage lies with a defending army. The rear-
guard of Marius held all the passes, and Sulla's
veterans had to fight as well as march every foot of
the way. To add to the difficulties the weather
was adverse ; storms of wind and rain overwhelmed
the troops, and for once Sulla was in a hurry. He
must have known how much depended on the speed
and success of his movements. He was expressly
anxious to fight that day : for he had had an important dream the night before, in which he thought
he saw old Marius warning his son to beware of
the morrow as a fatal day. He had already sent
out orders for a concentration preparatory to an
attack, when his principal officers intervened. They
pointed out the impossibility of executing his
orders : the men were dead beat, and had of their
own accord flung themselves upon the ground to
get a little rest, as soon as the march was halted.
Sulla never flogged a willing horse, and, as always,
he gave way ; but it was with the most intense
reluctance. Fortune had played false at the critical
moment.

But it was not Fortune that had played false :
the blame rested on human strength and endurance,
which could not rouse themselves to accomplish
the task Sulla had set them. Fortune came to the
rescue.

The actual course of events is variously told.
Plutarch had two versions of the tale—one probably
that of Sulla himself, in which Marius made an
attack in person ; the other that of Fenestella, in
which it was asserted that Marius never ordered
the attack, but, tired out, was snatching a little
sleep at the time. In any case, the attack was

made. The Sullan legionaries were engaged in
throwing up the earthwork which, by strictest and
most invariable command of the drill-book, never
failed to surround their camp at night. Caught
unawares, they snatched up their weapons and
fought.

Discipline, training and *moral* always tell in war ;
but they can never have told more than in the
short-sword fighting. Sulla's men, however dead
beat, were sufficiently alive to forget their fatigue,
and to scatter the new recruits of Marius before
them. One division of the consular army declined
to engage. Marius, according to Fenestella, was
awakened by the stream of fugitives which began
to pour through his bivouac. He had only time to
reach Praeneste ; the gates were already shut, and
he was drawn up to safety by a rope. It was indeed
a fatal day for him. Sulla's dream had come true.

The battle of Sacriportus cleared the road north.
While Marius sent urgent messages to the praetor,
Lucius Brutus Damasippus, to evacuate Rome,
leaving as few of the *Optimates* behind him as he
could, Sulla detached Quintus Ofella to blockade
Praeneste, and pushed on. Brutus carried out the
orders sent him, and when Sulla at last arrived
at Rome, to snatch a glance at the old city—which
he must often have wondered whether he would
ever see again—it was to meet the maddening news
of fresh massacre, Pelion heaped upon Ossa, in
which even the noblest and most honoured Roman
of his day had perished.

The murder of Quintus Mucius Scaevola was
in its day as shocking and scandalous as that of
Thomas Becket many centuries later. The old
man took refuge in the temple of Vesta, the holiest

spot in Rome, where the ever-burning fire stood.
The image of the goddess was drenched with his
blood ; his body was cast into the Tiber. He left
behind him his great work on the Civil Law, in
eighteen books, the basis from which all subsequent
study of law took its start. Sulla would have been
more than a soldier and a statesman—he would have
been a saint (a spiritual degree of which he had never
heard)—if such a deed had not roused his emotions
to fury. He was now the last of the group of
Optimates who had struggled to save the State from
all that was overwhelming it. Rutilius was still in
exile : Lucius Crassus had died, no one knew how ;
Drusus had been assassinated ; Scaevola murdered
on the altar : he himself had survived—how ? By
a series of miracles and chances—by Fortune.
    He had no time to waste. He pushed on north.
The three Sullan armies were closing upon Carbo,
who, at Clusium in Etruria, was held immobilised,
unable effectively to deal his blow at Metellus while
Sulla was coming up so rapidly. But Carbo was
in a powerful position ; and Sulla's advance came
gradually to pause. The moment had arrived for
fresh plans of campaign, and for a regrouping of
the various elements in the field.

VI

    The *Populares* were making every effort to relieve
young Marius in Praeneste, but thus far they had
been prevented from doing so. The war began to
centre upon the fate of Praeneste. Into this condition
of pause the Samnites (who might have moved
before) flung themselves, with the object of bearing
down the balance.
    A powerful force of Samnites and Lucanians,

under the Samnite general Pontius Telesinus, set out for the relief of Praeneste. Picking up the garrison of Capua on its way, it swelled to a formidable striking force of seventy thousand men, before which Sulla's detachments fell back. This serious news made it urgently necessary for Sulla to return southwards.

As Fortune would have it, he could go; for at this juncture his first plans matured of themselves. The proconsul Norbanus, carrying out what would, under more favourable circumstances, have been Carbo's counter-stroke, had masked Marcus Lucullus in Placentia, advanced upon the main force of Metellus Pius, and been defeated. Lucullus therefore left Placentia and ventured a pitched battle at Fidentia. He had sixteen cohorts against fifty. While he was waiting for a favourable opening the gale blew a quantity of flowers from the meadows near by, till the troops were involuntarily decorated with them. With something of Sulla's own quickness at turning such incidents to account, Lucullus pointed out to his men that they were already crowned with the chaplets of victory. They accepted the half-jesting omen, joined battle, and were completely successful. The whole of Cis-Alpine Gaul fell into the hands of Metellus as the result.

Carbo's powerful position was crumbling. Sulla accordingly felt free to return to Praeneste, which had become the chief point of danger. Sending word to Crassus to join him, he took post south of the city. Metellus was already on the march into Etruria, and Carbo threw up the game. He was never a man of strong nerves. He left secretly to take ship for Africa; the remnants of his army either dispersed home, or fell into the hands of Metellus.

The Samnites had entered the war too late : so late that they were the only combatants left in the field, with three Sullan armies to fight. One possible resource was left. They could destroy Rome, and go down fighting. The city was but one day's march away. Pontius Telesinus consulted his Lucanian colleague, Lamponius, who was willing. The associated leaders of the *Populares*, Lucius Brutus Damasippus and Carrinas, went with them.

It was not only the Samnites who were prepared to die fighting. If the roof of the world were to be pulled in, the slippered ancients, the boys, the loafers of the slums, and the odds and ends who were all that, for the moment, were left in Rome, were equally ready to be present at the occasion. Pontius camped that night by the Colline Gate, having cleverly dodged Sulla by a forced night march. At daybreak, the slippered ancients made their heroic sally, and were cut to pieces, as they probably expected to be, by the Samnite fighting men. Complete and unutterable panic reigned in the city : the women (Plutarch says) behaving as if it were already sacked. But the delay had sufficed. Before Pontius could follow up his easy victory, there were horsemen on the horizon—Balbus and seven hundred of Sulla's troopers, the advance guard of Sulla himself, who was coming up fast and furious behind. Balbus and his men only waited to wipe the sweat off their horses, and, rebridling, engaged the Samnites. Before noon, the foot-sloggers were at hand, and Sulla with them. He halted them, and ordered them to eat and drink while cohort after cohort wheeled into place.

Dolabella and Torquatus strongly counselled caution : they were not dealing with young Marius,
or Carbo, but with Samnites and Lucanians.
Sulla refused to listen. His blood was up. It was
four in the afternoon when the trumpets sounded
and the battle was joined.

VII

Dolabella and Torquatus, whether their counsel
was expedient or not, were right in their estimate of
the situation. The battle before the Colline Gate
was fought with a ferocity and desperation very
far from the standard of the Popular armies. The
left wing of the Sullans was at length broken, after
a sanguinary struggle, and Sulla rode to stop the
rout. His white charger was recognised, and two
Samnites simultaneously hurled javelins at him.
Only the watchfulness of his servant, who touched
the white horse forward, saved him, the javelins
falling behind his horse's tail. He flung himself
into the turmoil, entreating, threatening, catching
hold of men with his hands, but not even Sulla
could breast the stream of defeat. He was borne
along in the crowd, and carried, whether he would
or no, to the camp, where a considerable part of
the fugitives had taken refuge. Not only was the
wing broken up, but even many of the non-com-
batants, who had come out of the city to look on,
were involved, and killed or trampled underfoot.

In Rome, all was believed to be lost, and the
siege of Praeneste was supposed to be raised. Many
fugitives arrived at the head-quarters of Ofella's
investing army, to assure him that Sulla was dead,
and Rome in the hands of the Samnites. Ofella,
being out of the circle of excitement, must have

thought this a rather unlikely tale ; but the fugitives
were certainly a fact, since there they were before
him. He did not raise the siege, but wisely waited
for further information.

The battle must have broken up, and lost its
ordered coherence, after nightfall ; but it can have
been no happy night they spent, striving to patch
up some order out of the shattered remains of the
unbeaten Sullan legions, not knowing what Fortune
had in store. What Sulla thought of matters may
be better guessed, if the story of his prayer to Apollo
be true. He had a little golden image of Apollo,
bought from Delphi, which he always carried
about with him in battle. He drew it out, kissed
it, and said : " Oh, Apollo Pythius, who in so many
battles have raised to honour and greatness Lucius
Cornelius Sulla Felix, will you now cast him down,
and bring him to the gate of his own city to perish
shamefully with his fellow-citizens ? " And, indeed,
it must have looked very like that.

But about midnight messengers from Crassus
arrived with the sobering and restoring enquiry
whether Sulla had any supplies to spare. It then
appeared that the right wing, which Crassus had
commanded, had been entirely successful, and had
driven its opponents right off the field to Antemnae,
on the Tiber, north of Rome, outside which Crassus
was waiting. Apparently Fortune had not been
quite so fickle as she appeared, and the absence of
any pursuit was explained. Sulla reached Antemnae
by dawn, to see for himself how matters stood.

A body of three thousand of the enemy, whom
Crassus had penned in, sent out a herald to ask for
terms. Sulla granted them their lives on condition
that they changed sides. They accepted these

terms, and joined in an attack on their late allies. We are not told to what section they belonged. They can hardly have been Samnites.

The battle outside the Colline Gate, from first to last, lasted some sixteen hours or so, from the afternoon of one day to the morning of the next. Like all battles with the Samnites, it was a savage, stand-up, knock-down fight, in which endurance counted for more than science : and as with all unscientific battles, it is hard to trace exactly where it ended and when or how. During all those sixteen hours, the temple of Fortune, which stood in the angle of the wall close to the Colline Gate, looked down upon the combatants. In the upshot, the miserable wreck of Sulla's magnificent army had six thousand prisoners, including Pontius Telesinus, Brutus, and Carrinas : most of the rest of the Samnite fighters lay on the field.

VIII

This was the end. Sulla had come home.

CHAPTER XI

THE DICTATORSHIP OF SULLA

I

BUT to what home had he come ? To a world in ruins, a State in chaos, a mankind corrupted by revolution, war, passion, folly, until—even if the bricks of old Rome had been saved from the deathless fury of the Samnite—the spiritual, the archetypal Rome, immortal in the heavens, the city of Camillus and of Manius Curius, might well seem to be dissolved. Sulla was in the position of one who builds afresh from the foundations. The old Rome had come to an end : if Rome continued, it would be a new Rome. And Sulla would have been not a modest man but a fool if he had refused the task ; for there was no one else who could undertake it. Two feelings were in his mind : a sardonic scepticism about his own private ability to accomplish the work before him, and an almost equally sardonic conviction that Fortune would probably see him through.

The events of the last two years of his life were woven in too complex a web to allow of being narrated wholly in order of time. We have to disentangle them into a different kind of order ; and first we may take his official triumph.

It was a memorably splendid function, distinguished by the royal spoils of Mithradates—for Sulla had conquered a king—while in the rear

marched the exiles, crowned with garlands, hailing
him as Father and Restorer. After the procession
was over, Sulla delivered the formal official address,
in which he reported his actions and justified the
proceedings of his tenure of office. He deliberately
belittled the part played by his own foresight and
intelligence, and insisted throughout on the preponderant share of Fortune, enumerating in detail
the many hazards, and the miraculous conjunctions
of events, which had brought him home. He
finally requested to be granted the honorary title
of " Felix "—the Fortunate. And if there had
been, in the past, any considerable element of mere
jest in his attitude towards Fortune, there can have
been very little now. The moment was almost the
most solemn in the life of a Roman. The title he
requested was the judgment he asked from mankind.

II

He had not come home merely to wreak vengeance on political foes, though, being human, he
may have had no deep objection to the execution
of people he disliked, and, being a pagan Roman
in his moral training, vengeance was to him not a
luxury but a duty. But passion played so small
a part in his life that the blind fury of hatred probably had little to do with his motives. He had
come home of course to save himself ; but, for the
rest, to re-establish a principle and refound a State.
He had not created the circumstances : they were
given him, as a problem of chess is posited for
solution. And in all that follows we must strictly
remember the factors of circumstance which were
not external but internal conditions. Sulla did not
live after two thousand years of Christianity, nor

even in an age of developed human science and philosophy. He went by such rules as a man may derive from obvious common sense and ordinary worldly experience. Even the main point of Plato's teaching—that obvious common sense may be hopelessly fallacious, and ordinary worldly experience worthless—had not yet penetrated to the minds of men in Sulla's age. He unconsciously did as much as any man to drive home to mankind the practical importance of the Platonic standpoint : as will be clearer in the sequel.

The problem he had to solve was to restore the mystical, the ideal Rome—the state of mind and temper, the moral tension, which had constituted Roman greatness. The main process must lie in the re-creation of such an aristocracy as that which had first created Rome. To do this, he had on the one hand to collect the remnants of the old aristocracy, and to bring forward elements which might be fitting to supplement them ; on the other, he had to repress all adverse influences. The clearing of the stage came first in order, before the new actors could be introduced upon the scene.

Here the call of political theory coincided with the demands of prudence. The *Populares* themselves had made it extremely dangerous for Sulla to leave them alone : nor had they hitherto done anything to convince him that their genius was indispensable to the new Rome. They had borne their full share in creating that logic of events which is sometimes the blessing of men and sometimes their curse. For when great courses of action are once launched, they are as much out of control, even of the actors, as an avalanche is ; and men may fight madly against a necessity which sweeps them on to actions they abhor. It is the peculiar distinction of Sulla that he was not a man who fought against the logic of events. With a dry lucidity he carried out its dictates to the last letter. He was not mad, in the sense in which old Marius had certainly been mad ; there was no emotional frenzy in his mind : he was far too cynical to worry about injustice ; the acuteness of his intelligence was, if anything, sharpened ; he merely drove to its logical conclusion a process which other men had started, and to which there was no rational alternative in the field.

It began with the slaughter of the prisoners taken in the battle at the Colline Gate. They had been rounded up into the Circus Flaminius, which stood in the Campus Martius, and three days after the battle they were massacred by Sulla's orders.

He was addressing the Senate at the time in the temple of Bellona,[1] close to the circus ; and the shrieks and cries startled the nerves of the august assembly. The calm logician paused in his remarks, and reassured the nervous sentimentalists. It was, he observed acidly, merely the noise of a few offenders whose chastisement he had ordered. The senators did not accept his assurance with any kind of enthusiasm. Blood !—always more blood ! Where would it end ? Sulla might have asked the equally cogent question—Where did it begin ?

Since it was clear that Praeneste could never

[1] This temple, being technically outside the city, was the place where the Senate usually assembled to meet any one who, like Sulla, until his triumph was over, could not legally enter the city precincts. Foreign envoys were received at the temple of Bellona.

be relieved, young Marius and the leaders died by their own hands, and the town surrendered. Twelve thousand prisoners fell into the hands of Sulla. In accordance with his old promise, he dismissed all the ordinary citizens, both Roman and Praenestine, together with the women and children. The men of senatorial and official rank were detained. At first he proceeded against them by the legal method of individual prosecution, but finding that this would take more time than any one could spare, he anticipated the inevitable result by ordering them all to be executed. Praeneste was sacked. . . . Capua also surrendered. Naples was taken by storm. Many towns held out for long periods. Volaterrae, for one, defied a siege of nearly three years, and then surrendered only on terms. But by that time passions had run too high to be checked. Sulla's commander was slain by his own troops, and the garrison massacred as it marched out.

III

To do his work in the way he wanted, a legal office was necessary for Sulla. The power he possessed was, if it were anything, that of a proconsul in Asia : a very dubious official authority to exercise in Rome. One of the consuls for the year—the younger Marius—was dead ; the other, Carbo, was in exile, and an interrex was in office. But Sulla did not want the consulship. Its powers were far too restricted. He needed something much greater—something at once legal, and sufficiently wide in scope to accomplish his ends. He therefore proposed to the Senate the revival of the Dictatorship.

There was a touch of antiquarianism in the

suggestion. For a hundred and twenty years there
had been no Dictator ; it was an office almost as
obsolete as that of the Lord High Admiral in
modern England. But the idea had two virtues.
It was practical ;· and it went back to the days of
aristocratic supremacy, when men had no such
fear of Dictators as the oligarchy had always shown.
The Senate instructed the interrex, Lucius Valerius
Flaccus, to draft a law. Sulla was to be a novel
kind of dictator, technically " reipublicae constitu-
endae causa " ; and instead of holding the office
for a certain limited time (six months was the period
of the original office, technically " rei gerundae
causa "), it was to continue indefinitely, with practically unlimited power—even the power to make new
laws. The truth was, that this office was not the
Dictatorship, but was an absolute monarchy, in
which Sulla held all the power that had once belonged
to the kings. He had penetrated to one conception
which was historically accurate : namely, the truth
that, however much it may afterwards walk in
independence, an aristocracy is in its origin the
creation of a king.

Armed with this new power, Sulla proceeded
vigorously with the preliminary task of clearing the
stage. He despatched Pompeius to Sicily and
Africa, to recover those provinces and to resettle
them, while he himself took the task of dealing with
Italy. He declared that the very name of Samnium
ought to be blotted out ; and when he had finished
with it, Samnium was the wilderness it has remained
since that day.

Here, too, Sulla acted with consistence. The
Samnites had been a disruptive force ; their very
virtues, however admirable of their kind, did not

make for peace, security, or creativeness. They
had always been ready to wreck Roman government
in the interests of their own independence : and
the only question was whether this unbending spirit
of freedom was equally valuable to the world.   No
modern man dare answer such a question ; he can
only seek a way round the problem. For Sulla,
the answer was clearly implicit in the principles he
held. Believing, as he believed with his whole
heart, in the necessity and expedience of Roman
government, he did not hesitate at the logical conclusion. He did not hesitate when he faced the
still more difficult problem of the elements in Rome
itself which had continually sought the destruction
of Roman government. And here several rather
curious factors entered into the matter.

If Sulla had returned to a Rome which was in all
respects normal, his logic might have taken a turn
different from that which it did take : but he was
standing in the midst of a catastrophic wreck—in
which the public treasury, and the private fortunes
of his friends, not to speak of his own, had disappeared. Something of the former was recovered
by the capture of Praeneste, and the discovery of
Carbo's war-chest at Ariminum, but hardly sufficient
to put the finances of the government on a stable
basis. The majority of the refugees had no doubt
been carried on the pay-roll of the Sullan army :
ten years of war, revolution, and confiscation were
not likely to have left them much. Title deeds,
even when they survive such storms, do not bring
in money of themselves. If the treasury were to
be refilled, and compensation made to those who
had suffered, some quite extraordinary measure
must be resorted to.

The measure which Sulla evolved was to all intents a Capital Levy on the wealthy men who had stood behind the revolution. There was no fiscal machinery by which such a levy could be carried out as part of the ordinary administration of government. A Roman, moreover, would have been even less likely than a modern man to endorse the principle of a capital levy ; but presented to him in the shape of confiscation by the State of the property of political outlaws, it might pass muster. Again, it was neither possible, nor worth while, to split hairs over the scheme ; to take a man's property is to take his life, and it would be a more defensible plan to make a clean job of the business, and to wipe out all opportunity for conspiracy and revenge on the part of desperate men. Hence all the circumstances of the case pointed to one conclusion. The punishment of the guilty, the removal of dangerous sources of future rebellion, the refilling of the treasury, and the compensation of the sufferers, could all be made to follow from one act—the Great Proscription : which secured at the same time the removal of great amounts of wealth from hands which had misused it to others which would (at any rate in political theory) use it better.

Sulla's intention created an alarm among some of his friends which seems perhaps surprising,[1] if we do not realise that this " capital levy " was the

[1] Mommsen refers to " the indefiniteness of the proposed categories " as an explanation of this. The proscription was to include all civil and military officers, who had acted for the revolution since the convention with Scipio, which Sulla still maintained had been formally concluded. There is nothing indefinite about this. We must look elsewhere for an explanation.

core of the Great Proscription. They were reconciled to it chiefly by the careful presentment of the plan as an act of vengeance. They could accept it in that dress. But that many of them realised that the vast confiscations which accompanied it were an attack on property is shown by several facts. Some discredit attached to Sulla's action, not explicable in view of the ease with which mere proscriptions were glossed over in other instances.

Metellus Pius, a man thoroughly trusted by the average opinion of the oligarchy, and also a man high in Sulla's confidence, was put forward to interrogate him in a way which would have had no meaning if the measure had been purely a political proscription and nothing else. The Dictator was asked (a significant question) where the executions were to stop, and on what principle they were to be conducted. " We do not ask you," said Metellus, " to spare those whom you intend to destroy, but to free from doubt those you intend to spare." This was putting the matter plainly. Sulla replied ambiguously that he hardly knew whom he intended to spare. He was evidently reluctant to be drawn into public discussion. " Tell us whom you will not spare," said Metellus. . . . Pressed to this point, Sulla yielded : the first of the notorious proscription lists was published. It contained eighty names. The next day he posted two hundred and twenty additional names, and followed this with a third list of equal length.[1]

---

[1] The actual numbers proscribed by Sulla have been exaggerated. Valerius Maximus says 4,700. Appian says 40 senators and 1,600 *equites*. The latter figures are probably correct. They may not include the retrospective confiscation of the property of men who had already fallen, nor the executions

They were accompanied by an edict forfeiting to the State the property of the proscribed, excluding their children and grandchildren from civil office, setting a reward of twelve thousand denarii upon each head, and extending the proscription to any person who should harbour or protect one of the proscribed. The property of those who had already fallen was included in the confiscation.

The publication of the lists, while no doubt it safeguarded certain individuals, drew down on Sulla's head the criticism he probably anticipated. He had to shoulder the entire responsibility; he had to endure the public belief that the whole affair was merely another example of his cynicism and levity; public opinion, indeed, regarded this official publication and formal procedure as even worse than the frank personal vengeance of Marius. Sulla did not mollify his critics when he addressed them in the Forum. He assured them that he had put down all the names he could remember at the moment, but if he had forgotten any he would add them later! This produced silence, if not consent.

The real nature of the proscription is shown more clearly than even by the questions of Metellus, in the kind of story the Romans afterwards related concerning it. The less reputable elements among

which were military rather than political measures. It is the inclusion of the latter which swell the total to that given by Valerius Maximus. Mommsen suggests the figures :
　Proscription of Marius : 50 senators, 1,000 *equites*.
　Proscription of Sulla : 40 senators, 1,600 *equites*.
These figures illustrate the argument in the text. Sulla's proscription fell heaviest on the *equites*. Hence the legal witticism that the prosecutors and judges had been executed, and only the advocates left !

the Sullans had no doubt as to the objective in view. There was a rush to place upon the proscription list the name of every one who could profitably be plundered.   Plutarch distinctly says that those who suffered for political reasons were few in comparison with those whose only offence was their wealth.[1] It became the fashion, even among the Sullans, to say that this man had been killed by his house, that by his gardens, and another by his hot baths. One Quintus Aurelius, who took no part in politics, and imagined that all he had to do with public affairs was to sympathise with the misfortunes of others, strolled into the Forum to read the latest list. Finding his own name there, he cried out : " My Alban farm has informed against me ! " . . . The notorious Lucius Sergius Catilina, who had murdered his own brother, legalised his position by getting his brother's name included in the proscription list. . . .   The case of Sextus Roscius of Ameria was a particularly bad one, and is well known on account of Cicero's share in the proceedings which brought it to light.   By the complicity of Chrysogonus, Sulla's secretary, the name of the elder Roscius was placed upon the list of proscribed ; he was then murdered by two of his kinsmen, and his wealth seized.   When his fellow-townsmen

[1] We have no means of estimating the precise value of this assertion.   It may mean that those who had acted in civil or military office on behalf of the revolution were few in comparison with those who were proscribed for having been secret financial backers of Marius and Cinna.   Sulla had more means than the general public possessed of knowing the identity of these men. Those who had bought up the property of refugees, confiscated by Marius, certainly went upon the list : so that in the knock-out auctions the refugees must often have been simply buying back their own property.

took steps to have this scandal put right, the conspirators accused the younger Roscius of the murder of his father, and proceeded to suborn witnesses to prove it. It was unlucky for them that the young man who acted as advocate for Roscius was Marcus Tullius Cicero.

It is improbable that Sulla either intended, or would voluntarily have allowed, such disgraceful scandals as these; and they did not stand alone. He had intended something which, if unorthodox, was at any rate rational. There are faint indications that he resisted abuses where he could. Crassus received no further official employment after it was shown that he had illegally seized the property of a man who was not officially proscribed; but Sulla owed Crassus too much for severity to be possible—and in fact he owed a great many people too much.[1] There is nothing in Sulla's character —except the cynicism which was a question of manners rather than morals—to suggest that he would deliberately unravel with one hand the fabric of law and order he was attempting to weave with the other. . . . It was an integral part of the scheme that the confiscated property should be put up to public auction, where it was sold at knock-out prices. Vast properties in this way changed hands for next to nothing. The profits, nevertheless, filled the public treasury to overflowing. Sulla shared in the purchases, by way of setting the ball rolling, and also as a claimant justified in taking his share in this oblique scheme of compensation. Crassus did more. With his

---

[1] Sulla's " culpable indulgence " only means that he had not the power to restrain his servants, and did not risk his authority by trying to do so.

natural instinct for money, he bought on a huge scale, and laid by this means the foundations of his afterwards immense fortune. . . . Public opinion at large did not distinguish between any hypothetically legitimate or illegitimate method in these things : it seems to have taken the view that the whole scheme was a scandalous one, root and branch.

Posterity has accepted this view—perhaps without enquiry. It is true enough that. no amount of enquiry can square a political proscription with the laws of ethics ; nor is there any way of palliating the monstrous cases of which those of Catilina and of the kinsmen of Sextus Roscius are instances. Sulla paid the penalty. His name has ever since rested under a cloud which no one has been bold enough to lift.

In the outcome, the objects at which he had aimed were achieved. The men who had designed the revolution, and financed and inspired it, and contemplated its atrocities and profited by them, were swept away by a reign of terror which impressed the world—temporarily, at least—as it was meant to do ; the public treasury was refilled out of their confiscated property, and from the perhaps super-abundant surplus the exiles who had been ruined were handsomely compensated. . . . It was not the rich alone who profited. The bitter enquiry was made, whether the *Optimates* had fought the civil war for the sole purpose of enriching their slaves and freedmen. The question was intended to reach the address of Lucius Cornelius Sulla.

Certain irrational emotions intrude into the best ordered lives, not to speak of those which are less well disciplined. Marius had passed beyond vengeance—if any man could have wreaked it on that grim soldier. By Sulla's command his tomb was torn open, his bones scattered—a fate which has befallen many better men than he—and his memory outlawed. M. Marius Gratidianus, the adopted son of Marius's brother, was tortured to death at the tomb of Catulus, as a sacrifice to the *manes* of that admirable and well-meaning man. The heads of the proscribed senators were publicly piled at the corner of the Forum, where they were conveniently visible to their colleagues leaving the Senate House. . . . And so little are the mere feelings of men related to the facts of life, especially of politics, that amid all these gestures the man who, when Sulla was dead, was to succeed to the tradition of Marius and carry it to victory, passed unharmed. Gaius Julius Caesar was twenty-one years old in the year of Sulla's dictatorship.

IV

Sulla's creative measures belong to two types. He made an effort to collect about himself the core of a new aristocracy ; and he drafted extensive schemes of practical reform. He was particularly anxious to unite Pompeius to himself by the closest bonds. Every man has a touch of paternal feeling, and it may be that Sulla longed for a son of whom he could be as proud as he would have been of Pompeius. He had no daughter of marriageable age : but Metella had a daughter, Aemilia, by her former marriage with M. Aemilius Scaurus. Sulla proposed that Pompeius should marry her.

If ever Sulla showed folly and sentimentality, it was over Pompeius. Aemilia was married, and was expecting a child : Pompeius also was married, to Antistia, who had a tragic story. Her father had

GENEALOGY OF THE CAESAR FAMILY

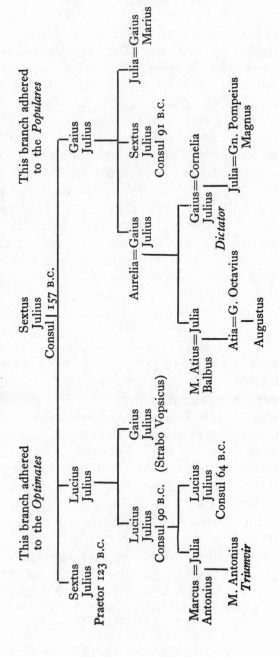

perished in the proscription the year before, when
Scaevola fell, and her mother had become insane
with grief, and killed herself. This tale might
well have been sufficient to ensure that Antistia
should be left in peace ; but since every man has
at least a weak spot, and must betray it at some
moment in his life, this proved to be the accidental
arrow which found the joint in Sulla's armour.
Some things he could not see. He could not see
that since an aristocracy is rooted in the quality
of its hereditary gifts, it is therefore rooted in the
purity of its family life ; he did not get hold of the
conception, which any old Roman patrician would
have shared with any modern puritan, that marriage
must not be tinkered with. He could not even
catch the notion of chastity as a tabu. Considering
the principle for which Sulla was standing, this
was more than a venial fault : it was a flaw that
ran right into the foundation of things. He thought
it a perfectly satisfactory arrangement that Pompeius
should divorce Antistia and marry Aemilia !

Pompeius, always amenable, allowed himself to
be persuaded. The match would be to his benefit.
The result was that Antistia was divorced, and
Aemilia married to him : whereupon Aemilia
promptly died. It was, of course, a pity ; but
Sulla had the stepson he wanted, and Pompeius
had the Sicilian command.

Another promising possibility for the new aristocracy was young Gaius Julius Caesar. Sulla had
marked him from the first. Caesar, however, was
the nephew of Marius and the son-in-law of Cinna.
Sulla proposed that he should divorce Cornelia.
Unlike Pompeius, Caesar was a genuine, if not a
perfect, aristocrat. He coldly declined. He dis-

approved of Sulla's politics, and probably of his
private character : and the fall of empires and the
crash of worlds, or even considerable personal in-
convenience, would not have made Caesar do anything he did not choose to do. Nor would Caesar
withdraw from his own activities. He put down
his name as a candidate for the priesthood—an
important official position in its way. Sulla at once
pulled the strings and saw that he was rejected.
He even contemplated placing Caesar's name on the
proscription list. Here, however, he encountered
the reality—as distinct from the theory—of aristocracy. Young Gaius was a remarkably important
person in the inner social world of Rome : his
descent was not merely blue-blooded, but azure
in its augustness : he was very rich, and very
charming in a curious, cold, impersonal way. He
pulled the strings himself. At once all the social
wheels were at work. The most highly-placed
people intervened to persuade Sulla : even the
college of Vestal Virgins took up the case. Sulla
was constrained : but he said, frankly, that they
were blind not to see many Mariuses in that boy.[1]

When this was reported to him (for he was the
kind of man who heard all the news going) Caesar
quietly effaced himself. He spent the time in
lounging from one to another of his country properties in the Sabine district, till one evening he
unexpectedly ran into a party of Sullan soldiers
who were looking for likely people. Caesar tipped
the commanding centurion two talents, a proceeding
which fulfilled all the necessities of the situation.

[1] Plutarch : *Caesar*, I ; Suetonius, *Div. Jul.* I. This story rests
on as good evidence as most such anecdotes. It may be a little
too good to be true : but Sulla was certainly an astute psychologist.

But feeling the Sabine district to be less restful than he had hoped, he decided to take a tour in the east, where he remained until Sulla was dead.

However, there was still Pompeius, the Perfect Aristocrat. Sulla had not lost hope.

The men whom Sulla could manage—men like Metellus Pius and the younger Catulus—were (perhaps just because he *could* manage them) in another way equally unsatisfactory. They had all the qualities which enable men to work together loyally and amicably : good sense, good temper, adequacy to the ordinary calls of government, sufficiency of stability and balance ; they admirably fulfilled some of the tests of aristocracy, but they lacked precisely the very power which is the determining factor in political success—ability to meet the unexpected. Such a man as Metellus had every gift except originality and adaptability. Whatsoever the cause may have been, aristocracy in Rome seemed to have reached a point at which intelligence and discipline were separating out as distinct and mutually exclusive elements. . . . How exclusive they were is clearly seen in the remarkable incident of the younger Cato. Sulla seems to have cast a hopeful eye on the juvenile population, and young Marcus Cato, among others, was frequently brought to Sulla's house by his tutor, where he took an observant interest in the proceedings. His final comment was : " Why does nobody kill this man ? " The alarmed tutor promptly terminated the visits. . . . In view of the later career of Cato, we are irresistibly led to the deduction that what he disliked in Sulla was what he disliked in Caesar, namely, intelligence.

Sulla's searching interest did not stop at the

oligarchy. Following his systematic principle of making one action serve many ends, he selected from the slaves of the proscribed—who came under the hammer with the rest of the property involved —the best men he could find, set them free, and incorporated them into a body known as the " Cornelians." They numbered about ten thousand. This step had precedents in the earlier history of Rome. It was no innovation. It represented a deliberate and careful choice of new blood for citizenship, and gave the new men a peculiarly strong interest in the maintenance of the new constitution which Sulla was creating.

V

The *Populares* had spent two years in power, without being able to think of any reforms to carry out. Sulla's period of dictatorship proved to be a torrent of practical reform. There was not the least trace of the spirit of Metternich about him. The most radical of the *Populares* was less radical than he, when faced by a necessity and an opportunity. The oligarchy looked on, humble and mystified, in the background.

He confirmed the grant of the franchise to the Italians, and brought to its full fruit the policy of Drusus. Henceforward, any citizen of an Italian community was a citizen of Rome, and all distinction between the old and the new citizens was swept away. On the day on which this was done, the old City State ceased to exist, and the modern nation was born. It was an infant, helpless and unconscious, destined to struggle for many a century before it grew up ; but it was born, and Sulla was the surgeon who ushered it into the world.

To accompany this measure, he made great changes in the local government of Italy. Hitherto, political conceptions had been limited by the principle, from which no thinker had been able to escape, of the city as the political unit. Prior to Sulla's day there had been, broadly speaking, only two methods of uniting the subject cities with Rome. They could be declared independent communities in alliance with Rome—when they retained their own separate government, and had no power of influencing Roman policy. Or, alternatively, they could be given the franchise, when they became part of Rome, and were, of course, governed by the Roman magistrates, while their citizens travelled to Rome to exercise the vote if they ever exercised it at all. Since all Italy was now in the Roman franchise, it had become a physical impossibility for the Roman magistrates to carry on the local affairs of the Italian cities, and the clumsy old arrangements had to give way. Sulla instituted a definite scheme of local self-government, each city being given a constitution, modelled on that of Rome, for the purpose of managing its own affairs ; while the Roman magistrates retained the power of control and special jurisdiction over those matters which involved general policy, such as are now exercised by a national government.

It was beyond Sulla—it was, indeed, beyond any man, until in the course of ages the problem was solved by a natural evolution—to devise a scheme by which the distant citizens could take their legal share in the election of the Roman magistrates, and in Roman legislation. They could, of course, go to Rome for the purpose, but probably few ever did so. It was, on general grounds, not even

desirable that they should go. This was the fatal
flaw which rendered democracy impossible in the
new Rome.

Nor was this all. With the forfeitures which
had accrued from the cities condemned for participa-
tion in the late civil war, and from the proscriptions,
Sulla set on foot great schemes of land-settlement.
He granted 120,000 small holdings to the discharged
soldiers of his armies, thus resettling Italy with
precisely the class of small farmer who was most
needed, and at the same time fortifying his new
arrangements with the zealous support of men
who had everything to lose by their alteration.
To strengthen the position of the new settlers, he
made their land inalienable, and he abolished the
corn dole which had done so much to destroy the
small Italian farmer. Everything he could do to
make the settlements permanent, he did.

Sulla next dealt with the *equites*, that class of
bankers and merchants whose political exploits we
have been chiefly engaged in surveying. He
abolished their control over the courts, and handed
the latter back to the senatorial order. He swept
away all the privileges that had made them a definite
class in the State. They had made much of their
money by the odious Gracchan system of farming
the taxes. Sulla, having seen for himself in Asia
what the tax-farming system was capable of producing, abolished it altogether, and converted the taxes
into fixed amounts. . . . He had seen the day
when great men were murdered for even suggesting
these measures. He had lived long enough to
pass them himself ; and the *equites* trembled and
obeyed.

Having taken the courts away from the *equites*

he proceeded to a fierce and stringent reform of
the courts themselves. He created eight different
judicial courts for the trial of various types of case.
He separated civil from criminal justice for the first
time in the history of law, and originated the system
by which civil cases were tried by a single judge,
and criminal cases by a bench of judges, or jury,
as we should call it. Since, among these courts,
he created one for the trial of cases of murder, he
practically abolished the death penalty, for the
citizen assembly retained its sole right to pronounce
sentence of death, and murder cases were now
withdrawn from its cognisance. Moreover, since
another of his courts was for the trial of cases of
treason, he made it much less likely that any special
partisan tribunal like that of Quintus Varius would
ever again be set up. . . . All these measures had
a purpose, and suggest that he had a good memory.
Every one of them covered the ground of some old
notorious scandal of Roman government. His court
" De Repetundis," for example, was largely the
fruit of his experience in Asia. It was intended to
make impossible, or, at any rate, less probable,
such proceedings as those which had caused the
Mithradatic war. The arguments of Archelaus and
of Mithradates had had their effect.

Finally, he turned to the Senate, into whose
control he had restored the courts ; and here his
reforms reached their culmination. The jurisdiction
of the censor had been used by the oligarchy to
pass its friends into the Senate, and to expel as
many men of enlightenment from it as possible.
Sulla avenged Publius Cornelius and his ten pounds
of silver plate by completely abolishing this censorial
power. He made senators irremovable. To restore

the balance, he caused entrance to the Senate to depend upon popular election. A seat in the Senate was to be the corollary of election to a magistracy. The supremacy of the citizen assembly Sulla left untouched ; but he provided that the only measures which should be proposed to it for legislation should be such as had passed the Senate, and were forwarded to it for ratification. He put the citizen assembly practically into the legislative position of a modern constitutional king, who has the right of assent or veto, but nothing more.

As part of this scheme, he reorganised the magistracies. He increased the numbers of the magistrates to enable them to deal with the increasing amount of business that passed through their hands. Two especial objects seem to have been before his mind. First, he attempted to keep apart the civil and the military powers, and to give the supremacy to the statesman rather than the soldier. He made it impossible for a civil magistrate to hold at the same time a military office. Secondly, he made it illegal to hold an office for several years in succession. He regulated and consolidated the laws relating to these matters, and enforced the old laws with regard to the age at which a candidate was eligible for office.

These measures had several aims. They prevented the magistracies from becoming the close preserve of a clique, who continued their friends in profitable posts year after year because there were not sufficient magistrates to make possible the yearly change in the provincial governorships. The increase in the number of magistracies enabled the work to be done by properly elected men who laid down office at the legal time, so that there was no further excuse for informal prolongations. And the increase provided the requisite number of qualified senators—men of official experience, who knew something of the business of administration. The amateur senator, whose only claim to the dignity was his social position in a wealthy oligarchy, was swept away.

One leading fact is betrayed by these reforms of the magistracies. Sulla was so careful to refurbish and restore the old republican machinery of government, with its limited annual tenure of office ; so careful to prevent the tribunes from holding the legislative initiative in the citizen assembly, as Gaius Gracchus had held it ; so particularly careful to render it impossible for any man to hold the consulship for several years in succession, as Marius had held it—that his motive in making these arrangements must have been especially strong. It is on the definiteness of his policy in this respect that we can build up the proof that his opposition to Marius was no mere question of personal ambition or party prejudice, but was rooted in a genuine difference of political principle. Sulla had a good deal more than the amount of intelligence necessary to imagine a simple logical extension of the six successive consulships of Marius. Why stop at six ? Why not, indeed, a permanent consulship ? Why not a monarchy ? This was the strategic point at which Sulla struck. He aimed at rendering it impossible ever to develop a Roman magistracy into monarchy. And this is again precisely the point on which Caesar sided with Marius, and against Sulla.

Thus far, however, the advantage in point of enlightenment must be adjudged to Sulla. Monarchy, as they knew it, was an old, outworn, reactionary, incompetent principle. A man who seriously proposed to renovate it as a necessary and vital element in political life would need to create a new form of monarchy, standing in a new relationship to the rest of the State. Sulla was certainly not called upon to provide his opponents with a political philosophy. He had little personal sympathy with monarchy. To him, as to most Romans, it seemed at the best a barbarous expedient for saving idle citizens from the trouble of exercising their own brains and shouldering their own responsibilities. He had no disposition to wear himself into an untimely grave by doing other people's work for them. He saw the problem before him as a question whether Rome should remain a growing, self-determined, political State, whose voice was found by the conference of all the classes and citizens who composed it, or become a State obeying the arbitrary will of a despot who, however enlightened he might chance to be, would nevertheless determine for men what men had hitherto determined for themselves.

VI

During the first year of his dictatorship, therefore, consuls were elected as usual, and the ordinary course of administration pursued its way, while he was engaged in creating the new constitution. For the second year, he himself came forward as a candidate, and exercised the normal office while still dictator for the purpose of his special functions. His colleague was Quintus Caecilius Metellus Pius, a stroke, Sulla ambiguously remarked, of Fortune, since Metellus was likely to be an amiable passenger.

And it is hardly possible to doubt his motives. Having reformed the constitution, he was determined to start it upon its new career by a year in office as an ordinary magistrate, giving a concrete example of how it should be worked, and seeing for himself what rough corners there might be in it. He still had the power to remedy these. There was, indeed, no external reason why he should ever surrender the dictatorship. But whatever other men might think, the mere fact of his consulship hinted at a personal bias against regarding his dictatorship as permanent.

It is distinctly apparent that in this, too, Sulla was allowing private feeling to blind him to the real state of the case. His supremacy was not so easily to be got rid of. That admirable condition of equality among themselves which had marked the old patricians, as it marks every true aristocracy, was based upon an actual equality of character and intelligence. But Sulla's position was based upon an actual inequality. There were not two Sullas, still less were there five hundred. . . . Whether he liked it or not, he had, in practice, to recognise its reality by many exceptional actions quite incompatible with his theory, and so was forced into inconsistencies which did not escape public criticism. Much was attributed to arbitrariness of temperament, and even to savage cynicism, which may have been due far more to a conscious effort to square two different conceptions of duty.

Sulla could not escape the dilemma. To restore law by despotic decree, and order by violence, is an inconsistency which attracts attention. No one took him seriously when he insisted on the necessity of discipline and obedience. No one even realised that he was wholly in earnest. Still less was it comprehended that this, and not his external reforms, was the core of his aims. The proscription lists hung round Sulla's neck. No one could distinctly see anything else. No one could see, or hear, or feel, or touch, or taste, anything about Sulla, except that he was the author of the Great Proscription.

The Perfect Aristocrat:
(Gnaeus Pompeius Magnus,)
as a young man.

Reconstructed from the Rome,
Naples and Copenhagen busts.

CHAPTER XII

THE DEATH OF SULLA

I

THE trend of affairs illustrates once more the logic of events which began to entangle Sulla. The Perfect Aristocrat had gone to Sicily, where the remains of the *Populares* were collecting. Perpenna had taken command of the exiles and refugees ; Carbo had collected a navy, while Gnaeus Domitius Ahenobarbus was raising an army in Africa. Perpenna did not wait long. He evacuated Sicily. Pompeius. was incorrigibly good-natured, and also incorrigibly lawless. He treated Sicily with liberality, and seems to have accepted a large number of excuses which would not have passed muster in Rome. He could not, indeed, avoid the necessity for many executions, when the notorious facts were too strong for him ; but whenever he could cultivate a blind eye, he did so.

Carbo, who fell into his hands, had a legal trial— a proceeding adversely commented upon in Rome, where it was argued that young Pompeius had no right to insult a man of consular dignity by solemnly sitting in judgment upon him, and that it would have been more respectful to have executed him out of hand. Quintus Valerius, a man of considerable learning, was another case. Instead of suffering immediate death, Valerius was brought to a personal interview with Pompeius, and it was only after a long conversation that Pompeius, finding him obdurate, reluctantly ordered his execution. These cases might conceivably be due to a young man's sense of prudence in dealing with political opponents who were far from being friendless, and very often far from being socially uninfluential; but such instances as that of the city of Himaera show that it was more than this. Himaera was so deeply involved in revolutionary activity that when Pompeius opened his tribunal it seemed certain that the city would receive heavy punishment. Sthenis, one of the leading citizens, publicly assured Pompeius that this would be to punish the innocent and let the guilty go free. Pompeius asked who, in that case, would accept responsibility for all that had been done : whereupon Sthenis answered that he would do so, who had compelled his friends by persuasion and his enemies by fear. This seems to have impressed Pompeius so favourably that he passed over the conduct of Himaera.

He kept very strict discipline, and when the conduct of his troops was made a subject of complaint, he had their swords officially sealed into the scabbards.

The suspicion always clung about Pompeius, to the end of his life, that he loved praise and admiration so much that he could not resist the temptation to curry favour with any human being, at the expense of more important considerations. The criticism was unjust, for a great deal—perhaps all—of his good nature was perfectly genuine. He lacked a certain severity of temperament which made the typical Roman both harsh and also law-abiding. The circumstances of the day had certainly discouraged the spirit of strict obedience to law : but Pompeius

showed a distinct tendency to disregard forms.
Among the incidents of his Sicilian command was
reported his remark to the Mamertines, when they
put in their Roman charter as a defence : " Will you
never stop talking of law to us, who carry swords ? "

There was much in all this that disappointed
Sulla, who was intent on the restoration of severe
discipline and the old patrician obedience. Caesar
was the man he really wanted ; but by the irony
of fate Caesar was one of the men with whom he
could not get on, or who could not get on with him.
He removed Pompeius to Africa. There was no
doubt of the military competence of the Perfect
Aristocrat ; and Domitius was assembling an army
that constituted a serious menace.

The reports of the Perfect Aristocrat grew worse.
His relations with the troops were admirably good,
too good to be altogether admirable in some eyes.
Shortly after their arrival in Africa, one of the
soldiers discovered a buried treasure : whereupon,
in spite of all orders, the whole army was soon
digging furiously, while Pompeius walked to and
fro and laughed at them. No further treasure
being found, the army came to its senses and
apologised ; and the way in which he took the
incident added much to his popularity. He defeated
Domitius, stormed his camp, and reduced Africa
to order within forty days of his landing ; and
then ascertaining that lions and elephants were
still existent in Numidia, went off on a big-game
hunting expedition.

Sulla now wrote to recall him. Capable though
Pompeius was, he was very young, and there was
in his actions an element of casualness perhaps
difficult to isolate and blame, yet not altogether

consistent with dignity.   Moreover, considering that he had never occupied any official post, but was merely a special military deputy, his personal popularity with the troops raised serious questions. Along such lines as were here possible, there would be no revival of the ideal Rome, but only some kind of Greek military tyranny.   Sulla was trying to suppress precisely this danger of military tyranny, and endeavouring to confirm the supremacy of law and civil government.   Pompeius had better come home, and be with Sulla for a while.   With experience and good companionship he would learn; and the military task had been accomplished with success.

Sulla was wise.   As soon as the order of recall was known, the troops broke out into a demonstration of loyalty to their commander which was only divided by the narrowest of margins from open rebellion.   The news was actually despatched to Sulla that Pompeius had raised the standard of revolt.   His bitter comment was : " It seems that it is my fate to strive with children in my old age." . . . But further and more reliable information put a somewhat different complexion on the matter. Pompeius and his army had carried on a highly emotional argument, accompanied by tears and speeches, which had ended in the army submitting to reason.   But the Perfect Aristocrat would have been more perfect than any aristocrat ever is, if he had not gained the justifiable impression that he could do nearly anything he liked with a crowd.

II

There were undercurrents. The lightness of Pompeius' hand in Sicily was known ; and the welcome prepared for him in Rome was equivalent

to a political demonstration against Sulla. Very
few people understood much, or cared much, about
the virtues of the new constitution, except that it
had in some way or other trenched on everybody's
rights and satisfied no one ; what they knew,
what obsessed them to the exclusion of most other
things, the label that stuck to Sulla, the medium
through which every one saw him, was that he had
been the author of the Great Proscription. It was
not easy for him to prevent a demonstration in
favour of his own favourite. Sulla did the only
thing that could be done : he took the wind out
of his enemies' sails by outdistancing them all
in the fervour of his enthusiasm. He was the
first to greet Pompeius and to fall upon his handsome neck, hailing him with the honorary title of
" Magnus "—the Great ;   and   commanding   all
present to acclaim him by that title. Pompeius,
in perhaps a slightly different spirit, did not take
this   title   any   more   seriously   than   that   of
" Imperator." It was a long while before he
added it to his signature ; but the name stuck ;
he was always " Pompeius Magnus." Sulla's sin-
cerity may not have been so obvious as on the
former occasion.

But the Perfect Aristocrat was not quite so
perfect as he had once appeared. He asked for
a Triumph. Sulla pointed out that he had held
no office. A triumph was an honour legally given
only to commanders of consular or praetorian rank—
so that even Scipio Africanus had not enjoyed a
triumph for his Spanish campaigns. If he granted
it, it would discredit his government and nullify
his efforts to restore the rule of law. Pompeius
was not convinced. He seemed to think these

arguments an additional reason why he should have
a triumph. It would be particularly good to have
what no one else had ever had. Sulla intimated that
he would use his authority to stop any such idea.

Pompeius reminded Sulla that more people
worship the rising than the setting sun. Sulla
had perhaps just resumed his seat in a mood of
annoyance, for he did not catch the remark; but
noticing by the obvious sensation around him that
something unusual must have been said, he enquired
what it was. When it was repeated to him, he
seemed thunderstruck, and then cried out : " Let
him Triumph ! Let him Triumph ! " . . . After
all, what did it matter ? There would never be
a new Rome : there was no Perfect Aristocrat :
let him Triumph. Sulla must have known from
that moment that his work was vain. He had
merely patched up the old oligarchic Rome.

So Pompeius enjoyed his triumph. He had a
great plan for having his triumphal car drawn by
elephants ; but unfortunately the gates were too
narrow, so that the old conventional method of
employing horses had to be retained. The triumph
was a little spoiled by the troops, who did not think
that Pompeius had given them a sufficient donation ;
but it was popular. Enthusiasm for Pompeius was
the easiest way of demonstrating against Sulla.

Pompeius, with the wisdom that is given to
babes and sucklings, had spoken the truth. Sulla's
sun was setting. . . . His work, for good or for
evil, had been done to the best of his abilities ;
but it was hard that its doom should be pronounced
by the very man whose example and person were
to have ushered in the new era. Caesar was an
enemy, too powerful to be crushed ; and Pompeius

—O ! Pompeius was a fool, a gilded soldier, a Greek tyrant ! The labour of restoration was to have been only the framework for the task of creation : . . . and this was all that was left of the new aristocracy !

III

Sulla was not a man to enact a private tragedy. He was more the kind of man who, in trouble, goes out and gets drunk. He grew sharper and more cynical, and more Bohemian in his private enjoyments.

He now made up his mind, and prepared to resign the Dictatorship. The work he had done others must carry on. He had tried to restore a spiritual state, an atmosphere ; he had not tried to make himself a monarch. The Romans could therefore carry on his intentions, or not, as they chose ; and have Pompeius, if they liked Pompeius better.

Sulla dedicated a tenth of his fortune to Hercules, the Doer of Great Deeds, and gave a public feast of many days' duration. He silently underlined the occasion by producing nothing less than the " Opimian " wine—the immortal vintage of that year when Gaius Gracchus fell. He had spent most of his mature life in fighting the results of the Gracchan policy, particularly that aspect of it which had wrested the control of government from the responsible, political authorities, and given it into the unofficial, irresponsible hands of financiers and traders. He would toast himself out of office on the appropriate vintage. . . . His meaning seems to have been recognised, for many people—probably the financiers—held aloof, so that every day of the feast much food had to be thrown

into the river for want of eaters. The bankers were
not beaten yet.

Fortune herself held aloof from that feast; the
ill-luck which dogged all those who had to do with
the fall of the Gracchi pursued even Sulla when he
invited it by this broad gesture. In the midst of
the feasting, Metella fell sick, and lay dying. For-
bidden by the official ritual from visiting the sick,
or polluting his house with mourning, he sent her
a divorce and caused her to be removed to another
house. Though he accepted the ceremonial necessity with a calm which somewhat disturbed his
critics, it was not from indifference; for as soon
as he was absolved from its jurisdiction he gave her
a magnificent funeral, in which he defiantly broke
his own sumptuary law limiting the expenditure
permissible on such occasions.

Sulla began to go down-hill after his breach
with Pompeius and the death of Metella. He did
not observe his own sumptuary laws even in his
own private entertainments. His parties of unconventional friends grew more numerous, and
more costly. But he was still a man of business,
who could wear the mask well enough in business
hours, and throw it off cheerfully after them. A
few months after Metella's death he was sitting
in the theatre when some one, in passing, plucked
a few hairs from his woollen cloak. It was a
handsome girl. Sulla looked up in surprise, and
asked what that meant. There was no harm, she
answered, in sharing in his Fortune : and she went
on to her seat. Sulla was intrigued, and made
enquiries. She was Valeria Messalla, the sister of
Hortensius the orator. He kept his eye upon her ;
and they carried on the kind of affair that can so

easily be conducted by looks alone. A Valeria of
the great Messallan family was as good as a Cornelius
of the Sullan branch, and Sulla was attracted. He
made overtures, was accepted, and married her.
But he made little change in his manner of life.
He saw enough of social distinction and formal
greatness during business hours, to enjoy the
company of a different sort of person in his leisure
moments. There is no sign that Valeria influenced
him, or engaged more than a passing interest.

IV

The time came round, and with it the elections
and the vacation of office by the old magistrates.
Pompeius had set an example, and Ofella now
followed it. He came forward as a candidate for
the consulship, for which he was not legally eligible.
Sulla prohibited the candidature, but Ofella persisted,
and appeared in the Forum with an armed bodyguard. But Ofella was not Pompeius. Sulla, sitting
in the Temple of Concord, from which he overlooked the whole Forum as from a gallery, sent
a centurion across to cut down Ofella. When
the uproar had subsided, Sulla rose and addressed
the crowd. He was making a last appeal to their
sense of obedience to law. He told them that he
had authorised the act, which was therefore a
legal execution and not a murder ; and he commanded them to release the centurion. He explained
to them precisely what Ofella had done.

" There was once a husbandman," he concluded
dryly, " who was much troubled by vermin. Twice
he took off his shirt and shook it. On the third
occasion he burned the shirt. Take care that the
city of Rome is not like that shirt."

With this grim and prophetical parable, he ended his career as a public speaker.

Pompeius was canvassing in person for another candidate, Marcus Aemilius Lepidus, whereas Sulla was supporting Quintus Lutatius Catulus, the son of his old friend and commander. Lepidus was the kind of man particularly obnoxious to Sulla, an ex-governor of Sicily, who, to escape a prosecution for extortion, had left the *Optimates* for the *Populares* : a violent and fluent speaker, of doubtful character, and still more doubtful wisdom. Lepidus had little chance of election without help. The popularity of Pompeius was the factor which turned the scale in his favour. As they were leaving the Forum afterwards, Sulla came forward and spoke to Pompeius.

" Young man," he said, " I see that you rejoice in your victory, and no doubt you think it a matter for congratulation that that scoundrel Lepidus is elected before an honourable man such as Catulus. But have a care for yourself, for you are strengthening an enemy at your own expense."

These, as far as we know, were the last words which ever passed between Sulla and his ideal aristocrat ; and they might have formed the epitaph of Pompeius. He strengthened his enemies at his own expense.

With the opening of the new official year, Sulla divested himself of the Dictatorship. Those who hoped, and those who feared, that he never would do so, were alike disappointed. His resignation impressed his contemporaries. There was something great in the proceeding ; but men were not agreed as to the exact nature of the greatness. Considered as a " gesture," was it the noble act of

a public-spirited man too large for the little glories
of kingship ?—or was it the contemptuous act of
a cynic weary of doing good to Rome ? They could
not tell, for none of them understood Sulla.

Both motives may have had their part. Sulla
not only resigned, but, self-stripped of his sanctity
as Dictator, walked publicly in the Forum, a private
man again, so that any one who chose could call
him to account for his acts. No one did so. No
one questioned him. . . . But a young man followed him home, denouncing him and all his
works, which Sulla endured with fortitude. . . .
It is surmised by historians that the proceeding
was carefully staged by Sulla's orders, and the
surmise is possible. It would have been like
Sulla's perverse humour to stage an opposition of
one man : the joke would have been good. But
then it would have been only a joke ; and Sulla's
sense of humour was ample enough to have enjoyed
far more the amusing reality of being actually
abused by one young man.

We are none the wiser for the remark he made as
he re-entered his house : " This young man will
prevent any future holder of such power as mine
from laying it down again " : a truly Delphic comment—on which two thousand years of puzzled
silence fell.

Having done this much, he retired to his Campanian villa, and the world had little more to hear
of him. The career of Lucius Cornelius Sulla was
over.

V

It was over in more senses than one. Sickness
was creeping over him, in no way fended off by
his habits. He had not at first noticed its approach,

but it revealed itself more and more. It was an intestinal ulceration. Its symptoms, as related by his biographer, are obscure; but the probability is that he was attacked by one of those internal parasites which are known to modern medical science, though beyond the control of the physicians of his own day. He may have acquired it in Asia. He was ordered a course of hot baths, without result.

During this, his last year of life, he hunted, occupied himself in reorganising the municipal affairs of the neighbouring city of Puteoli—a task which he took as seriously as the reorganisation of Rome—and completed his autobiography, dedicated to Lucius Lucullus, and finished only a few days before his death. In it he mentioned that the Chaldaeans (probably those who accompanied the Parthian ambassador in the days of his Cilician propraetorship) had foretold him a life of honour, to conclude in the fullness of prosperity. . . . It may have been as well not to drag it out. . . . He had apparently no regrets. And he said that he had had a dream, in which he had seen his son stand by him in mourning attire, bidding him cast off further care and come with him to Metella, to live in peace and comfort with her.

The day before his death, he heard that one Granius, a public official of Puteoli, had, in the expectation of his demise, declined to discharge a public debt. Sulla was not dead yet, and the news touched all his most violent prejudices. . . . Disobedience !—dishonesty !—only waiting for him to go. . . . He had Granius summoned to his presence, and strangled. But in the excitement (for he seems to have spoken heatedly) he burst a blood-vessel. He passed the night in acute pain, and died probably towards morning.

He left behind him two children, Faustus and Fausta, by Metella ; and after his death Valeria was delivered of a daughter.

When his will was read, it was noticed that Pompeius was passed over in silence. Lucullus was his executor, and the guardian of his children. No word came across the grave to the Perfect Aristocrat. But Pompeius had no ill-feeling. There was a widespread movement to prevent Sulla receiving a public funeral : and when it was decided (against the traditional usage of the Cornelian house) to cremate the body, Lepidus intervened to stop the deposition of the ashes in the Campus Martius. Pompeius came in person to Campania, took charge of the body, and conveyed it to Rome. All his power and influence were employed to protect the defenceless dead man who had been so powerful in life. Even Lepidus could not interfere with Pompeius. The women folk of the *Optimates* contributed the funeral-spices for their party chief. Such vast amounts were subscribed that in addition to what was borne on two hundred and ten litters, a large figure of Sulla, attended by a lictor (the mark of the dictator), was made out of the frankincense and cinnamon.

It was a dull, threatening day, and those in charge were doubtful about carrying out the corpse. At about three o'clock in the afternoon they at last risked it, still fearing that rain would prevent the ceremony. Sulla's body was borne on a golden bier with royal splendour, preceded by horsemen and trumpeters. The pall-bearers were senators. His standards and fasces went before. The procession was enormous. Over two thousand golden crowns were carried in it, the gifts of cities, legions, or individual friends. All the guilds of priests and priestesses followed ; the entire Senate ; the whole body of magistrates ; a great number of *equites* in regalia ; and all his veterans in their due legionary ranks, bearing their full-dress golden ensigns and silver-mounted shields. Young Faustus was not of age to deliver the funeral oration, so the first public speakers of the day accepted the office on his behalf. The cheers of farewell were raised by the ranks in order, beginning with the senators and ending with the plebeians. The wind blew up the flame, and the pyre burned splendidly ; everything was consumed in good time, and the fire was dying to its embers when at last the rain came and continued till nightfall. . . . So, as Plutarch says, his Fortune continued with him to the last, and even officiated at his funeral.

His monument was erected in the Campus Martius, with the epitaph, composed by himself, that no man had excelled him in doing a good turn to his friends or a bad one to his foes.

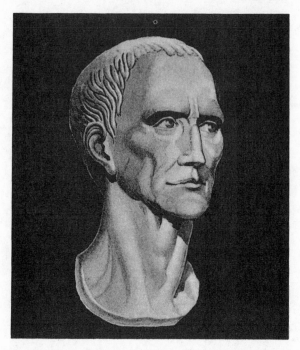

Gaius Julius Caesar.
After the portrait bust in the
British Museum.

CHAPTER XIII

THE DEATH OF SULLA'S WORLD

I

NO sooner was Sulla dead than all the powers and forces which he had held in check were once more set free. How powerful they were we can see by the promptitude of their action. The utmost that Sulla had done had not destroyed, nor even seriously weakened them. But they were forces that could not act directly ; they needed a representative, and they could as then find none better than Lepidus. The struggle was not a long one. Before many months were out, Pompeius was able to inform the Senate that the danger was over. Lepidus was dead ; his armies were dissolved. Sulla's work had marked a period. To undo what he had done, the *equites* would need to find and finance a man greater than Lepidus ; greater than Pompeius ; perhaps greater than Marius—if such a man could be found.

To understand the career of Sulla we must continue the story a little further, and review the processes by which his work was undermined and destroyed. He had been right when he quoted the Chaldaean prediction that he should die in the fullness of prosperity. With his invariable good fortune, that is what he had done. Had he lived, it would have been to see his own failure develop with an inevitable necessity out of the circumstances he had left. For he had failed in the essential task—the creation of a new aristocracy. He had only restored an oligarchy, and there it was, without difference or improvement. His real success lay in the fact that he had dragged Rome by the short hairs through the most dangerous series of crises she had ever had to face : he had succeeded as a practical statesman : he had at least left Rome pretty much as he found it, instead of a silent city of ruins, fast being forgotten : but he was destined to fail as a creative idealist. . . . This is a habit Fortune has. She is willing to help men to great practical successes : but she reserves the task of creation for herself.

The *equites* had reasons for anxiety which increased with time. Stripped of all the advantages and privileges which Gaius Gracchus had given them, they were faced with conditions slipping steadily from bad to worse. The old oligarchy had been of angelic light and wisdom compared with the new oligarchy which Sulla left behind him. Beside the men of the new senatorial courts who acquitted Gnaeus Dolabella, the men of the old equestrian juries who condemned Publius Rutilius Rufus might justly feel themselves patterns of judicial virtue. The scandals of misgovernment which began with the two Dolabellas found their towering peak of iniquity in the notorious case of Verres. Such misgovernment could not fail to reflect itself in damage to commercial interests which gave a sharper edge to opposition than simple righteous indignation could have given.

There were several loose ends to Sulla's work from any or all of which it might be unravelled.

He had left the east hardly pacified. Mithradates was steadily rebuilding his power. The seas, after half a generation of anarchy, were swarming with organised piracy. It was still conceivable that Rome might lose the east. And (complete though Sulla's victory may have seemed) the most brilliant of all the *Populares* was still defending the last ditch. Quintus Sertorius, driven out of Italy, had taken to a roving life, as a captain of what later ages would have called Free Companions. After many remarkable adventures, which may be read in Plutarch's life of him, he formed a government in Lusitania which he conducted with admirable ability and success. For some eight years he held his own against all the forces which the oligarchy could send against him. He had genius as a soldier, and perhaps genius as a statesman, as we can see by the interesting account which Plutarch gives of the college he founded for the sons of Lusitanian chiefs, an educational institution none the less real because the youths were not only students but also hostages for their parents' loyalty. . . . Quintus Metellus Pius entirely failed to deal with Sertorius.

From the personal point of view, the career of Sertorius in Spain was a romantic tragedy ending in failure and death ; but in its political aspect it was a triumph of unconventional genius which altered the course of history. The consequences were incalculable. The Senate was compelled at last, much against its will, to send Pompeius to Spain with proconsular power. Even Pompeius met his match in Sertorius. Mithradates seized the opportunity to re-open the war in the east. On top of this the gladiators broke out of the training school at Capua, elected a Thracian named

Spartacus as their leader, and planted war in the midst of Italy itself.

Spartacus, the slave-Napoleon, is an illustration of the danger and difficulty of dealing with the European as a slave. Here, thrown up accidentally, was a man of military genius at least equal to Sertorius, equal, for all we know, to Hannibal ; for Spartacus was never defeated in a strictly military sense. For two whole years he defeated every army which the oligarchy could raise. He could have broken out of Italy and gone free to the wide, if his men would have followed him. But Spartacus illustrates another thesis also—the importance of political, as distinct from military factors in war. He fell because his slave army had not the close-knit disciplinary construction of the Roman State.

When we disentangle the events of these years between the death of Sulla and the rise of Caesar, a number of interesting truths emerge. The Roman State, when confronted by mere force, or external danger, was still rigid enough and solid enough to defy all assault. Her internal coherence resisted the fourfold strain put upon it by Sertorius, Spartacus, Mithradates, and the Cilician corsairs. It was her own evolution, her own processes of internal growth, that were the difficulty : over these, she was constricted, crippled and strangled. She blundered through to victory under circumstances of the most scandalous nature, which shocked and disgusted her best citizens, and convinced them that vast changes were imperative.

The downfall of Sertorius was the first to come. It demonstrated once more the inherent weakness of the popular party—its inability to keep itself proof against internal treachery : its lack of cohesion.

Sertorius was assassinated by members of his own party, fellow-exiles who were jealous of him with the feeble-minded jealousy of those who envy a man they cannot replace, and whose work they cannot do. When the conspirators promptly fell into the hands of Pompeius and the lawful government, Pompeius had a delicate problem to deal with. They offered, as ransom for their lives, the correspondence of Sertorius, containing many letters completely incriminating a large number of important individuals in Italy. It is perfectly obvious that the popular party was far from dead ; that the movement against the oligarchy afterwards headed by Caesar was already in being ; and that Sertorius was a forerunner of Caesar, though an unlucky one without " Caesar's fortune " either material or spiritual.

Pompeius chose a course for which he deserves every praise as a wise and right-minded man. He burnt the correspondence unread and unrevealed, on the ground that enough blood had been shed, and that it was time to let ill alone. . . . Had Pompeius been more short-sightedly prudent in a partisan sense, he might have stamped out the Caesarian revolution ; but had he done so, he might have stamped out Rome as well. Very little margin, in the end, saved the Mediterranean civilisation from dissolution into anarchy.

Another hint of importance is given us by the circumstances of Sertorius's death and the revelation it brought about. We can see that the precise type of the Caesarian revolution—its militaristic nature—arose naturally out of such facts as these. It was impossible to make a water-tight party out of the *Populares* save by means of military discipline.

The powerful pressure of interest kept the oligarchy unfalteringly united. The *Populares* had no such motives to bind them together. Caesar must have seen in these years that the only possible solution of the problem was to bind them in the strong bonds of soldierly association : and there was no other solution within the reach of a practical statesman who must produce immediate results.

Pompeius returned from Spain in the following year to find that as regards Spartacus, the oligarchy had been driven to place itself in the hands of Crassus as a sort of political liquidator in bankruptcy. Crassus was excellently adapted for the task. Though not a great soldier, he had precisely the faculties required : he organised the war as if it had been a bank or a business, and overwhelmed Spartacus by mobilising against him the resources which a civilised political State can command. When Pompeius arrived, just in time to help in wiping the servile army off the earth, both these old disciples of Sulla were in a changed mood. They had begun to see matters from a different point of view.

They were not, as it happened, friends. A third power, anonymous and indefinite, intervened to make a link between them, while their armies still stood intact. This third power seemed to know the change in their minds ; it seemed to have the power of saying and doing the things which would bring Crassus and Pompeius together ; it seemed to possess the diplomatic ability to secure for itself a price for its intervention.

II

Crassus and Pompeius held the consulship together for the ensuing official year. Their joint power, once united with that of the anonymous third factor, who controlled the electors of the old party of the *Populares*, was sufficient to compel the oligarchy. Besides the consulship, Pompeius received a triumph, and Crassus an ovation ; and (judging by subsequent events) there may well have been secret clauses to the agreement which only time would reveal. In return the *Populares* received their price. The Sullan constitution was abolished. Pompeius himself introduced the law which sent the tribunes back to the Assembly with all their old powers. The courts were once more handed over (though not so absolutely as before) to the *equites*. The tax-farming system was revived : the censorship was restored. We have no difficulty in perceiving whose interests were served by these changes. . . . The anonymous third power did more than this : it ushered Crassus and Pompeius out of office again without a breach : it sent Pompeius into retirement afterwards, there to wait for events which should in due time happen.

These were very strange proceedings, without a parallel in Roman politics. Since when had the *Populares* possessed these gifts of diplomacy ? Since when, moreover, had they gained the power of playing the intricate chess-play which from this point began on the political board ? It started from the position in Asia, where Lucullus was carrying on a series of wonderful campaigns against Mithradates. More than any other man, Lucullus was the successor and the representative of Sulla. But he had less political instinct than Sulla, and he was being felt for by a foe more dangerous than any that Sulla ever had to face.

Lucullus, who could probably have survived any military difficulties, could not survive the powerful financial influences which were at work against him, both in Asia and at Rome. The *equites* were in power again. His last campaigns were wrecked and rendered futile. After exploits which few soldiers have ever surpassed, he began to stand unaccountably in the position of a failure.

III

Two years after the eventful consulship of Crassus and Pompeius, Gaius Julius Caesar stood as a candidate for the quaestorship, his first official post. His year of office was distinguished by a remarkable episode. His aunt Julia, the widow of Gaius Marius, died. She was one of the few surviving links which connected that generation with the world of Gaius Gracchus, and although we know nothing of her personality or of the influence which she exercised, Caesar did not seem to think the occasion meaningless. He himself not only delivered the funeral oration—a much admired one in its day—but he did something more significant : he formally exhibited the ancestral images, including that of the outlawed Marius. So popular was this daring action that he could afford to ignore the protests made against it.

He was away in Spain the following year, so it would be difficult to bring home to him any responsibility for the progress of the cabal against Lucullus. The logic of events probably saved him much trouble, both then and later. The abolition of Sulla's constitution had been but a preliminary to practical business. The *equites* meant

to have Lucullus out of Asia. He was superseded [1]
and replaced by a fresh commander. . . . Meanwhile, under the government of the oligarchy the
Cilician corsairs had actually produced famine in
Rome itself, by intercepting the corn ships—a consummation that can hardly have been altogether
unexpected in some quarters. Ways and means
were ready. A tribune was put forward to propose
a measure of emergency. This, of course, was
perfectly in order ; but the measure of emergency
he proposed was a deep and carefully thought out
scheme which very few tribunes known to us had
the brains to produce on their own responsibility :
it was that Pompeius should be appointed with full
powers—carefully specified—for three years, to
take every necessary step required by the situation.
Pompeius was, in fact, made military dictator.

The price of corn dropped as soon as the emergency law was passed. The success of Pompeius
against the corsairs was swift and complete. In
three months he did what the oligarchy had not
done in ten years. His treatment of his prisoners
was, as usual, humane and sensible. He settled
them in colonies in Asia Minor.

Caesar, meanwhile, continued his own course
with perfect calm : reflecting, it may be, on the
admirable example Pompeius had given to the
world of the superiority of a single, personal ruler
to a Senate, and reflecting, also, probably, on the

[1] Publius Claudius Pulcher, the notorious " Clodius," afterwards well known as one of Caesar's principal henchmen, was
in Asia with Lucullus, and actively intriguing against him.
The line taken by Clodius does not quite agree with Plutarch's
idea that his motive was merely personal resentment against
Lucullus.

denseness of the oligarchs whose only method of expressing their political disagreement was to annoy Pompeius. So convinced were the majority of Romans as to the advantages of Pompeius's dictatorship that a new measure was passed, giving him the command against Mithradates. Here too the success of Pompeius was a striking illustration of the advantages of a single, personal ruler. He took only some three years to sweep Mithradates off the board and to carry out a permanent resettlement of Asia.

Caesar regarded all these things with approval. The absence of Pompeius gave him, perhaps, additional scope. His aedileship was a rocket-flight of brilliance, without regard for expense.[1] When his own means gave out, he borrowed on a vast scale which proves that no accommodating loan from friends was in question : only the great Roman financiers could have produced the money Caesar spent like water. As aedile he had charge of the public buildings of Rome. One morning the statues and trophies of Marius stood again on the Capitol, bright with colours and gold, with inscriptions relating the victories of Marius over the Cimbri and Teutones. All Rome rushed to see them. As a test of public opinion, and an open declaration of faith, it was successful. We get an interesting glimpse of the change of feeling that was spreading, when we read Plutarch's account of the episode : the anger and indignation of some, the tears of joy that arose in others ; the instant general identification of Caesar as the only possible person responsible for it ; the impeachment of

[1] Caesar was in debt 1,300 talents *before* his quaestorship. The interesting question arises, on what did Caesar spend this immense sum ?

Caesar in the Senate by Catulus ; Caesar's cool and satisfactory defence. As well as a test and a declaration, it was a reminder that the policy of military dictatorship, which was showing its value in the successes of Pompeius in the east, was far better represented by the political tradition of Marius. The reminder was one that could be conveyed without words.

Other policies and impulses, however, were at work among the *Populares*. There are signs that divisions existed in the secret counsels of the party. It had never been intended that Pompeius, on his return home, should continue to be a shining example of either the virtues or the vices of monarchy : but the method of preventing it was not yet clear. The dissensions were indicated by a number of different projects, none of which had the whole weight of the party behind it. There was an attempt (the " Servilian Rogation ") to set up a commission with supreme power, a board of dictatorship. Caesar himself tried to get a personal commission to settle affairs in Egypt. Neither of these plans succeeded. A third section attempted a revolution which became famous as the " Conspiracy of Catilina." It was betrayed. The very mysterious circumstances of Catilina's conspiracy may be considerably illuminated if we recollect a few cardinal facts. Caesar was both connected with the conspiracy and yet not one of the conspirators. He neither betrayed it nor endorsed it. He endeavoured to prevent the illegal execution of Catilina's accomplices. The truth was that they were political allies of his own,[1] of whose policy

[1] Caesar and Crassus supported the candidature of Catilina for the consulship. In prosecuting the Sullan agents who

he disapproved. The oligarchy was allowed to suppress the conspiracy on condition that it did not drag in the rest of the party. Caesar probably had good reason for his passivity. The execution of the Catilinarian leaders swept the party clear of an undesirable but powerful element and gave Caesar absolute control : so that from this time onward we know without question the identity of the anonymous diplomatist who arranged the coalition of Pompeius and Crassus, and we can guess what policy inspired it. The mysterious " No. 1 " of the *Populares* was Caesar himself.

With Caesar in sole control, the party steadied to a perfectly lucid policy. He could depend upon the stupidity of the oligarchy, and its readiness to insult and frustrate Pompeius. The return of the latter was imminent. When he arrived, all fell out as had been expected. The Senate refused him the consulship ; refused him land for his troops ; refused to ratify his reorganisation of the east. The *Populares* were aloof, until Pompeius was driven to desperation. Then Caesar stepped forward. The coalition was re-formed. Pompeius was to receive all that he had asked from the Senate ; through Crassus, the *equites* were promised a reduction of one-third in the purchase money they had contracted to pay for the Asiatic taxes ; Caesar was to have the consulship, and afterwards a governorship for five years, where perhaps he could recruit his shattered fortunes. The wealthy land of Egypt was not mentioned. The governorship was to be in the comparatively poor and barbarous

carried out the Proscription, Caesar allowed the escape of the worst of them—Catilina. The only possible explanation is obvious.

country of Gaul. This satisfied all the parties to the coalition.

We know the result. The agreement was carried out by the disciplined masses of Caesar's voters, the soldiers of Pompeius, and the financial backing of Crassus and his friends. Caesar left for the north, there to begin the creation of the Caesarian army which was a more splendid military machine than even Sulla's, and that famous conquest of Gaul which is the start of the history of western Europe. He kept the organisation of the *Populares* firmly in his own hands. Its leaders were his protégés—often men whom he had rescued from ruin. He found five years insufficient for the work. The triumvirate was reconstructed ; his time of office extended to ten years. Then came the death of Crassus, the break with the oligarchy, the battle of Pharsalus, the fall of Pompeius, the dictatorship of Caesar, and his assassination at the hands of an oligarchic conspiracy. . . . If Sulla's be a strange and remote age ; if Marius be a name to us and little more, the career of Caesar in Gaul, and his death, are familiar and almost modern history.

In going to Gaul, Caesar was following a political tradition. Marius had been praetor in Spain : so was Caesar. Marius had made his military fame in Gaul : so did Caesar. Like Marius, Caesar was a " westerner," a man with faith in Europe, or at any rate with his interests centred upon it. When he crossed the Rubicon he was leading the young, healthy, rising provinces of the west to the rescue of the old, ruined and dying Italy ; and perhaps he knew it.

IV

The assassination of Caesar was a crisis, in the
most strict and solemn sense of the word. The two
Gracchi, Saturninus, Glaucia, Drusus—numberless
men, great and small—had fallen in the struggle,
and the world had, with agitation, pursued its way.
But it did not pursue its way after the fall of Caesar.
The oligarchy was at length at the judgment seat,
and it was condemned to political death. Octavianus
and Antonius were the judges, and half a million
marching, fighting, engineering Roman legionaries
were the jury which fought out and returned the
verdict.

And now, after many years, the movement begun
by Tiberius Gracchus reached its goal. He had
handed on the tradition to his brilliant and creative
brother, who handed it on to the rough, low-born
soldier who proved to be the greatest military genius
Rome ever produced ; and he, in turn, handed it
on to the keen, cold, lucid statesman who invented
a new type of monarchy to fit the ideal. From him
it passed to the first of the Roman emperors, who,
on the failures of many men of genius, erected a
power destined to be permanent. Augustus had
a genius which consisted largely in the absence of
all the gifts which men commonly associate with
genius. He saw all things in the sober, clear light
of perpetual afternoon. All his life he had the
qualities of a good chairman of committees. Under
the refreshing stream of his mere good sense the
Roman world revived. Other men had laid out
and planted that garden : he conducted its maintenance. Its faults and beauties were not of his
making. He was not the architect of its grandeur
nor of its baseness.

V

We come now to review and judgment. Rome had passed a political verdict adverse to Sulla. We are bound to ask ourselves the reason, and to consider how far it was justified.

The first and most obvious reason is, of course, that which has already been given, namely, the worthlessness of the oligarchy, and Sulla's failure to find the aristocracy he desired : but this is too vague and general a statement to be particularly useful. Why was the oligarchy worthless ?—and what was it that really prevented Sulla from reviving aristocracy ? On what especial points—if at all— did the methods of Caesar offer better results ?

The factor which made all the difference was the purest Fortune : the character of Caesar. No human contrivance could possibly have secured that he should automatically, and merely by being himself, solve the otherwise insoluble problem of inventing the type of monarchy necessary to justify the policy he inherited from his predecessors. He was almost the last of the great Roman aristocrats. If only one aristocrat were left, and he continued spontaneously, effectively and without flinching to act as an aristocrat—what would happen ? The answer is, that he would become a monarch. There is no avoiding this conclusion without altering the meaning of the terms.

It was the peculiar virtue of Caesar that he did act throughout in perfect consistence with his own character. His power was not imaginary nor accidental. He really did, by one means or another, dominate all who came into contact with him ; he really had the quiet unbending courage which is never flurried nor frightened ; he really had the austere self-mastery which is the infallible index to a man's power of mastering other men. To these qualities (most of which Sulla had possessed in at least equal measure) he really did add the dry lucidity which sees things precisely as they are : and therefore he never hesitated to face the truths which Sulla had elected to ignore. Having to choose between being a chief without a clan, and making the world his household, he calmly chose the latter course. As the last of the Roman fathers, he set out to put his giant household in order, and to command his multitudinous tribesmen for their good.

He was not quite sure what legal form his monarchy would take. Augustus had more to do with the final determination of the details than Gaius Julius ; but it was Gaius Julius who rough-hewed the conceptions that were to be embodied in constitutional forms : the ideal of a new type of ruler, neither an oriental despot nor a mere magistrate, but one who could accept the existence of the political State, the " respublica," as a necessary part of right human life, and could fulfil the function of regulating it.

Once the preliminary difficulty of conceiving a rational monarchy, suitable for a political State, was overcome, Caesar was faced with the same problem with which Sulla had sought to grapple, namely, the necessity for a real unity of feeling and outlook in those who represented the general direction of the vast Roman State. A gentile aristocracy, whose similarity is to a great degree one of actual common descent, has this unity ready made from within. The difficulty is (as Sulla found) that once such an aristocracy degenerates or dwindles

it is impossible to recreate it artificially. There
is a further difficulty, that a gentile aristocracy,
being a natural product usually evolved in days
prior to the political state, is more or less alien to
the institutions of a community rapidly discarding
gentile links in favour of contract, agreement and
voluntary nexus. Caesar's solution of the problem
was to blend together the hints contained in the
policies of his predecessors—the goodwill of Tiberius
with the personal monarchy of Gaius Gracchus and
the military professionalism created by Marius.

He removed political control altogether from the
oligarchy and from the Assembly of the People,
vesting it in a body of men distinct from either.
The fault inherent in the oligarchic system lay in
the fatal method by which it elected men into its
own ranks : and the existence of this method was
due to its neglect of the qualifications which made
for political strength. It could do nothing with
men like Sertorius on the one hand or Spartacus
on the other, but exterminate them ; but every
scoundrel with money could buy his way into its
ranks. The policy of Caesar was to make the
carrière ouverte aux talens through the army. In
the army every Sertorius, every Spartacus, had the
opening to his natural destiny. The army, therefore,
became something between an aristocracy and a
bureaucracy. It was not an aristocracy, since it
made no attempt to breed the type of man it wanted ;
it was not a bureaucracy, for it hedged its members
with rigid discipline. It was a military order,
whose chief held in his hands the political control
of the Roman dominion. The *Populares* had been
transformed from a political party into a military
guild.

By doing this, Caesar rendered all his ample concessions to the *equites* absolutely delusive. The political control was now beyond their power to influence. Money would still talk, as it always does, but that leverage which the great bankers had exercised over the provincial governors was rendered impossible. The governors became responsible to the emperor alone. The empire succeeded in asserting the absolute supremacy of the political control over all other forms of dominion.

This result would have been impossible had it not been very much to the benefit of the commercial interests themselves. They had sought the Great State, and the empire gave it to them. Under the emperors of the second century—Trajan, Hadrian and the Antonines—that Great State came to the fullest degree of peace, happiness and prosperity that it had enjoyed. It did not stop, nor begin to decline, until it had reached the utmost limits that the resources of the age allowed a single government to deal with. Political power ended by outstripping economic power. Not until the age of the steamship, the railroad and the telephone could a larger political unit be made stable : and the world had to wait until they were invented.

VI

But although Caesar was more successful in stamping his ideas upon the world, were those ideas inherently better than Sulla's ?—or, on the other hand, were they no more than a substitute to fill the gap left by the failure of better designs ? Some of Caesar's policies might not have won their way so readily but for the failure of Sulla's. And in any case, let us remember that Caesar's methods did bring about precisely the results which Sulla tried to prevent : they did close the door finally upon the political evolution of Rome ; they did end the era of individuality and liberty ; they did remove government from the hands of the civil authorities, and hand it over to the soldier.

Caesar was justified in so far as he was indeed compelled, as a statesman, to produce immediate results ; but military discipline as a basis for social conduct has this defect about it, that it is produced by external pressure on character. It may usefully mould character, and that is something. But simply to *mould* character is not enough. Whence is to come the character it moulds ? A power is necessary which shall literally *generate* or create action—inspire the being and the deeds of men from within to a common associate end, without any external force. This is beyond the power of any statesman. For a man who is using the instruments of ordinary government is to some extent bound by them : he must not look too far ahead, or he may ruin his own power for good : he plays the short game of instant action and prompt results. Another kind of man, and another kind of action, is required for the long game which reaches far forward and waits for its results : the religious thinker and the institutes of faith.

Men do not rest permanently content with discipline alone, because it is not possible to cope with the practical difficulties of life without some freedom of action and range of individual discretion. While they will, and do, sacrifice a great deal for the sake of material prosperity, they are rightly told by some inward spiritual faculty that freedom is more precious, and even, ultimately, more profitable. All inventiveness, all energy—practically all that makes men materially wealthy—springs from this spiritual freedom, as we can see by the growing paralysis which falls upon them when they lose it. This energy of mind and body is not overrated when we call it holy. The dumb demand of the Roman world was for one more thing, deeper and greater than the gift of immediate organisation which Caesar bestowed. Forty years after his death, it came. It was not altogether an accident that the empire and Christianity arrived in the Roman world almost together. They were both of them answers to an insistent problem : they supplied a demand made with all the heart and soul of millions of desperate and miserable human beings : the demand for worldly order and for immortal hope.

Nevertheless, this is a criticism as well as an explanation of the facts. Caesar's policy was so inadequate to meet the full demands of the day that a complementary movement was absolutely necessary. And, moreover, that victory of the political principle over the gentile principle which was marked and illustrated by the success of Caesar was equally shown in the organisation of the new religion : it grew up, not as a priestly caste, Levitical or Magian or Brahman, but as a Church, a separate organised body of faithful whose mutual bond was one of agreement, and whose members were similarly drawn from every class and race without distinction. Hence, there was from the first a divorce between the two bodies. Christ and Caesar seemed to be not merely distinct but even antagonistic. It takes no great philosophic gift to perceive that this antagonism is a questionable benefit. We have not even yet completely resolved it. We are still haunted by a dualism beyond our power to transcend. The State with its material interests, the Church with its spiritual interests, are obviously enough both of them necessary to human well-being. They are clearly intended to work to a common end ; they are parts of some common whole which we do not perfectly grasp. We see the advantages of their separation. It is not easy to dispense with it ; it has so often been a benefit to civilisation that one should have the power of exerting external influence on the other. Both, at times, are liable to demand an exclusive allegiance. . . . And yet, for all that, we cannot be satisfied with it. The dualism is a radical fault, though we may not be able to see how it could be avoided. We are driven to the belief that somehow, under some circum- stances, in some way, these two things may yet be one thing : human society is not meant to rest permanently satisfied with less. . . . And therefore Sulla is not to be ignored or despised.

He saw many things—some of them things far more remote, more difficult, than he supposed them to be. He had defects due to the mental quality of the age he lived in ; other defects, personal to himself ; his vision proved to be out of per- spective. But it was not an untrue vision. There were inconsistencies in what he did ; cross-purposes in the circumstances around him ; some things in his world could not be right, because they were posited wrongly to begin with. He looked too much to the past, because the social unity there was nearer than the social unity in front of him. But he did hold it better that the determination of policy should rest with the civil power rather than the military, and be discovered by the consensus of men deliberating in common, rather than by the edict of a princeps. He did side with the conception of life in which political, economic, and spiritual authority are united in the same hands. If there is any fault in such a conception, it is not its meanness, but its seemingly impossible idealism. He came of a race of men who had actually wielded such a unity of power, so he did not grant its impossibility ; nor are we able to declare, in the light of such a fact, that it is impossible.

The truth may be that there are alternations in the process of human history—periods of involution, when all the forces run towards unity, and periods of evolution, when with unanimity they depart from it. They were departing from it in the age of Sulla. The creation of the Great State involved the destruction of the old smaller unities, and the building up (often very much on faith) of vaster and much vaguer unities. Authority was becoming dispersed ; the old solid faith was becoming broken up by the philosophers ; power was beginning to have its seat outside the old appointed bounds. Sulla fought in vain against a tide which set irresistibly against him, and on which he himself, sceptical, loose-living, unconventional, often drifted. . . . It was impossible to get outside the logic of events by which the Roman aristocracy had levelled up to themselves the successive subject classes. The centre of authority and power was inevitably dispersed by the natural development of the process. Hence, an attempt to restore aristocracy was, in a way, an attempt to undo the work of aristocracy. Aristocracy could never, *ex hypothesi*, be restored until the unity of the Great State was impaired, and its component parts had diverged and differentiated, when the process of levelling-up would once more become possible. Aristocracy may be defined as a political process of uniting differentiated types. As soon as the union is accomplished, its function automatically ceases.

All these considerations suggest that the history of Sulla and his times is a part of a process of which we have not even yet seen the whole. Until we have done so, there can be no final judgment of his work. If this be the case, we must regard it as indissolubly united with our own history—a stage in the development of the life we see about us and live in. However remote he may be, or seem, he functions vividly in us. Rome was not on a side path of human evolution, but on the great main highway.

We might deduce from all that has here been said that, whether or not Sulla's real aims " failed," they were aims by no means doomed to ultimate failure, nor foolishly held. He was right in supposing aristocracy to be important, though he could neither save it nor restore it. He was right because, being an aristocrat himself, he felt its virtues in him ; wrong, because he too was grit of the grindstone, part of the logic of events, himself degenerate together with the aristocracy he sprang from. The Roman aristocracy created Rome. After it died out, Rome continued to develop until the impulse given it by the old aristocracy was spent ; and then it dissolved. Such is the tale of all civilisations unless they can renew in some adequate shape the force which originated them.

INDEX

Adherbal, 91
Aemilia, 267–269
Alexander the Great, 42
  Empire of, 42, 153
Antistia, 267–269
Antullius, 62
Apellicon the Teian, Library of, 237
Aquae Sextiae, Battle of, 123
Arausio, Battle of, 116
Archelaus, 189, 192, 193, 195, 196, 199, 200, 201, 203, 204, 220, 221, 222, 224–228
Ardyaeans, 211, 214, 216
Aristion, 189, 193, 194, 195, 226
Aristocracy, Roman, 44, 46–50, 68–70, 73–76
  Definition of, 317
Aristocrat, The Perfect (*see* Pompeius Magnus)
Aristotle's works, 237
Asia, Province of, 59, 146, 149, 150, 152, 175–176, 223, 226, 232–234, 304, 306
Asiatic taxes, 59, 233, 274, 301, 306
Athens, Siege of, 29, 193–195
Augustus, 97, 308, 310

Baltic, 21, 114
Bellona, Temple of, 257
Bocchus, King of Mauretania, 101–110, 151, 157
Bonds of good behaviour (offered by Sulla's army), 239
Britain, 19 *et seq.*
Brundusium, 170, 185, 239

Caecilia Metella, 39, 179, 193, 288, 292
Caepio, Q. Servilius, 114–117, 148 f.n.
Caesar, Gaius Julius, 27, 240, 267, 269–271, 283, 299, 302–317
  Lucius Julius (Consul), 165, 169, 170, 214

Calliphon, 195
Cannae, Battle of, 52, 116
Caphis, 192
Capital Levy, 261, 266
Capua, 240, 249, 258
Carbo, Gn. Papirius (father), 92
  (Son), 235, 243, 245, 248, 249, 251, 258, 281
Catilina, L. Sergius, 264, 266, 305–306
Cato, M. Porcius, the Younger, 271
Catulus, Q. Lutatius (father), 121, 122, 125–126, 127, 129, 130, 131, 138, 139, 214, 267
  (Son), 271, 290
Censorinus, G. Marcius, 157
Chaeronea, 191
  Battle of, 198–204
Christianity, 255, 313
Chrysogonus, 264
Cicero, M. Tullius, 86, 264
Cilicia, 152–156
Cimbri, 22, 92–93, 113–116, 125–130
Cinna, L. Cornelius, 186, 208–213, 235, 241, 269
City State, 40–45, 164, 173–174, 272
Claudius, Appius, 55
Claudius Pulcher, P. (" Clodius "), 303
Concord, Temple of (Rome), 289
Corfinium ("Italia"), 164, 166
Cornelii, in Consulship, 27 f.n.
Courts, Judicial, 58, 115, 117, 141, 143, 148–150, 158–160, 185, 208, 274, 301
Crassus, Lucius Licinius, 148, 158, 159, 248
  Marcus Licinius, 240, 241, 244, 245, 249, 252, 265, 300, 301, 302, 306, 307

Delphi, 191–192, 209
Dentatus, M. Curius, 32 f.n.
Dictatorship, 5–8, 258, 287

Dorylaus, 220
Drusus, M. Livius (father), 61–62
 (Son), 157–160, 165, 248, 272,
 308
Dyrrachium, 189, 238

Empire, The, 308, 312
Equites, 58, 59, 76, 94, 114, 115,
 117, 139, 141, 143, 144, 145,
 149, 157, 164, 165, 170, 174,
 177–185, 207–209, 233, 261–
 264, 274–275, 296, 301–303,
 304, 312
Europe, 19
European, The, 80–81, 298

Faustus and Fausta (Sulla's children), 189, 293, 294
Fimbria, G. Flavius, 218, 222–224,
 226, 227, 228, 230–232
Flaccus, M. Fulvius, 63
 L. Valerius (Consul), 140, 218–
 220, 222–223, 224 f.n.
 L. Valerius (Interrex), 259
Flora the Courtesan, 32
Fortune, 29, 33, 39, 108, 153, 170,
 179, 189, 190, 192, 194, 195,
 197, 200, 204, 207, 217, 222,
 238, 240, 241, 246, 248, 254,
 255, 288, 294, 296
 Temple of, 253
Franchise, 24, 60, 62, 75, 83, 140,
 145, 147–148, 158–160, 163–
 165, 168–170, 173, 178, 207–
 209, 211, 217, 234, 239,
 272–274
Freedman, The (Sulla's overhead
 neighbour), 31
Frisians, 20–21

Gabinius, 200–203
Gaul, 22–23, 53, 90, 92–93, 99,
 113–117, 121–125, 126, 307
Germany, 21
Glaucia, G. Servilius, 117, 140,
 141, 143, 144
Gracchus, G. Sempronius, 31,
 57–64, 65, 66, 82, 85, 115,
 157, 287, 296, 302, 308
 T. Sempronius, 55–57, 308
"Group, The," 148, 150, 151, 158,
 165, 248

Haliae, Fishermen of, 237
Hannibal, 51, 53, 169
Hiempsal, 91
Hortensius, 196, 198, 201, 203

" Italia " (*see* Corfinium)
Italy, a nation, 164

Jugurtha, 91, 93, 99–110, 118
Julia, Wife of Gaius Marius, 90,
 302

Lamponius, 250
Lebadea, Oracle of, 199
Lepidus, M. Aemilius, 290, 293,
 295
Lex Servilia, 115, 117
Longinus, L. Cassius, 99
Lucullus, L. Licinius, 28, 147, 189,
 190, 192, 196–198, 218, 219,
 223, 228, 234, 292–293, 301–
 303
 M. Licinius, 245, 249
Lupus, P. Rutilius, 165, 166

Maecenas, C. Cilnius, 70
Marius, Gaius, 32, 85–90, 93, 94–
 106, 113, 117–131, 133, 135–
 147, 149, 152–153, 155, 157,
 166–167, 170–171, 180, 181,
 183, 207, 209, 210–216, 218,
 224 f.n., 246, 266, 267, 277,
 295, 302, 304, 305, 307, 308
Marius, Gaius, the Younger, 243,
 245, 246, 247, 248, 251, 258
 Gratidianus, M., 267
Marseilles, 23
Metella, Caecilia (*see* Caecilia)
Metellus (Dalmaticus) L. Caecilius, 39, 88–89, 95, 179, 190
 (Numidicus), Q. Caecilius, 93–
 95, 99, 103, 139–140, 142–143,
 190
 (Pius), Q. Caecilius, 185, 211,
 212, 243, 244, 245, 248, 249,
 262, 271, 297
Metrobius (the actor), 34
Midias, 195
Mithradates VI, King of Pontus,
 146, 149, 154–156, 174–176,
 184, 189–190, 193, 207, 217,
 218, 219, 220, 223–230, 232,
 275, 297, 298, 304
Monarchy, 82–83, 277–278, 308–
 312
Murena, L. Licinius, 201–203,
 234

Nero, emperor, 27, 28, 195
Nicopolis, lady, 33
Norbanus, Gaius, 117, 148 f.n.,
 235, 240, 249

320   INDEX

Octavius, Gaius (tribune), 56
  Gnaeus (Consul), 186, 209–212, 214
Ofella, Q. Lucretius, 247, 251, 289
Oligarchy, 57, 68–70, 311
Opimian wine, 64, 287
Opimius, L., 62–64, 70
Ostia, 211–212

Parthia, 156
Peasantry, Roman, ruin of, 53, 54
  To be restored by T. Gracchus, 56
Perpenna Vento, M., 281
Piraeus, burned by Sulla, 196
Pisa, 23–24
" Political," defined, 41
Pompeius Magnus, Gn., 28, 32, 240–242, 244, 245, 259, 267–269, 281–287, 289–290, 293, 295, 297, 299–307
Populares, 134–135
  Become a military guild, 311
Proscription, Marian, 212–216, 262 f.n.
  Sullan, 261–267, 279–280

Rome, 23–26
  Change in character, 164
  Fall of the spiritual Rome, 254
  History, 43–55
Roscius, Sextus (of Ameria), 264–265
Rufinus, P. Cornelius (ancestor of Sulla), 32
Rufus, Q. Pompeius (Consul with Sulla), 178, 180, 186
  P. Rutilius, 93, 120, 136, 150–152, 157, 248
  P. Sulpicius, 177–183

Sacred Mount, Secession to, 46, 50
Sacriportus, Battle of, 245–247
Samnites, 32, 160, 166, 172–173, 207, 211, 248–253, 257
Samnium, 166, 173, 240, 259
Saturninus, L. Appuleius, 56, 117, 121, 140–144, 308
Satyr, discovered, 238

Scaurus, M. Aemilius, 150, 158, 165
  M. Aurelius, 115
Scaevola, P. Mucius, 56, 57
  Q. Mucius, 148, 150–152, 165, 214, 247
Scipio Asiaticus, Lucius Cornelius, 235, 240, 242–243
Scipio Nasica, P., 57, 64, 68, 70
Sertorius, Q., 116, 128, 210, 213, 216, 218, 235, 243, 297–299, 311
Servilian Rogation, 305
Servius Tullius, King, 44, 97
Slavery, 24, 77, 79–80, 298
Social War, 163–174, 177, 185
Spartacus, 298, 300, 311
State, The Great, 42, 76, 312
  Rationalised, 43
Stepmother, Sulla's, 33
Strabo, Gn. Pompeius, 166, 170–173, 185, 186, 211, 240, 241
Sulla, L. Cornelius (father), 33, 224
Sulla, L. Cornelius (son), (the Dictator), appearance, 27–29 ; early poverty, 29–31 ; family, 26–27, 30–32 ; character, 34–39, 83–85 ; earlier marriages, 35–36 ; his principles inferred, 65–83, 277 ; love of drama, 34–35 ; marriage to Caecilia Metella, 179 ; his sincere affection for her, 180, 193, 288, 292 ; his cynical humour, 185, 191–192, 200, 204, 263, 287, 289, 291 ; criticism of his ideals, 315–317 ; his own verdict on himself, 255, 294

Taxiles, 196, 198, 199, 203
Telesinus, Pontius, 249–253, 257
Teutones, 113–116, 121, 123–125, 126, 127, 140

Valeria Messalla, 288–289, 292
Varian Tribunal, 165, 169, 275
Varius Hybrida, Q., 165, 169, 214
Vercellæ, Battle of, 127–130, 138
Via Aurelia, 24, 212